THE BOY WHO DARED TO ROCK:
THE DEFINITIVE
ELVIS

THE BOY WHO DARED

TO ROCK:

THE

DEFINITIVE

ELVIS

by Paul Lichter

DOLPHIN BOOKS, Doubleday & Company, Inc., Garden City, New York, 1978

Library of Congress Cataloging in Publication Data

Lichter, Paul, 1944–
The boy who dared to rock.

Includes index.
CONTENTS: Book 1. The story.—Book 2. Standing
room only.—Book 3. Recording sessions [etc.]

1. Presley, Elvis Aron. 2. Presley, Elvis Aron
—Bibliography. 3. Singers—United States—
Biography. I. Title.
ML420.P96L52   784′.092′4   [B]
ISBN: 0-385-12636-0
Library of Congress Catalog Card Number 76–52006

ACKNOWLEDGMENTS

I'd like to thank the following people
for their help, friendship, and/or inspiration.

I'd like to express my sincere appreciation to my wife, Janice,
and children, Kyle and Danielle, for being so understanding
while I was writing this book.

RCA Records
Joan Deary—Director of Administration, RCA Records, West Coast
Alan Cress, Esq.—RCA Records
Lois Quinn—RCA Records
Paula Douma—RCA Records
Larry Snyder—Tempo Records
Al Gallico—Music Corporation
Joel Whitburn—*Billboard* Magazine
Jim Menick—Doubleday
Elaine Chubb—Doubleday
Dee Ratterree—Simon & Schuster

Mr. Lichter's staff photographers:

Robert Kirschner
Blake Roberts
Glen Griffin
Ronald Lawrence
Bob Heis

Thanks also to friends and supporters, without whom . . .

Muhammad Ali
John Lennon
Paul McCartney
Johnny Burnette

Joan Border
Jocelyn Lane
Geraldo Rivera
Roy Leonard
Michael Radbill, Esq.
Matt Demsker
Jackie Wilson
George Krosunger
Marvin Berg
Manny Lichter
Marsha Cohen
Elton John
Martha Berg
Rod Stewart
Sylvia Lichter
Joe Esposito
Jerry Hopkins

I'd also like to thank the man
who has been the greatest inspiration in my career,
Colonel Thomas A. Parker.

Special thanks to Elvis Presley for his friendship
and ability to bring happiness to so many!

On August 16, 1977, I received a phone call from RCA and heard the sad and unexpected news that Elvis Presley had died in Memphis of a heart attack. The short life of the the King of Rock and Roll had come to an end.

The sad irony of having THE BOY WHO DARED TO ROCK already at the printers was made doubly sad by now having to include the final chapter of Elvis' life. I had hoped to be able to present him personally with the book when it was published, but a book that had been intended as a tribute to a living legend had suddenly become a memorial.

I like to think that Elvis would have enjoyed the book had he lived to see it. I would like to dedicate THE BOY WHO DARED TO ROCK to the young Tennessee truck-driver singer who made rock and roll what it is today, and to his legion of fans who made him the King of Rock and Roll that he was, and always will be.

PAUL LICHTER

Janice, this one's for you, baby!

Contents

BOOK 1 THE STORY • 1

The Chosen / 3

Memphis / 8

The Hillbilly Cat / 11

Golden Boy / 20

Pvt. US 53310761 / 46

Elvis Is Back / 52

The Love Years / 69

The King of the Jungle / 78

The Myth, the Legend, the Man / 83

Aloha / 111

BOOK 2 STANDING ROOM ONLY • 113

That's the Way It Was / 115

That's the Way It Is / 117

Live Appearances / 147

BOOK 3 RECORDING SESSIONS • 155

BOOK 4 DISCOGRAPHY AND FILMS • 199

American Records / 201

Rare Records / 250

Bootlegs / 268

Foreign Records / 283

The Hollywood Years / 299

About Paul Lichter / 301

THE BOY WHO DARED TO ROCK:
THE DEFINITIVE
ELVIS

BOOK 1

THE STORY

Vernon Elvis Presley and Gladys Smith Presley.

The Chosen

It is difficult for a northerner to understand the effect that the Civil War had on the South. Elvis Aron Presley was born in the heart of the South, in Tupelo, Mississippi. Tupelo was known as a hard-luck town. Very few of the township's small population were able to rise above their difficulties. For the many "just ordinary" folks, all hope for an easy, comfortable life was lost. The Great Depression of the thirties put an extra weight on their backs; and many found that a stubborn, independent pride was their only defense. They found joy in strong family ties.

Vernon Elvis Presley, Elvis' father, was the son of a farmer; even as a young boy he did the work of a man. He never made it further than the fifth grade, when he had to leave school to help out at home.

Gladys Smith Presley, Elvis' mother, also came from a farming family. She was one of eight children, five sisters and three brothers.

It was in Tupelo that Vernon and Gladys fell in love. They went together for only a short time before they decided to get married. The year was 1933. Vernon, who was seventeen, and Gladys, who was four years older, went to Verona to be wed. They made a handsome couple, Vernon with his blond good looks and Gladys with her dark beauty. They lived with their in-laws, first the Smiths and then the Presleys. Vernon continued to do farm work and Gladys was employed by the Tupelo Garment Company. They both started their day at 6:00 A.M. They worked twelve hours a day, six days a week. Their combined earnings for a week's work amounted to twenty-six dollars.

3

LEFT: Vernon and his father built this house in Tupelo, where Elvis was born. RIGHT: The First Assembly of God Church, where Elvis was first exposed to music.

In 1934 Vernon and his father built a small two-room house for Vernon and Gladys to live in. The front room was the bedroom and the back room was the kitchen. They had no running water. Outside there was a pump next to the outhouse.

During the summer of 1934 Gladys learned that she was pregnant. She had to quit her job, and Vernon got a job driving a milk truck.

Shortly after noon on January 8, 1935, just two years after they married, Gladys gave birth to identical twins in their little house. They were given matching names: Elvis Aron and Jesse Garon. Elvis' twin, Jesse, was delivered only minutes after Elvis. He was perfectly formed, but something had gone wrong and he was born dead. Little Jesse Garon was laid out in a tiny coffin in the front room. They buried Jesse the following day. His resting place was an unmarked grave in the Priceville Cemetery. Gladys worshiped her surviving son and she treated him as though the Lord had somehow let her know that little Elvis was indeed "the chosen."

4

Minnie Presley, Elvis' greatest fan and grandmother.

When Elvis was a year old, a tornado hit Tupelo, leaving hundreds dead and tearing the heart from the Mississippi town. The twister had missed the Presley home by only one mile. Vernon and Gladys thanked God while grieving for friends. Elvis would spend his early years in the chaos and ruin of Tupelo, Mississippi.

Gladys took Elvis everywhere she went and friends say she never let him out of her sight. The Presleys taught their son politeness. He was instructed that he shouldn't interrupt or argue, and that if you didn't have something nice to say, you didn't say anything. He learned his manners so well that even as an adult he addressed his elders as "sir" or "ma'am."

Elvis first showed his love for music at the age of two. The Presleys belonged to the First Assembly of God Church, which was located just one block from their home. One of their greatest joys was singing together in church. There were no stained-glass masterpieces, no silver or gold altar furnishings in the tiny frame building, but it was in this building that the Presleys and their neighbors found the beauty of love. For them "O come, let us sing unto the Lord, let us heartily rejoice in the strength of our salvation" was no empty phrase—it was a way of life. As the choir stood and sang, little Elvis couldn't contain himself. He began to twitch and stir in his mother's lap. He would wriggle off and run down the aisle to the platform

5

where the singers stood. There he stood trying to sing along with them, his small body swaying to the rhythm.

As Elvis grew, he and his parents sang at camp meetings and revivals, but only as part of the congregation. The Presleys never sang as a popular trio and, while they enjoyed attending church, they were never fanatical, as has been reported in several biographies. Years later, when Elvis was asked how he got his famous wiggle, he said, "There were these singers, perfectly fine singers, but nobody responded to them. Then there were the preachers and they cut up all over the place, jumping on the piano, moving every which way. The crowd responded to them. I guess I learned from them."

Elvis was a happy, normal boy. He played all the regular boys' games and would come home all bruised, with holes in the knees of his pants. He always got along well with the other children. He hated to argue. To avoid trouble, he would sometimes give his toys to the other kids. Of course, a bully would come along once in a while to give him a hard time. Vernon told Elvis that he would have to take care of himself. The next time the bully started with Elvis, the boy had the hell beat out of him. Needless to say, the child never bothered Elvis again.

When Elvis was five, his mother began walking him to class, a practice that would continue until his final year in high school. Like most parents, Vernon and Gladys wanted to give their son all of the advantages that they had missed. Elvis wanted a brother or sister very badly. Vernon recalled years later, "That was just one of those things that could never be. Sometimes you wonder when you see other families with several kids, why it couldn't be the same with you. Hard up as we were, we spent a lot of money on doctors trying to change it, but there wasn't anything we could do."

Vernon worked hard at a variety of jobs, but the Presleys were always in debt. But even though they were struggling, they made sure that Elvis always had a good Christmas and they always dressed him as well as they could. Even when the family didn't have a dime, Elvis still believed that one day it would be different.

Gladys and Elvis were left alone in Tupelo during most of the war years. Vernon had gone to Memphis, where there were better jobs and a chance to earn more money. On Sundays he would tramp all over town, attempting to find a room for his family. Whenever he did, the first question they would ask was, "You got any children?" When Vernon answered, they'd say, "We don't want any children here," and shut the door. Vernon didn't have to worry, though; he knew Gladys would take good care of herself and Elvis. But the separation was breaking their hearts, and no matter how many times Vernon visited with them, he couldn't help longing for his family.

Elvis met his first girl friend when he was nine. Her name was Caroline Ballard; her father, the Reverend James Ballard, was the pastor at their church. The Ballards later moved to Jackson, Mississippi, and the last Elvis heard of Caroline, she was attending classes at a Texas university.

When he was in the fifth grade, his home room teacher was Mrs. J. C. Grimes. "He was a good student," Mrs. Grimes recalled. "You remember when they're not! Sweet—that's the word. And average. Sweet and average. Each morning we'd have chapel, and one morning I asked the kids if any of them could say a prayer. No one answered. I looked around and there was Elvis with his hand raised. He said he could say a prayer, and he recited a prayer and sang several songs. I remember one of them, and it wasn't really right for chapel, but he sang it so sweetly, it made me cry." The song Elvis sang was "Old Shep," a sad song about a boy and his dog.

Mrs. Grimes was so impressed with Elvis' singing that she asked the school's principal, J. D. Cole, to listen to Elvis' voice. He liked his singing so much that he took little Elvis to the annual Mississippi-Alabama Fair, held nearby. He entered him in the talent show, which was broadcast over station WELO. Elvis had to stand on a chair to reach the microphone, and he had to perform without music because the guitar players there were reluctant to help any of the competition. Elvis sang "Old Shep." Vernon, who was driving his truck a few miles from the fair, cried with joy as he heard his son's sweet, boyish soprano over the truck's radio. Elvis won second prize—five dollars and free admission to all of the amusement rides. "I can still remember it," Elvis said; "Caroline Ballard and I rode every ride at the fair that night."

The Presleys' financial problems continued, and they lost their home. This brought about several moves. They were able to feed themselves, although the food was not the most nutritious. Their normal diet consisted of peas, tomatoes, corn, and apples. Vernon's brother, Vester, who had married Gladys' younger sister, Cletis, would come by and play the guitar. Elvis loved the sounds that came from Vester's guitar. His uncle knew only a few chords, but he taught Elvis what he knew.

When Elvis was thirteen, he asked his parents for a bicycle. The Presleys couldn't afford to buy him a bike, so Gladys asked if perhaps he wouldn't prefer a guitar. She explained how it would help him with his singing. Elvis replied that if he could get a guitar, he wouldn't ask for the bicycle again for a year. He loved that guitar and took it everywhere he went. He'd listen to radio shows and try to copy the sounds he heard. Among his favorites were Jimmie Rodgers, Otis Spann, B. B. King, Howlin' Wolf, Arthur Crudup, and Muddy Waters. Elvis combined their sound with the spirituals he had always loved. Slowly he was developing the sound that would one day change the music world forever.

Elvis, pre-greatness.

Memphis

Vernon Presley didn't want to leave Tupelo, where he had lived all his life. He knew that things weren't getting easier, however, and that he and his family would have better job opportunities living in a big city. The Presleys left Tupelo overnight for Memphis. Vernon and Gladys loaded their clothes and a few belongings in their 1939 Plymouth. They left town on a Saturday, so that Elvis wouldn't have to miss even one day of school.

Memphis on September 12, 1948, when the Presleys arrived, had a population of almost 300,000. It had grown during the war years and was only one hundred miles from Tupelo. But the family's problems didn't improve with the move to Memphis. If anything, they were worse. They found shelter in a one-room apartment at 572 Poplar Avenue. They had no kitchen and shared a common bath with three other families. They used a hotplate to prepare their food. The city was big and strange to Elvis, and he didn't know anyone to make friends with.

Vernon went to the L. C. Humes High School to arrange Elvis' registration with the principal, T. C. Brindley. The principal had come into the Memphis school system as a football coach and he, too, was new to Humes High that year. Mr. Brindley had this to say about his most famous former student: "The only credit that this school can claim for Elvis' success is that we did not try to compress him into an academic mold. We let him follow his own beat."

Meanwhile, Vernon and Gladys walked the streets looking for work. Vernon found employment as a laborer at the United Paint Company; he earned eighty-three cents an hour, grossing $38.50 in a good week. Mrs. Presley began work as a nurse's aide at St. Joseph's Hospital. Elvis would mow lawns after school, a field dominated by grown Negro yard boys. Elvis' father bought him a hand lawn mower, and Elvis would give all of his earnings to his parents.

Mrs. Jane Richardson of the Memphis Housing Authority visited the Presleys on June 17, 1949. The Presleys had asked for public assistance, and Mrs. Richardson was there to see if they qualified. In August, shortly after Elvis had completed his first year at Humes, the Presleys were accepted for residence at the Lauderdale Courts, a federally funded project.

Elvis was a boy who needed friends because of his shyness and poor English, and he made very few during his first year at Humes. None of his classmates or teachers can remember very much about him. They didn't know Elvis well enough to talk about him. Like most high school students, he went unnoticed.

The young Presley really loved football, and he demonstrated his skills during his second year at Humes, when he played end for the Humes High Tigers. Gladys was worried that he would be injured, so she asked him to give up the game. This caused a real conflict for the boy, but in his desire to be a good son he told his coach, "I don't want to worry my mother—I'm quitting the team."

Gladys had begun to gain weight, and her health was failing. In order to help the family income, Elvis found employment as an usher at the Loew's State Theater. This job was short-lived, however, as one of the other ushers told Arthur Groom, the manager of the theater, that Elvis was sitting and watching the films when he should have been ushering. Mr. Groom called Elvis on the carpet, and Elvis had a good idea of how his employer had found out. He confronted the other usher, and the boy said something that made Elvis so angry that he knocked the boy down. Mr. Groom then fired both of them.

Elvis' next job was with the Marl Metal Products Company. He worked a full shift, from three in the afternoon until eleven-thirty in the evening, all the while keeping up with his studies. His schoolwork was suffering from his heavy work load, so Gladys forced him to quit his job. Despite her poor health, she returned to her job at the hospital.

When Elvis first entered high school, he wore his hair in a flat-top style (short, almost crew-cut on top, and much longer on the sides and in the back). Now, at the age of sixteen, he felt the need to be different. Much to his parents' dismay, he began to let his hair grow long, combing it high in the front and sweeping the hair at the sides into a D.A. at the back. He also grew long, fuzzy sideburns. He began to dress in wild clothing that featured unlikely colors such as pink or Kelly green. He wanted to be noticed, and he was! Elvis seldom had spare money to spend on clothing, but when he did, he spent it at the Lansky Brothers shop on Beale Street. The Lanskys specialized in pink sport coats, royal blue high-rise pants with a white stripe

Elvis and schoolboy
friend George Klein.

running the length of the leg, and bright yellow corduroy jackets trimmed in imitation leopard. Bernard Lansky remembers Elvis well: "He used to come and stare in our window. One day I asked him to come in. 'No, sir, I ain't got no money.' Well, after he got some money, he began to buy here. When he hit the big money as a singer, he bought us out."

Elvis was still shy, but he was slowly developing his own identity. It wouldn't be until the latter part of his senior year that he would show the self-confidence that became so much his trademark.

George Klein, who is Memphis' top disc jockey today, remained one of Elvis' closest friends. He recalls their high school days: "I think Elvis was more comfortable with his teachers than his fellow students. I hardly got to know him until our senior year. One thing I'll never forget was the first time I heard him sing—he sang 'Cold, Cold, Icy Fingers,' which was a popular country tune at the time. It was then that I realized how gifted Elvis was." In his senior year, Gladys loosened her apron strings somewhat and Elvis began to run with the boys. He also began to date, although not often. When he had spare cash, he usually took his date to a movie or to the local carnival. Elvis really dug the movies, and Tony Curtis was his idol.

During his final year of school, he joined ROTC. He enjoyed it immensely, and after his first success he bought new uniforms for the school's ROTC drill team. Mildred Scrivener was Elvis' home room teacher during his senior year and was also the producer of the school show, which raised funds for needy students. She put Elvis in the show, among thirty other acts. The student who received the most applause would have an encore at the end of the show. All of the performing students tried their best to win that encore. Elvis, wearing a red flannel shirt, sang a sad love song; he received the most applause, to win the privilege of doing another song.

On June 14, 1953, he received his high school diploma. The photo in his yearbook shows him in a dark sport jacket, white shirt, and light tie. It also shows him to be the only member of his class to have a large spit curl in the middle of his forehead.

Vernon was having back problems and was frequently forced to miss work. He has often said that this was the lowest period of his life. He had no way of knowing then that in less than two years his son would retire him to a life of millionaire splendor.

The Hillbilly Cat

One thing can be said for Gladys' loving son, and that is this shy young man was a unique human being. His manners were still soft, his friendships few. His appearance, however, was most bizarre. This soft-spoken adolescent was dressing more outrageously than any street-wise pimp. In 1953 no one dressed in this style, which would later become common to everyone. Elvis went to work for the Crown Electric Company, driving one of two trucks, delivering electrical supplies to the forty-five electricians employed by Crown. His work, which he liked very much, earned him somewhere around forty-one dollars each week. James Tipler remembers how Elvis came to work for him. "I called Tennessee unemployment, and they told me about the boy. They also warned me about his appearance. After he started working here, my wife would make appointments at the beauty shop for him."

One spring day, as Elvis was driving the Ford pickup, he passed the Memphis Recording Service, a small but lucrative sideline of the Sun Record Company. Since he was on his lunch hour, he decided to park his truck across the street from the studio. He had four dollars in the pocket of his worn jeans, just the right amount to make a private recording. As he stood there trying to summon the courage to cross the street, he nervously fingered the dollar bills. Eventually the tall youngster crossed the road and stood in front of the Sun Record Company.

Sam Phillips, the president of Sun Records, hadn't returned from lunch. Elvis was greeted by Mrs. Marion Keisker (who had formerly worked as Miss Radio of Memphis), who smiled and asked, "Can I help you?" "My name is Elvis Presley and I want to make a record."

No one, including eighteen-year-old Elvis, would have thought of this moment as having any significance. In retrospect, one can see that this serious young man was the first white vocalist to sing a song the way he felt it.

"The day Elvis walked into Sun Records' office," says Mrs. Keisker, "he was wearing faded work clothes and he was dirty." He told her he wanted to make the record as a birthday present for his mother. Marion Keisker asked him, "Who do you sing like?" His reply was "I don't sing like nobody but me, I reckon." He had no music to accompany him, but his battered guitar hung across his back. He never bothered with a case like the rest of the boys. He would record two songs that day, "My Happiness," backed by "That's When Your Heartaches Begin." Sam Phillips returned shortly before Elvis had completed his ten-minute recording session. Elvis paid his four dollars and left with his prized record.

After Elvis had gone, Mrs. Keisker picked up a note that Sam had left on her desk. It read: *Elvis Presley . . . Good ballad singer. Save this.*

Sam Phillips was raised on an Alabama plantation, where he had heard the blacks sing the blues since he was a small boy. Sam felt that Negro songs were the only music left that was still free and alive with emotion. He had recorded many of the finest black vocalists in the South: among them, Bobby "Blue" Bland, Howlin' Wolf, Jackie Brenston, Little Junior Parker, and the Prisonaires.

Several months later, Elvis returned to the tiny Sun recording studio to make another private record. Sam was at the controls as Elvis laid down vocal tracks for "Casual Love Affair" and "I'll Never Stand in Your Way." Elvis' voice was a mixture of two definite styles, pop and country. To this day, neither of the songs Elvis recorded during his second visit to a recording studio has been heard by the public.

Sam Phillips journeyed to Nashville in search of new talent. While there, he bought a demo record of a song titled "Without Love (There Is Nothing)." It was a great ballad, but Sam was unable to find the identity of the Negro vocalist who had performed it. Phillips was faced with a decision. Who would he find to record it? Mrs. Keisker reminded Sam, "Remember Elvis Presley?" "Yes, indeed," Phillips recalled. "Give him a call." Marion called Elvis at Crown Electric Company and told him Sam Phillips wished to see him. Elvis dropped what he was doing and rushed to the tiny studio. Mrs. Keisker recalls, "I turned around and there was Elvis. He flashed that crooked smile that would later become famous."

Elvis tried his best to make a good recording of "Without Love," but the material proved to be too much for the youngster's vocal range. After Elvis had become famous he would return to Sun and try his hand again at recording "Without Love." His dedication was so great that, some fifteen years later, Elvis, now under contract to RCA, finally recorded and released "Without Love (There Is Nothing)."

Although Sam didn't know what it was, something about this young man fascinated him. He asked Elvis to sing every song he knew. Elvis did just that for nearly three hours.

The Blue Moon Boys—Bill Black (left), Elvis (center), and Scotty Moore.

Scotty Moore and Bill Black, along with Johnny Burnette, had been play-ing music in the Memphis area for a few years: Scotty on lead guitar, Bill on bass fiddle, and Johnny on vocals. Scotty and Bill would eventually join forces with Elvis and help shape the sound that rocked the world. Strangely, it was Johnny Burnette who knew the teen-age Elvis best. Before his tragic death, Johnny would write and record such hits as "Dreaming," "You're Sixteen," and "The Fool" (which Elvis would record on his 1971 *Elvis Country* album).

In an early interview, Johnny had this to say about Elvis:

13

You looked in the front door and saw straight out the back. I must have seen his house a million times, but he wouldn't let me go inside that house. He used to wear the wildest clothes! Whenever I saw him, and that was often, he'd be wearing purple pants with black stripes down the side, white buck shoes and a pink sports jacket. He'd always have his shirt collar turned up and would wear his hair real long. There never was anything false about him. He didn't talk much, he never knew what he was capable of. He used to go down to the fire house and he'd sing to the boys there. They were the only ones around Memphis, and they seemed to have a lot of listening time. Every now and then he'd go into one of the cafes or bars and slouch across a chair. He never sat up straight, he'd just sort of lie there with a mean look on his face. Then some folks would say, "Let's hear you sing, boy," and Elvis would stand up all of a sudden, he'd slide his guitar 'round to his front and he'd raise hell with that rockin' sound of his.

Scotty Moore had done some session work at the Sun studio. Sam called him and asked Bill Black to come along, and together they headed for the studio. Once there they met Elvis and the three of them began to run through all of the songs they knew. "I don't think any of us was too impressed with the other," Bill Black notes. "We just happened to like each other."

The trio rehearsed for a few months and then returned to the Sun studio to see if they could get it together. Once again they ran through every song they could remember. They tried hard, but the sound Sam Phillips was looking for just wasn't there. The boys took a break and enjoyed some cold bot-

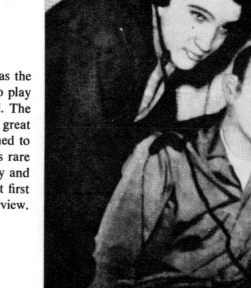

Dewey Phillips was the first disc jockey to play an Elvis record. The response was so great that Elvis was rushed to the studio. This rare photo shows Dewey and Elvis doing that first interview.

tles of pop. Suddenly it happened. Elvis began singing the first chorus of "That's All Right (Mama)" and all at once Phillips had discovered a white man with the vocal emotions of a Negro! The pounding beat, the freshness, the vocal modulations, that magic something was there.

Although Elvis, Bill, and Scotty knew they had discovered their own groove, it wasn't until they heard the playback that they realized just how great the sound they had created was. They chose an old country standard, "Blue Moon of Kentucky," for the flip side. Bill Monroe had written and recorded this song many years before.

Sam Phillips could hardly contain his excitement. His mind was reeling as he tried to decide how to get his dub played. Finally he remembered Dewey Phillips, who was the top disc jockey at radio station WHBQ in Memphis. Dewey was ahead of his time and had been playing the so-called race music for years before the rock and roll craze. Dewey played "That's All Right" on his show, and the sensuous voice with its rock and country inflections went soaring into the night. "That will get them," said Dewey, who had a style of speaking that was his alone. "Yessir, that'll get them."

Dewey Phillips remained a close friend of Elvis until his death in September 1968. Elvis always got a kick out of the music that Dewey was the first to play in every instance. Some of his favorites were "My Baby Left Me," "I Got a Woman," "Blueberry Hill," and "Tutti Frutti." Elvis would jump on his big Harley-Davidson bike and ride down to the station with hoagies for himself and Dewey. When he arrived, Dewey would shout into the mike, "Hey, Elvis, you got my hoagie?" Elvis would yell back, "You better believe it."

The front of the studio featured a picture window, and the fans would watch Dewey and Elvis broadcasting. Dewey had the walls lined with girlie photos, and he would joke how Elvis was looking at his fine collection of fillies. That was the summer of 1954.

In the first seven days following the initial airing of "That's All Right," Sun received more than five thousand orders for their new artist's first recording. They had yet to press a commercial record. Sam Phillips realized that something really big was happening. Sleepy Eye John was a country music disc jockey who had the largest listening audience on station WHHM. Sam brought Elvis' record to Sleepy Eye and asked him to play it. He played "Blue Moon of Kentucky." Sleepy Eye was the first to play this side, although he didn't personally care for the song. Sleepy Eye John hadn't any intention of playing Elvis' record again; however, he left for a vacation the following day. When his substitute arrived, he found the disc on the turntable and kept it spinning.

Rhythm and blues disc jockeys refused to play Elvis' records because they felt his sound was country and western. On the other hand, the country disc jockeys felt his tunes were R & B.

Elvis had a record the public was buying, but, because record royalties are paid twice yearly, he was still broke.

Sam Phillips decided that the best way to sell his records was for Elvis to promote them himself. Bob Neal was the head of a local booking agency

Elvis' first big public performance (Dewey Phillips on the left).

and was organizing a show that would feature Carl Smith and Slim Whitman. The show would take place at the Overton Park Shell auditorium in Memphis on August 10, 1954. Sam asked Bob to find a spot for Elvis in the show. Presley would appear as a warm-up act for country star Webb Pierce and would receive no billing. The audience greeted him with polite applause when he was introduced. He sang "Old Shep" and "That's When Your Heartaches Begin." He was disillusioned by the crowd's lack of passion toward him and told both Dewey and Sam what had happened to him during the afternoon show. Dewey informed Elvis that he would be deemed nothing special if he sang only country songs. He advised him to do "That's All Right (Mama)" and some other rockers at the evening performance and leave the country tunes to the other singers on the bill.

That evening, Dewey introduced him to the audience. The curtain parted and, standing on center stage, Elvis was a sight to behold. He wore a black sports coat trimmed with pink darts and black high-rise pants that featured pink pocket flaps and pink lightning bolts lining the outside seam of the leg. He threw one arm above his head and began to move his leg in the now famous corkscrew motion, his smoldering blue eyes peering out at the audience, his thick lips curled in a sexy snarl. He hadn't sung his first note and

16

Elvis giving a rocking performance in Tupelo.

they were already screaming. Elvis shouted, "Well-ll-ll," and went right into "Good Rockin' Tonight." There was chaos in the audience. As the song ended, the screaming covered the beginning of "That's All Right (Mama)." Elvis was grinning. He braced himself against the microphone stand and suddenly started to thrust his pelvis, which he managed to circle and grind slowly while caressing the mike stand. He threw his head back and let out one clear scream that was high, intense, and purely animal. The crowd screamed, dug their fingernails into their temples, and bit their bottom lips before releasing an exhilarating sigh. Elvis completed his song, and there wasn't a cold heart left in the auditorium. He made his way backstage, meeting Webb Pierce, who had been waiting to close the show. Webb didn't understand what he had just witnessed. He did understand, however, that there was no reason for him to go on stage any more, as the show was over.

The owner of a men's clothing shop in Memphis remembers the day Elvis was standing outside his store and some boys passed by. Elvis' name was becoming familiar by then, and the boys were jealous of the success Elvis was having with the female population. They barely acknowledged him, while keeping an even stride. Elvis watched as they walked by; he turned to the shopkeeper and said, "What's the matter? Those fellows went to school with me and they were my friends; they didn't even stop to talk!"

"That's All Right" had sold steadily, although today no record exists of just how well. In July of 1954 Sam Phillips hadn't begun to keep track of Elvis' record sales.

Following the success of the Overton shows, Bob Neal began to handle Elvis' career. Bob put Elvis, Scotty, and Bill on the road. The trio would travel some twenty-five thousand miles. They went across country in a secondhand Lincoln, often using the back seat as their bed. A typical week's schedule would have them in New Orleans on Friday, Shreveport on Saturday, Memphis Auditorium on Sunday, Ripley, Mississippi, on Monday, and Alpine, Texas, on the following Friday and Saturday.

Elvis Presley, the Hillbilly Cat, and his Blue Moon Boys: that's how the marquee read at the Silver Palms bar, located in Pocahontas, Arkansas. There weren't too many people who entered the Silver Palms roadhouse who had ever heard of the Blue Moon Boys, and you had to be listening to the right radio station to know who Elvis was. The female customers panted, moaned, and squealed all around the bandstand. The farmers and truck drivers weren't too crazy about the Hillbilly Cat. They were appreciative later on, though, when Elvis had put their women in the mood for love and made them much more agreeable to their own advances.

Elvis' second record, "I Don't Care If the Sun Don't Shine," backed by "Good Rockin' Tonight," was released at the same time as his third single, "Milkcow Blues Boogie," paired with "You're a Heartbreaker."

It was late 1954 and Elvis was on fire. His personal appearances had made him the hottest act in the South. He was getting fan mail from young ladies who had seen him on tour and couldn't wait for him to return to their part of the country.

Bob Neal began to travel with Elvis and the boys. "He was always wonderful to handle," Bob recalls, "and we had lots of laughs, especially over his eating habits. He'd developed a real passion for peanut butter and banana sandwiches." Even then Elvis was battling the curse of insomnia. "He was always keyed up. Sometimes he wouldn't unwind until five in the morning. I'd sit around with him and we'd talk about the future. He always did a bob-dance when he sang. The more they screamed, the more turned on he'd become."

The Memphis *Press-Scimitar* ran the following headline on its front page: "He's Sex!" Memphis' largest newspaper also displayed a three-column picture of its hometown boy. The story mentioned that Elvis was sexy, lazy, tough, and good-looking. The article gave Elvis' career added momentum.

Elvis' latest singles weren't selling as well as had been expected. Dewey Phillips was the only disc jockey in Memphis who played them. Following the news article, all of the stations began to play Elvis' records and for the first

Elvis performing at his alma mater, Humes High School.

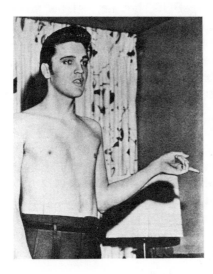

Back in his hotel room after a wild performance in Texas, where the fans rushed the stage and tore Elvis' shirt right off his back. (Note the high-rise pants that helped give birth to the name fans had begun to call him—the Hillbilly Cat!)

time Memphis realized it had a hometown phenomenon. The story reprinted in newspapers throughout the South and, if things were moving fast before, they were racing now.

Before each show Elvis paced like a caged tiger. Once on stage, he was like an animal turned loose. He'd grind and the audience would sigh. Elvis turned it on hotter, burning, and his followers melted. Their screams and passions rang in his ears.

19

Golden Boy

In early 1955 Bob Neal was still managing Elvis, but he had his problems. He was trying to hold down his own job as a disc jockey, manage Elvis, and keep a wife and five boys happy at home. The latter was the most difficult because keeping up with Elvis meant being out of town frequently. "He had gotten so big that it meant I would have to give up everything and go with him." Then Bob exclaimed, "I weighed it . . . I needed more time with my family."

Thomas Andrew Parker was born to parents who were traveling with a carnival. He had lost both of his parents by the time he was ten. Tom was raised by his uncle, whose carnival show was known as "The Great Parker Pony Circus." When Tom was seventeen, he had his own circus act, which featured a pony and a monkey. He would later become a press agent for several traveling shows. He entered the show business world when he took over as manager of Gene Austin, who had a hit recording with "My Blue Heaven." He had already made stars of Eddy Arnold and Hank Snow when he first set eyes on Elvis Presley in Texarkana, Arkansas.

It was just before a matinee break when Parker slipped into a seat to catch the act that was driving the audience mad. He watched the young stud carry the crowd with him as he worked himself to the point of exhaustion. Parker glanced around him to see the people pounding the seats and floors with rhythmic approval, causing the rafters to ring with their screams. At that moment, all of the years of experience gained from the thousands of days and nights with the sideshows, the carnivals, the circus, and the one-night stands hit "the Colonel" with a mad rush. Tom Parker could see that whatever Elvis had, it was real and vital, it was solid talent. It was a kind of magic that comes along once in a lifetime. The poor boy from Tupelo and the old carny met backstage and the greatest union in show business history was formed.

On November 22, 1955, this story appeared in the Memphis *Press-Scimitar:*

Elvis Presley, 20, Memphis recording star and entertainer who zoomed into big-time and big money overnight, has been released from his contract with Sun Record Company of Memphis, and will record exclusively for RCA Victor.

Both Sam Phillips and RCA officials said at the time that the money involved was believed to be the highest ever paid for a contract release. What made it more unusual was the fact that Elvis, still just twenty, had only one more year to go on his contract with Sun. *Billboard* reported that the price was "a reported payoff of $40,000." With the contract, RCA obtained the rights to the five released Sun singles. Colonel Parker, Bob Neal, and Phillips, along with Coleman Tiley III, were involved in the deal. Colonel Parker also arranged for the establishment of Elvis Presley Music, a publishing firm, in collaboration with Hill and Range Music, Inc., of New York.

After the new contract Elvis, accompanied by the Colonel and country legend Hank Snow, arrived at the Country and Western D.J. Convention in Nashville. As country star Minnie Pearl put it, "They had him on display." Mercury had offered Elvis $10,000, Columbia bid $15,000, while Atlantic put down $25,000 with the kitchen sink thrown in. But Elvis was now in RCA's pocket and, when this convention ended, deejays from the North knew of the South's best-kept musical secret.

On January 10, 1956, just two days after his twenty-first birthday, Elvis went into RCA's Nashville studio on McGavock Street to cut his first side for his new label. The first number put on tape was "I Got a Woman," followed by a song Elvis had discovered while touring the South, "Heartbreak Hotel." His voice had become more assured and much deeper since his last Sun recordings. Scotty Moore and Bill Black were joined by drummer D. J. Fontana, pianist Floyd Cramer, and guitarist Chet Atkins. "Elvis had on a pair of pink britches," Chet recalls, "and when he was singing 'Heartbreak Hotel' he split 'em right down the back. He had to take them off and put on another pair. I threw the old ones outside the studio. One of the girls who worked there at the studio asked who they belonged to. I told her Elvis and said, 'Pick 'em up and keep 'em, they'll be worth a fortune soon.'" The following day Elvis recorded "I'm Counting on You" and "I Was the One." The Jordanaires sang backup for Elvis—this was their first session together.

Before going any further, I think it would be interesting to note how Colonel Parker's mind was already a finely tuned instrument in 1955. Let's go back a few months to the time when the Colonel's master plan was still in the formative stage. Parker invited the general manager of Edward B.

Marks Music Corporation over to have dinner at his home in Madison, Tennessee. After a most enjoyable evening, the Colonel and his beautiful wife, Marie, asked their guest to spend the night. The next morning the Colonel and the record executive went to the office, located at the rear of the house. Piled next to a phonograph was a stack of records, of which one had a yellow and brown label. The record man had never heard of the Sun label, or of the singer Elvis Presley. Colonel Tom began to play the discs and his guest noted that the voice had negroid qualities. He was surprised to learn that Presley was a white kid from Tupelo, Mississippi. The Colonel informed him that he expected to become Presley's manager, adding, "No one has heard of him north of the Mason-Dixon line, but he's the biggest thing to hit the South in years. I don't know whether city folk in the North are ready for Elvis, but you're such a hot music man, I'm sure you can get him played in the city."

The Colonel's friend returned to New York and went to see Bill Randle, a deejay who did a live show from New York on Saturday night and was on WERE in Cleveland during the week. He felt Elvis would be too much for his New York audience, but agreed to play his records for his Cleveland listeners. Bill Randle was swamped with calls, each one shouting, "He's dynamite." As a result of the attention Randle was giving Elvis' records, the Colonel began getting calls from every New York label. By this time the Colonel had come to New York with a telegram from Elvis' parents giving him the power to negotiate a contract for their son. For years the Colonel, as manager of Eddy Arnold, had worked with RCA. Elvis' recording contract, including the Sun masters, went to RCA. What Bill Randle had done for the Colonel was help raise the ante for a deal he had been trying to negotiate (at a later date it was learned that the Colonel had been unsuccessful in pitching Elvis at RCA for some time).

Colonel Parker landed Elvis a six-time deal on "Stage Show," the Dorsey Brothers TV show presented by Jackie Gleason. CBS began giving Elvis a build-up as Tommy Dorsey's "discovery." Both *Billboard* and *Cash Box* named Elvis "most promising new singer in the country and western field for the year." On January 28, 1956, Elvis made his debut on national television. The show also featured Tommy and Jimmy Dorsey, George "Bullets" Durgom, and Jaye P. Morgan. The William Morris Agency had arranged the deal for Elvis and he would receive $1,250 for each of his six appearances. He sang "Blue Suede Shoes" and introduced "Heartbreak Hotel" (the Dorsey orchestra providing him with backing). Elvis' first network appearance caused quite a sensation. CBS was flooded with phone calls and letters. Dorothy Kilgallen's column carried an item on Dorsey's "discovery." Jackie Gleason said, "The kid has no right behaving like a sex maniac on a national show." There was even talk of canceling his remaining appearances. However, he made his second appearance on February 4, 1956. On this show he sang a wild version of "Tutti Frutti" and introduced what would be the flip side of "Heartbreak Hotel," a sensuous ballad entitled "I Was the One." The doorman at CBS-TV in New York was quoted as saying, "I have never seen anything like it."

Elvis with Jimmy and Tommy Dorsey.

This photo was taken only moments before Elvis
was to make his first network TV appearance.

It was during this period that Elvis' popularity shifted significantly. Elvis was no longer a country star, he was a rhythm and blues *and* a pop star. RCA reported that its new celebrity's single "I Was the One"/"Heartbreak Hotel" was selling faster than any record in the company's history. Strangely, it was "I was the One" that became number one overnight on the Memphis radio stations. It was much later that "Heartbreak Hotel" would take over the number one rating in Memphis.

Elvis made four more appearances on the Dorsey Brothers show. On February 11, 1956, he sang "Shake, Rattle and Roll" (he ended it with a verse of "Flip, Flop and Fly") and "I Got a Woman." He made his fourth, fifth, and sixth appearances on February 18, March 17, and March 24, 1956. On the fourth show he sang the Sun recording "Baby, Let's Play House" and "Tutti Frutti," and on the last two shows he performed "Blue Suede Shoes," "Heartbreak Hotel," and "Money Honey." This was recorded by one of the New York papers regarding the Dorsey show appearance: "Presley puts intensity into his songs. Overemotional? Yes, but he projects. He sells!!" Elvis had definitely arrived. "Heartbreak Hotel" continued to sell like wildfire, and so did everything else Elvis recorded. His first album was released and went directly to the top of *Billboard*'s charts. The album contained a collection of unissued Sun tracks, as well as some newer material. In the space of one month it sold more than 362,000 copies, breaking all of RCA's previous sales records; to be exact, it was three times the total of RCA's previous top sellers (one thing is certain: if Richard Rodgers never got to hear Elvis' bizarre version of "Blue Moon," Bob Dylan certainly did. Dylan sang it on one of his own records.)

From the beginning of his national exposure on TV, Elvis became controversial. His personal appearances did very little to change this image; in fact, they added to it. Two turnaway audiences of over 5,000 people paid $15,000 to hear him sing eight songs in the San Diego Arena. The arena manager had to call out the police and a platoon of shore patrol to handle the mob who pursued Elvis to his dressing room. In El Paso he was mauled pretty badly. They had already started trying to get at him, and he considered himself lucky to keep the shirt on his back. "One girl took a swipe at me and really clawed my side," he said; "it stung pretty bad for a while." A reporter reviewing his show in San Antonio, Texas, wrote: "He's fascinating!—like a snake."

Parents from all over the country shared a common bond—their disapproval of the "Presley menace." One fourteen-year-old girl from Long Island told reporters, "They locked up my Elvis records and my father broke my record player." The most amusing story about the effect Elvis was having on his fans was found in *Confidential* (a popular scandal magazine in the fifties). Writer Lou Anderson told how teen-age girls were getting Elvis to autograph their breasts. They said he would sign Elvis on the right one, and Presley on the left. "You've never read it in your local gazettes," Anderson wrote, "but reporters in the know can tell you there are any number of chicks who've sported Presley's print on their superstructure. They can't

A sensuous study of the face that was melting female hearts everywhere.

A gold record for "Heartbreak Hotel." This would be the first of 117 gold discs he was awarded.

By the time he made his sixth and final appearance on the Dorsey Brothers show, the legend that is Elvis Presley had been formed.

cash themselves in like a check, but it's fun while it lasts. It's nice pen-pushing if you can get it, and how this wacky stunt got started is anyone's guess. As you might imagine, no one seems to enjoy this unofficial custom more than Elvis!"

Every day the newspapers would report another "serious" romance involving the young man from Tennessee and:

JUDY SPRECKELS: The former Judy Powell, who was the sixth wife of Adolf Spreckels, ordinarily referred to by the newspaper reporters as "the sugar king."

JUNE JUANICO: Who met Elvis when he made a personal appearance in her home town of Biloxi.

NATALIE WOOD: The beautiful movie star, who flew to Memphis to meet his parents.

BARBARA HEARN: The girl back home; the fan magazines gave her the inside track to Elvis' heart.

Milton Berle had been the king of television to millions of viewers in the fifties, but in 1956 his ratings began to slip. In an attempt to cash in on the daily publicity Elvis was receiving, he signed Elvis to appear on his show, which aired on Tuesday nights. On April 3, 1956, live from the flight deck of the U.S.S. *Hancock,* Elvis appeared along with Esther Williams, Harry James, Buddy Rich, and Arnold Stang. The Berle show came on at 8:00 P.M. and was broadcast in color. Elvis' performance on the "Uncle Milty" show was perhaps the wildest TV performance he ever gave. The critics shouted cries of "Lewd" and "Obscene." Forty million people watched the show and, love it or loathe it, I'm sure they never forgot it.

The Colonel booked Elvis into the New Frontier Hotel in Las Vegas for a two-week stand beginning on April 23. It was here that Elvis suffered his first and last failure as a professional entertainer. The newspapers reported: "Elvis Presley wound up his first nightclub date, a two-week stand at the New Frontier Hotel. Elvis was somewhat like a jug of corn liquor at a champagne party. He hollered songs like 'Blue Suede Shoes' and 'Tutti Frutti' and his bodily movements were embarrassingly direct. Most of the high rollers breathed a sigh of relief when his set ended." Elvis recalled, "An audience like this doesn't show their appreciation. They're eating when I come on. I wasn't a flop—they don't keep a flop for two weeks." While performing in Vegas, Elvis was visited by the famed Hollywood producer Hal Wallis. The Colonel and Wallis arranged a visit to Hollywood for Elvis for a screen test. Later in the month of April, Elvis and seasoned actor Frank Faylen performed a scene from *The Rainmaker.* The response to the screen test was overwhelming: he signed a three-picture deal with Hal Wallis and 20th Century-Fox.

Elvis made his second appearance on "The Milton Berle Show" on June 5, 1956, along with Arnold Stang, Irish McCalla ("Sheena, Queen of the Jungle"), and Debra Paget, the beautiful young lady who would costar with him in his first film. Elvis offered a rousing new song, heard for the first

This photo was taken moments before Elvis was to appear on "The Milton Berle Show." Many still feel that Elvis' two appearances on the show were the wildest performances he ever gave on TV.

Elvis and Gladys in front of their home on Audubon Drive.

Elvis with Uncle Milty. The show was seen by 40 million people—one out of every four people in the United States at that time.

Elvis' first Vegas appearance,
at the New Frontier Hotel.

Relaxing in Vegas.

time: "Hound Dog." While performing the now-classic rocker, he pulled out all stops. The morning papers read: "Is He a Fad? Or the Beginning of a Long Line of Entertainers? Is He a Good Influence? Or Bad? Is He Dangerous?" The headline in the New York *Times* looked like this on June 6, 1956: "T.V.: New Phenomenon!" Jack Gould wrote in his review: "Elvis Presley is currently the entertainment world's most astonishing figure. The young man with the sideburns and mobile hips is the rage of the squealing teenagers and his records are a top item in the never-never land of juke box operators and disc jockeys. By any reasonable standards of success, he is big business."

In the entire history of show business, no entertainer has had such a meteoric rise and such sudden, frantic, widespread adulation and vicious condemnation as Elvis. Elvis' private life was just as hectic. Once he pulled into a gas station and got into a fight with two of the attendants. The fisticuffs flared when Ed Hopper, the manager, became irate because a crowd drawn by Elvis and his $10,000 car was blocking the pumps and so delaying business. Hopper slapped Elvis on the back of the head and told him to move

Elvis and Natalie Wood.

Elvis signing his first Hollywood
contract (Hal Wallis on the right)

on. Elvis jumped out of the car and crossed a right that set Hopper on his
heels. Another attendant, Aubrey Brown, a six-foot-four 220-pounder,
moved in and also drew a right from Presley. Elvis appeared in Memphis
City Court along with the two service station men who had been outfought.
Presley was cleared, but his two opponents were fined on assault and battery
charges.

In Chicago, at the International Amphitheater, thirteen thousand came to
see Elvis, who proudly wore a suit of gold lamé. This was the first time his
legendary suit of gold had been seen.

Today Pat Boone sells milk and preaches religion, but in 1956 he was
Elvis' biggest rival. The clean-cut youth had a long string of hits, including
"April Love," "Love Letters in the Sand," and a cover version of Fats
Domino's "Ain't That a Shame." The adults created him as an alternative to
the long-haired hood, but in reality he and Elvis were close friends.

Elvis appeared in tails on "The Steve Allen Show," on July 1, 1956,
standing perfectly still as he sang "I Want You, I Need You, I Love You."
He was involved in a comedy skit with Imogene Coca, Allen, and Andy

LEFT TO RIGHT: Glen Derringer, Steve Allen, Imogene Coca, Elvis.

Elvis and his good friend the late actor Nick Adams.

Griffith, and he sang a few lines about Tonto candy bars. He also sang "Hound Dog" to a basset hound. It was Steve Allen's idea to have Elvis dress in formal attire and to tone him down. Just after the show went off the air, Dewey Phillips' telephone rang.

"Hello, you bastard," Dewey said.

"How'd you know it was me?" asked Elvis.

"You'd better call home and get straight, boy. What were you doing in that monkey suit?"

He returned home and bought Vernon and Gladys a beautiful green and white ranch home surrounded by trees. While Elvis was resting in Memphis, the "Great Elvis Presley Industry" was grossing between $19 million and $24 million. Colonel Parker hired Hank Saperstein to handle all of the mar-

"I Want You,
I Need You,
I Love You."

Elvis waiting to appear on "The Steve Allen
Show."

keting and exploitation for the 188 Elvis gadgets being manufactured by
Elvis Presley Enterprises. Saperstein had promoted products endorsed by
the "Lassie," "Wyatt Earp," "Ding Dong School," and "The Lone Ranger"
shows. He was also the merchandising genius for the Kellogg people. He
says, "The Presley thing makes them all look pale; it's the most successful
operation I've ever been a part of." The demand for Elvis products is still so
great that the manufacturers are not able to keep up with the demand for
them. Promoters with new ideas line up to present them to Saperstein. The
marketers granted licenses to make Presley items are very limited: they have
so much work that they have to farm out their contracts to subcontractors.
Elvis' estate, the Colonel, and Saperstein collect a royalty of 4 to 11 per cent
of the manufacturer's sale price. Some items that have been carried with the

31

Elvis Presley name are T-shirts, black jeans, sneakers, caps, charm bracelets, Elvis pictures that shine at night, pens and pencils, compacts, leather jackets, perfumes, shirts, stuffed animals, watches, candy, bubble gum cards, glasses, Elvis busts, and Hound Dog Orange lipstick, as well as anything you could imagine.

While the Presleys were happy at their new residence on Audubon Drive, they would soon fall victim to Elvis' tremendous popularity. The fans were causing huge traffic jams, and the Presleys' new neighbors were complaining bitterly about the situation. Elvis began to look around for a more secluded property, and in early 1957, ten days after Graceland was offered to him, he signed the check for $100,000 that made it his. Graceland was constructed some thirty-five years ago, and the beautiful thirteen-and-three-quarter-acre estate was legendary throughout the South. The two-story stone house is a classic example of southern architecture. Upon entering through the famed sculptured gates, you found yourself traveling along a three-quarter-mile curved driveway bordered by well-tended lawns that swept by majestically. The house was surrounded by perfectly manicured trees. In the evening, pale blue lights illuminated the driveway and reflected off the house's exterior. The carport, located in the rear of Graceland, housed Elvis' many cars, motorcycles, and three-wheeled go-carts. A short distance from the house were an office building and a kennel for his many pets. The flagstone patio featured a giant television, guitars, drums, and furniture. From the patio you descended the flagstone steps to the first level of the terrace, where you found a fireplace and kidney-shaped swimming pool. At either side of the terrace were tall white pillars. The entire area was housed in pink and yellow fiberglass, and in the evening the lights gave off a rainbow glow that was an unbelievable visual experience.

The lower level of the house was completely covered in a thick white carpet. The den and game room could be found here. The walls were of softly burnished oak, almost every inch covered with the awards of a fantastic career. The main floor consisted of a music room (in this room were over 25,000 record albums, part of Elvis' fabulous collection), living and dining rooms, and the kitchen and the maids' quarters. Vernon and Gladys' rooms were on the second floor, but in later years all of the rooms had been converted for Elvis' use. Elvis had a bedroom—sitting room, bathroom, and dressing room equipped with a barber salon. A private conference room was designed by Elvis and contained a large oval oak table.

Elvis may have come from humble beginnings, but at his peak the King lived in a palace.

Ed Sullivan was quoted as saying he would never put Presley on his show. I imagine he changed his mind on the day following Elvis' appearance on "The Steve Allen Show." When old smiley looked at the morning papers, he found that Elvis' presence had helped Allen crush him in the ratings war.

In 1955, when Bob Neal was still managing Elvis, he had had him fly to New York—it was Elvis' first time on an airplane—to audition for "Arthur Godfrey's Talent Scouts," the most important new-talent showcase on televi-

The famous Ed Sullivan Press Conference. Mr. Sullivan is standing to Elvis'
right. The man on the right wearing the Elvis shirt is Colonel Tom Parker,
Elvis' legendary manager. Right behind Parker is Nick Adams.

"Hound Dog."

sion. Godfrey, then one of CBS's big shots, proved his vast ability to judge new talent when he rejected Elvis. He nearly broke the kid's heart. It's ironic, though, that Sullivan, with CBS backing, offered Elvis $50,000 for just three appearances on his Sunday night show. On September 9, 1955, Elvis appeared on "The Ed Sullivan Show." Ed's ratings for the evening were a record 82.6 per cent of the TV viewing public, and there were over 25,000 requests for seats for this show. The King sang "Don't Be Cruel" and "Ready Teddy," plus a few lines of "Hound Dog." He was shown on the home screen from the waist up. The only way viewers could tell when (or what) he was moving was to listen to the screams of the girls in the studio audience.

Elvis' portion of the show was broadcast from Hollywood. Charles Laughton, the guest host, referred to the film Elvis was making by its original title, *The Reno Brothers*. This was his first film, released as *Love Me Tender*.

Jack Gould of the New York *Times* wrote: "When Presley injected movements of the tongue and indulged in wordless singing, that was singularly distasteful on the Sullivan show; enough was enough. When Presley executes his bumps and grinds, it must be remembered by the Columbia Broadcasting System that even the twelve-year-old's curiosity may be overstimulated." Gould closed his review with: "In the long run perhaps Presley will do everyone a favor by pointing up the need for early sex education so that neither his successors nor TV can capitalize on the idea that his type of routine is somehow highly tempting, yet forbidden fruit."

On the October 28, 1956, "Ed Sullivan Show" Elvis introduced the title song from his film *Love Me Tender,* adding a verse that is not on the RCA recording. He announced that the film would be in the theaters by Thanksgiving. He also sang "Love Me" and "Don't Be Cruel" and closed the second show with these words: "Ladies and gentlemen, I'd like to do a sad song for you; it has very beautiful lyrics." Then he proceeded to perform the best version of "Hound Dog" he ever did on TV.

Elvis' final Sullivan appearance took place on January 6, 1957. On this show he sang a gospel tune, "Peace in the Valley," for the first time. Elvis told the audience that he'd received 282 teddy bears that Christmas. He also stated that he wished he could buy every one of his fans a brand new Lincoln. Elvis then sang "Hound Dog," "Too Much," "Paralyzed," and "When My Blue Moon Turns to Gold Again." Ed thanked Elvis and said that it was a pleasure to have had him on the show.

While making his first film, Elvis was interviewed by Patricia Vernon of the New York *Herald Tribune*. Her chronicle said in part:

I walked into his dressing room. "Hi!" he said. His hand grasped mine in a firm grip. Then he went back to his couch, where he had been reading a story about himself in a magazine with his picture on the cover. I ask him about it. "You know, stories like this make me madder than anything," he said; "Ah don't think this guy who wrote it ever saw me. Why, there was this woman the other day—she said I danced vulgar. She'd never talked to me, and I bet she never saw me sing, she had

Elvis in rehearsal for
"The Ed Sullivan Show."

The cameras showed Elvis
from the waist up on
"The Ed Sullivan Show."
Here's what you missed
on your TV.

"Why Me, Lord?"

Elvis, Gladys, and Vernon.

no right to print those lies about me. I don't do anything vulgar. My mom wouldn't want me to. Writers ask my opinion on things like Suez. I don't like that. Sure, I'd like to be able to keep up, but I've been moving fast these past two years, mighty fast, and I don't have time to do what I want, not counting what I should!" Elvis had worked himself up to quite a pitch. I mentioned that he got good money for it, whatever it was he did. "I don't care about the money," he said, "I can't earn much more this year anyhow. This is my first picture, and it's got to be good." A press agent came by to tell me I had enough time with Elvis. I started to leave, and Elvis, who was still sprawled on the couch, darted out his hand and caught my foot. "Maybe she's shy, maybe she'd like to be alone with me," he said. The press agent shrugged and left. I asked Elvis to take his hand off my foot. "Okay," he said looking up under heavy lids, "Ah'm just spoofin' you." I asked Elvis how he felt about girls who throw themselves at him. Again, the heavy-lidded look. "I usually take them," he said, watching my face for the shock value of his words. He grinned, "Hell, you know I'm kind of having fun with you because you're smart." I asked Elvis why he thought he was a success now. "Because God let me come along at this time," he said. He started nibbling on his fingernails and I asked why he did that. "I'm so nervous," he said, "I've always been nervous, ever since I was a little kid." I asked Elvis if he thought he was a sex symbol to kids, as some psychiatrists say. "Someone should put those psychos on a long couch and tell them a thing or two," he said. "They all think I'm a sex maniac. They're really just frustrated old types anyway. I'm just natural." He gave me the heavy-lidded look again, "You don't love me," he said,

Four rare never-before-seen photos of Elvis ripping them up at the University of Dayton, Ohio, at the Fieldhouse, 1956.

"Love Me."

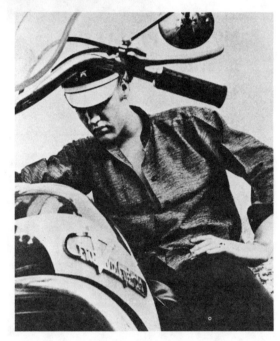

The wild one!

accusingly. I told him I didn't love anyone on such short notice. "I bet you'd like me if I tried," he said, "I'm just teasin' now, but I'd be sweet and you'd like me because I was sweet, wouldn't you?" He was teasing, but underneath I sensed the desire of a small boy seeking approval. Then he went to meet two young fans who wanted their picture taken with him. He told me to stay where I was, that he'd be right back. I ran for my life!

The King of Hearts.

Elvis did another interview, for *TV Guide*. This interview was put on wax and RCA titled the disc *TV Guide Presents Elvis Presley*. The custom-made record was shipped to five hundred radio stations across the country. Deejays also received a two-page printed sheet that contained the questions that made up the open-end interview. The radio stations were instructed that the disc was to be used between September 6 and September 14, 1956, and was to be returned to RCA immediately. One of the questions Elvis answered on the disc was what Elvis thought about the nickname he'd been given. He answered, "I don't like to be called Elvis the Pelvis, but, uh . . . I mean, it's one of the most childish expressions I ever heard coming from an adult." The *TV Guide Presents Elvis Presley* 45 rpm record is one of the most valuable pieces of vinyl in recording history. Collectors literally get in line to purchase this rarity at the price of $5,000. Extraordinary, yes!—but a bargain to many if they could find it.

In my first book, *Elvis in Hollywood,* I gave a detailed accounting of all thirty-three of Elvis' films, so I will go into a minimum of detail concerning this aspect of his career.

Love Me Tender opened at New York's Paramount Theater, and there was a tremendous mass of people on hand for the premiere. The demand for this film was so great that 20th Century-Fox had more prints shipped and made of *Love Me Tender* than any other film in the studio's history. Once again, the nation's reporters tore into Elvis and had nothing but derogatory things to say about his performance. I will not dwell on this but instead offer an opinion of my own. In this, his first film, Elvis more than held his own. His handsome face showed the full spectrum of emotions and, much like his singing, his acting was totally Elvis. As such, his debut was a unique experience.

The title song from the film became his sixth million-seller and the flip side, "Any Way You Want Me," his seventh. Before reporting to Paramount to begin work on his second film, *Loving You,* Elvis gave a concert at the huge outdoor Cotton Bowl stadium in Dallas, Texas. The Colonel was seen at the main gate selling autographed pictures. His high regard for money had even led to charging writers, disc jockeys, and local dignitaries for the privilege of viewing Elvis in concert. This policy caused Elvis a great deal of embarrassment in later years. Disc jockeys were reluctant to play his latest release because of the animosity they felt toward the entire Presley organization; furthermore, reporters who were accustomed to the professional courtesy extended to them by the entire industry took out their grievances toward Colonel Parker's unprofessional and selfish business policies on Elvis. I believe this to be the reason you could usually count on reading an unflattering review on the morning following Elvis' concert in your town.

Elvis' second film, *Loving You,* was in color and showed Elvis with black hair for the first time. The film caught Elvis' early stage act better than any that came before or after. Elvis had Vernon and Gladys flown to Hollywood for a bit part in the film. If you look closely as Elvis sings the film's finale, "Got a Lot o' Livin' to Do," you can spot his parents sitting in the third row, on the left-hand side of the screen.

Elvis was starting to live the life of an immensely rich, hugely popular, and attractive young star. He was staying at a Hollywood hotel along with an entourage of six Memphis buddies, three musicians, three personal assistants, and five secretaries. His third film, MGM's *Jailhouse Rock,* came in at number three in the top-grossing films of 1957. His performance in this brought an eerie remembrance of the late James Dean to mind. The standout scene, and probably the best musical production number in his career, was the title number, "Jailhouse Rock."

I once asked Elvis what film of his had given him the most gratification. He answered, "Paul, without question, *King Creole* is the one I'm most proud of." The facts surrounding how Elvis came to get the role of Danny Fisher in Paramount's *King Creole* are most interesting. Hal Wallis, the man responsible for bringing Elvis to the big screen, went to see famed director Michael Curtiz. Curtiz had been the mastermind of a number of Hollywood's classic films, including *Casablanca.* Wallis asked Curtiz if he would consider directing Elvis. The answer was no. He said he was used to working with stars who possessed a certain dignity and that he didn't think Elvis Presley and dignity were exactly roommates.

Hal was not to be discouraged, so he asked Mike at least to look at the script he had in mind. The film was to be based on Harold Robbins' *A Stone for Danny Fisher.* It had been bought for James Dean and shelved when the young star met his tragic death. Wallis continued, "You can give Presley the thing he wants most." "What's that?" asked an unsmiling Curtiz. Wallis replied, "What the boy wants more than anything else in the world—the re-

Three views of Elvis'
performance in Florida on
August 3, 1956. The police
stopped the show.

By the time this photo was taken, Presleymania was at an all-time high. Elvis' films were breaking box office records, and his discs topped all the nation's charts. Colonel Parker had more than one hundred different Elvis items on the market. All of these items were marked Elvis Presley Enterprises and are worth a fortune to collectors today.

Both these shots were taken on the set of *Loving You*. Notice the striking resemblance between mother and son.

Elvis in his suit of gold.

Two views of Elvis' mansion, Graceland.

Elvis' final personal appearance before entering the U. S. Army.

spect of older people." Mike told Wallis he would do the film if he had Elvis' complete co-operation. When he met Elvis, he told him to cut his hair and to lose seven or eight pounds. He expected a blow-up, but none came. Curtiz told the kid that his God-given personality fit the part, and to play the role naturally. He also told Elvis that although he would sing in the film, it would be done with very little movement. Curtiz waited for another temper tantrum, but Elvis said, "You're the boss, Mr. Curtiz."

Mike found that his young star was a warm, humble, and good human being. He drove Elvis hard, and his ability to act became very apparent. When *King Creole* was completed, Mike Curtiz was proud of the dignified performance turned in by Elvis.

King Creole would be Elvis' last film for a little more than two years. He had given his fans and his critics something to remember him by while he served his country. He left the critics shouting "Oscar!"—and to his fans Elvis had given a performance that he would never duplicate.

45

Pvt. US 53310761

In the early months of 1953, shortly after his eighteenth birthday, a Memphis boy registered for the draft. It was a routine, insignificant event that no one remembered much about. Within five years, Elvis Presley's views on the Army were front-page news. The year 1958 marked an end and a beginning. In 1958 the boy Elvis became a man. Just because he was the most publicized celebrity of our day, Elvis did not expect special treatment from the Army. When he received his greetings from Uncle Sam, he said, "I'm kind of proud. It's a duty I've got to fill, and I'm going to do it." The Colonel was more upset with the thought of Elvis' salary dropping from the hundreds of thousands a year to $78.00 a month.

Paramount and Elvis both wrote letters to his draft board in Memphis asking them to delay his induction until the studio finished the filming of *King Creole*. Elvis' departure in January would have meant a loss of $300,000 already spent in preparing the film. The deferment was granted until March, at which time he would be enrolled as a private.

His good nature helped him learn to put up with a lot of jealous hecklers, but the gibes from the G.I.s did prove to be hard to swallow. Taunts about his singing style, his wealth, his fame, his teddy bears, rolled off his back. He kept his temper. He ignored them and got his work done. Men who came to sneer remained to admire. It cost the United States $500,000 a year in lost income taxes to make Elvis Pvt. US 53310761. When he arrived at Fort Chaffee, Arkansas, he visited the barber, where his sideburns were removed. He was then given seven dollars to tide him over until payday.

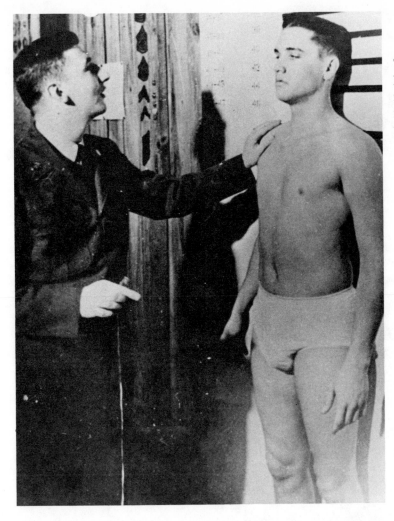

This is one of the rarest Elvis photos ever. The nation's teen-agers were in an uproar when Elvis was inducted.

Elvis' mother and father had been staying with him (near Fort Hood, Texas, where he had been transferred), and for several days Mrs. Presley hadn't been feeling well. Vernon and Elvis thought that she should go back home to Memphis to be with her own doctor. The Memphis doctors said that she was suffering from acute hepatitis, and they had her admitted to the Methodist Hospital, insisting that there wasn't any need to send for Elvis. Two days later, they changed their minds and called Fort Hood, requesting that Elvis be given an emergency furlough. They told Gladys that Elvis was on his way to be with her, and in the midst of her great suffering she remained the protective mother: "I don't like him to take planes." Elvis arrived at the hospital at 7:00 P.M. Tuesday, August 12. Four specialists had been called in to assist the Presley family doctor. No one was able to determine the cause of the infection.

On Wednesday, August 13, Gladys seemed a little better and Elvis went home at 9 P.M. to get some sleep. Vernon had a cot put in the hospital room and he stayed with his wife. Vernon woke up at about three in the morning. His wife was struggling for breath. "I got to her as quick as I could and raised her head. I called a nurse and told her to get a doctor. They put her

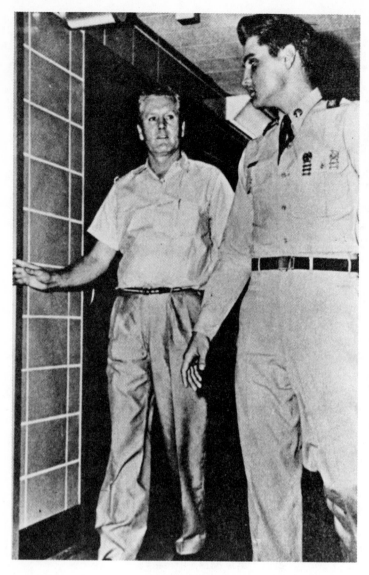

Vernon and Elvis
stricken with grief as
they enter Gladys'
hospital room. She
would pass away before
daybreak.

in an oxygen tent—but it was too late." Gladys Presley had suffered a heart attack. She died at the age of forty-two.

The next day her body was moved to the music room at Graceland. Friends stopped by to offer sympathy and pay their respects. Elvis wanted to have the funeral at home with the estate open to all who wanted to come. "Mama loved my fans. I want them to have a last look at her." Colonel Parker's counsel had been negative to this idea, and Elvis decided to take his advice. Mrs. Presley's body was moved from Graceland to the National Funeral Home.

Telegrams of condolence poured in. Marlon Brando wired; so did Ricky Nelson, the governor of Tennessee, Ernie Ford, Dolores Hart, and Cecil B. DeMille; Nick Adams flew in to be with his friend at this sorrowful time. Flowers crowded the church, the house, and the funeral parlor. Outside the funeral parlor on that Friday afternoon, some three thousand people stood, grieving for Elvis, who mourned the mother whom he adored. In the family

"Soldier boy."

Rock legend Bill Haley visits with Elvis while touring Germany.

room, screened from the eyes of the crowd, Elvis and his family listened as the Blackwood Brothers (J. D. Sumner was a member of the group) sang Gladys Presley's favorite song, "Precious Memories," and her favorite hymn, "Rock of Ages." Numb with crying, Elvis sat beside his father. He was dressed in a black suit, black shoes, black tie, and white shirt.

Along the ten-mile drive to Forest Hill Cemetery, the streets were lined with spectators. The curious crowded the grave site. Five hundred policemen kept the crowds at a distance. An honor guard stood by the grave as Elvis and Vernon said their good-bys. Flowers were piled everywhere, but their beauty could not hide the fresh wound in the earth. "Good-by, darling, good-by," whispered the boy to his mother, "I love you, I love you so much." No human ear could have made out the broken words, but one would like to believe that somewhere Gladys Presley heard them. They would have meant more than mansions and minks to this gentle woman who asked for nothing and was rewarded with the gift of her son's heart.

Thus, in 1958, Gladys Smith Presley was prematurely taken from her loving son and husband. It left a wound in Elvis' heart that would never heal.

After basic training, the G.I.s were assigned their tours of duty. Private Presley, his hair bleached by a summer in the Texas sun, stood on the top deck of the Europe-bound troopship *General Randal* and posed for photographs. Directly below, an army band played a medley of Elvis' hits. The pier was filled with three hundred newsmen. Elvis held a forty-five-minute press conference (RCA EP *Elvis Sails*). Elvis said that he was looking forward to meeting Brigitte Bardot when he got to Paris. When word reached Elvis that the Sex Kitten wasn't going to be courted by any Hound Dog, he quickly bowed out.

On October 1, 1958, Elvis arrived in Germany, and fifteen hundred fans were waiting for him. The press reported that he was shopping for a castle. Elvis said he needed a big place to house his friends, his father, his workers, and his grandmother. He didn't find a castle; instead, he settled for a three-story house on Goethestrasse in Bad Nauheim.

49

Elvis on leave in a Paris night club. After the club
closed, Elvis sang "Willow, Weep for Me."

While in Germany, Elvis met a pretty, petite teen-ager. She was an armed
forces brat, the daughter of an air force captain, Priscilla Beaulieu. In 1958,
no one could imagine the boy from Mississippi and the girl from New Jersey
would one day become man and wife.

Meanwhile, back in the U.S.A., the Colonel made sure that Elvis' name
was appearing almost daily in newspapers across the country. Although
Elvis made no appearances and recorded no new material, he remained a
highly commercial property. The Colonel told reporters that Elvis had made
over $2 million in 1958, and that in 1959 he would earn even more.

Elvis left a limited amount of material that RCA had to release very spar-
ingly. In 1959 it released the *Elvis Sails* extended play and two soundtrack
EPs from *King Creole*. The *Creole* EPs remained best sellers for a period of
over eighteen months. In February *Billboard* noted that Elvis didn't have a
solitary single in the top 100, the first time in three years that he was absent
from the nation's charts. In March a new single titled "A Fool Such as I"/"I
Need Your Love Tonight" was released. It quickly became Elvis' nineteenth
consecutive million-seller. In June, RCA released the last song Elvis had
recorded before leaving for his army stint. "A Big Hunk o' Love" sold over
one million copies and reached the number one position.

Elvis was really dedicated to his new way of life. When pressed for a
statement, he replied that he wished to prove himself a good soldier and
"stay out of crap games because I have to set a good example for my fans."
Elvis spent his days reading maps, scouting, and patrolling. Wherever his
platoon sergeant went, Elvis drove him. The sergeant spoke highly of his
chauffeur. "He's a good driver. He's had lots of practice. He's had lots of
cars."

In September RCA released the album *A Date with Elvis*. The title referred to the date Elvis would become a civilian. There were several extras
and souvenir bonuses accompanying this package, including a fold-out 1960

calendar, which, when opened, showed Elvis' discharge date, circled in black.

Elvis continued his army routine in Germany. He would shine his boots and entertain his army buddies by singing songs such as "Danny Boy" and "I'll Take You Home Again, Kathleen" (both of these songs appeared on LPs in the mid-seventies). While in the service, he never took the easy way out. He showed exceptionally good sense for a kid worth millions. He had survived the shock of stepping from a world of absolute fantasy into the olive-drab routine of army life. He had become a number. He had neatly deposited his colossal personality in a foot locker for nearly two years. His army record won Elvis Presley a badge of respectability that he had been unable to buy as a civilian millionaire. The Army helped make him an institution. By behaving like any other soldier, he showed the world the importance of being Elvis.

Elvis in his custom-made army dress uniform.

Elvis arriving for the taping
of the Frank Sinatra
TV special.

Elvis Is Back

The day on which Elvis would return to the United States was near. On the day before his departure from Europe he and the Army staged a giant press conference. He arrived wearing a custom-made uniform, with stripes and gold braids. On the next day, Elvis and Priscilla went to the airport. After kissing her good-by, he boarded the plane.

One reporter called Elvis' discharge the most publicized return of a soldier since General MacArthur's. His plane landed in the midst of a raging snowstorm at Fort Dix, New Jersey. In spite of the nasty weather, there were two thousand fans, TV crews, newsmen, and photographers waiting to greet him. He smiled and waved to the crowd. Nancy Sinatra was on hand to give him a gift from her famous dad. There was a flag-bedecked press conference. During the interview a woman reporter told Elvis that he was the sexiest man that she had ever seen. While all this went on, Colonel Parker stood close by, chewing on the butt of his cigar. A few days later, March 5 to be exact, Elvis was once again a civilian. Amid cheers and cries of "Go get 'em, Elvis," he left Fort Dix.

Elvis and Nancy Sinatra at his discharge at Fort Dix, New Jersey.

The private railroad car that was occupied by Elvis, the Colonel, Tom Diskin, Parker's right-hand man, and others who had accompanied him to Germany arrived in Memphis. The King was wearing his custom uniform, complete with white gloves. He was given a police escort as his car sped along the highway leading to Graceland. He took a deep breath as he slowly entered his silent, waiting home, where he had shared so many happy moments with his mother. He knew the minute he entered the house that Gladys would never really be gone, not as long as his heart was beating.

On March 26 the Grand Ballroom of the Fontainebleau Hotel in Miami Beach, Florida, played host to the taping of the Frank Sinatra television show "Welcome Home, Elvis." Seating for the show was strictly by invitation. Some seven hundred lucky persons clutched their precious tickets as if they were gold. Sixteen off-duty policemen plus twenty-six uniformed officers tried to control the unticketed masses.

On May 12 the ABC network televised the show. It began with the entire cast singing "You'd Be So Nice to Come Home To," only the lyrics had been changed ("It's Nice to Go Traveling") to fit the "Welcome Home, Elvis" theme. Elvis, in his full dress uniform, sang, "It was nice to go traveling, but oh, so nice to come home." He then left the stage while his costars (Sinatra; Frank's daughter Nancy; Sammy Davis, Jr.; Joey Bishop; and Peter Lawford, to the accompaniment of Nelson Riddle and his orchestra) sang and danced in an attempt to show Elvis the musical happenings of the past two years.

After nearly forty minutes, Elvis turned to the musicians, raised his hand, and went into his latest RCA release, "Fame and Fortune." As the song ended, he pointed his finger in the direction of the Jordanaires; and with a nod and the ever-famous smile, they went into "Stuck on You." The heat was on! This was it, the minute everyone was waiting for. He quivered, shook, and shimmied. His hair fell across his eyes. He was all of the things they hoped for—pure Elvis. He was theirs once again. Elvis then sang a

Frank Sinatra and Elvis
sing a duet on Frank's
"Welcome Home,
Elvis'" special.

"Stuck on You."

duet with Sinatra. Frank toyed with "Love Me Tender," while Elvis sang a little bit of "Witchcraft."

Presley was on nationwide television for six minutes, and he was paid $125,000 for the chore. In regard to this appearance on the Sinatra special, the critics wrote, "Although Elvis was a good soldier, he's still a lousy singer."

Following the TV special, Elvis went to Nashville to record *Elvis Is Back!* Today it still ranks as one of his finest LPs, consisting of solid down-to-roots blues. Phil Spector, who went on to become a legend in the rock music field, was one of the producers. Elvis then reported to Paramount to begin work on the fifth motion picture of his career, *G.I. Blues*. The film contained eleven songs and was greeted by long lines at the box office.

54

This photo is from Elvis' personal photo album and shows him at home.

Colonel Parker told the world that Elvis' TV price was now $150,000. He said, "I don't want Elvis competing with his own movies." Elvis would not appear on TV again until 1968.

It was announced that on July 3, 1960, Vernon Presley would marry Dee Elliott. This news didn't exactly thrill Elvis. His relationship with his stepmother would grow warmer in the coming years, but in 1960 he chose not to attend the wedding ceremony. Dee had begun dating Vernon while Elvis was in Germany. She was stationed there along with her army sergeant husband and their three sons, Billy, Ricky, and David.

That same week, RCA released Elvis' second single since his discharge. The *Guinness Book of World Records* credits "It's Now or Never" with sales in excess of twenty million units. Another single released in 1960 would quickly become the nation's best seller; its title is "Are You Lonesome Tonight?" As the year came to an end, Elvis released *His Hand in Mine*. This was a religious LP, giving him a chance to sing his favorite type of music. The album remained on the charts for half a year and became another gold disc for Elvis.

55

Elvis and Vernon.

Elvis in his office at Graceland.

There was a new film at the end of 1960, and two new films in 1961, each released during a holiday season. The Colonel's battle plan was fully formed and it made sense to release Elvis' films while the nation's youths were home from school. The first release of the three was 20th Century-Fox's *Flaming Star,* in which Elvis played a role that was originally written for Marlon Brando. *Flaming Star* was a Western, and although it was a good one, the box office suffered because fans were not prepared to see Elvis in a dramatic role. His next appearance on the silver screen was in the 20th Century-Fox release *Wild in the Country*. Once again, Elvis' acting was praised but the film was slow at the box office.

The rejection of these two films changed the shape of Elvis' acting career for all time. Their failure indicated to the Colonel that the public would accept Elvis only with a guitar in his hand and a song on his lips. If Parker needed any further convincing, it came with the release of Paramount's *Blue Hawaii*. This film was destined to be the most successful movie Elvis would ever appear in. I'm sure that both Annette Funicello and Frankie Avalon are still grateful to *Blue Hawaii,* the father of *Muscle Beach Party, Beach Blanket Bingo,* and the never-ending succession of beach films produced by American International in the mid-sixties. The soundtrack recording from this film has sold over $6 million worth of LPs. Although the film was a financial success, I wish it had never been made. It was the first Presley film to feature too many songs. Elvis sang a song every time you blinked. It seemed to have marked the beginning of a series of films with less plot, less originality—what would quickly become known as the "Elvis Presley film."

In 1961 Elvis would make his last live appearances for almost eight years. While the entire entertainment world was begging for personal appearances at name-your-own prices, Elvis and the Colonel chose to do three charity shows, with the proceeds benefiting the needy. On February 25, after turning down millions of dollars' worth of offers to appear in concert, Elvis performed before nine thousand people during two sold-out performances at the Ellis Auditorium in Memphis. A $100-a-plate luncheon was held in Elvis' honor. There were 225 people attending the luncheon; the Claridge Hotel donated the entire meal so that the proceeds would go to charity. Elvis arrived at 12:45 P.M. (about fifteen minutes late), wearing a black silk and mohair suit. RCA presented him with a plaque for achieving sales in excess of 76,000,000 records! Dick Clark honored him with the "American Bandstand" award for being the top male vocalist. The *Music Reporter* magazine also presented Colonel Parker with the "Showman of the Year" award. Juliet Prowse, Hal Wallis, and Sam Phillips wired their congratulations. The luncheon, which ended at 1:30 P.M., was followed by a press conference. Here are some excerpts:

Q: How's your love life?

A: I'll let you know.

Q: What's your favorite record?

A: "It's Now or Never," sir.

Q: Are you happy?

A: I don't know. —Just nervous.

Q: What was your best movie role?

A: *King Creole*.

Q: Are you going to move to Hollywood?

A: No sir, I'll stay in Memphis.

Q: Are you going to be doing any more TV?

A: I'm too tied up. Too much television hurts movies.

Q: Do you smoke?

A: Cigars . . . rarely. Usually when the Colonel gives me one.

Q: Why did you cut your sideburns?

A: I just outgrew them.

Q: What about the girls in your life, Anita Wood in particular?

A: Anita's just a friend. If I take anyone out a couple of times, the newspapers make a big deal out of it.

Q: Will you be touring soon?

A: Colonel Parker will have to answer that one. Eventually, I'll tour Europe.

Q: Do you keep any pets?

A: I've just added a couple of mules.

Q: How many cars do you own?

A: Two at the moment. I'm going to keep the pink one, the one Mother liked best—a Cadillac. It's the first I've ever owned.

Q: What has been your biggest thrill in show business?

A: Getting my first gold record.

Vernon checking the sight on his new rifle.

After forty-five minutes and loads of questions, the press conference ended. The audience was filled with excitement and great anticipation. While Elvis was extremely nervous at the prospect of facing a live audience again after such a long absence, the butterflies disappeared the minute he stepped on stage. Tall and beautiful in his white jacket, he held the audience spellbound for the entire forty-nine minutes he performed. All in all, he sang twenty songs, including "All Shook Up," "I Got a Woman," "Don't," "Fever," "Reconsider, Baby," and "Love Me." When he sang "One Night"

Elvis and Nipper, two old friends, are reunited for Elvis' 1961 Hawaii charity show.

and came to the line "I ain't never did no wrong," he gave the crowd a wicked grin and shouted, "I ain't never, never, never did no wrong." He closed the set with a torrid version of "Hound Dog." The audience all but drowned him out during his finale. When all was said and done, Elvis had raised $51,000 for various Memphis charities.

On March 8, 1961, Elvis appeared by special invitation before the General Assembly of the Legislature of Tennessee. He was honored for his outstanding contributions to the world of entertainment and as a credit to the young people he represented. Governor Buford Ellington made Elvis an honorary colonel while praising him for his sense of values. Elvis then mounted the rostrum and spoke a few words to the assembly. He thanked them for inviting him to speak and, laughing, mentioned that he was not as funny as Tennessee Ernie Ford, who had been the guest of the general assembly the week before. The nation's press gave the event very little coverage. What the honor meant to Elvis was summed up as he said, "May God bless you as He has blessed me."

Elvis' next concert took place in Hawaii, where he helped raise $60,000 for the U.S.S. *Arizona* War Memorial. He sang sixteen songs during the performance. He was dressed in a gold jacket and at one point fell to his knees as he serenaded Nipper, the RCA dog. The Honolulu *Star-Bulletin* reported: ". . . less sub-navel activity, but he's just as dynamic as the last time [1957]."

By 1962 Elvis' life had settled into a pretty standard format. He would make three films a year, and almost all of his records released would be soundtracks. The Elvis entourage had been formed and the newspapers referred to the members as the "Memphis Mafia." Joe Esposito, an old army buddy from Chicago, was a member of the "Mafia." I have had the pleasure of meeting Joe many times; he's a perfect gentleman. He handled all of Elvis' business matters and is as shrewd as anyone, the Colonel included. Red West was with Elvis from the beginning as a bodyguard. He appeared in many of his films and wrote some fine songs ("If Every Day Was Like Christmas," "If You Talk in Your Sleep"). Red, like his boss, was an expert at the art of karate and owned a karate school in Memphis. Sonny West, who is a cousin of Red's, served Elvis in the same capacity. Charlie Hodge is known to the fans as the man who gave Elvis his scarves and water when the King was onstage. Offstage, he was possibly Elvis' closest friend. There were others, of course, but you'd need a scoreboard to keep track. It was a shame when some of these friends turned against Elvis at the end, all for the sake of publishing a scandalous book. But the less said about that, the better. Most of his true friends were at his side all the way.

Around this time Elvis purchased a 1960 Cadillac limousine, which became known as his "Solid Gold Cadillac." After he bought the car, he took it to the top customizer in the world, Mr. George Barris. George lengthened the top and covered it with pearl Naugahyde. The body was sprayed with forty coats of paint that contained (among other things) crushed diamonds. There were gold records embedded in the ceiling of the car, and all of the trim was fourteen-karat gold. Included in the interior of this Presleymobile were a gold phone, gold razor, gold bar, and gold television. For trips to Los Angeles he bought a customized bus.

The King received a call from Dick Clark, and on January 8, 1962, "American Bandstand" celebrated Elvis' birthday by featuring a forty-five-minute tribute.

Elvis then returned to Hawaii to film *Girls! Girls! Girls!* (The film had undergone two previous title changes; at first the choices had been *Welcome Aboard* and *A Girl in Every Port*.) When his plane landed in Hawaii, he was met by eight thousand fans. The Hawaiian people had great respect and admiration for Elvis. They hadn't forgotten his benefit concert the year before, and the publicity *Blue Hawaii* was giving the islands made him quite a hero. The interior filming was done in Hollywood, and it was back to Memphis upon completion.

Elvis and the boys rented the fairgrounds in Memphis, and everyone had a ball. He showed midnight movies and ran *West Side Story* at least a dozen times. His habit of eating things like bacon and mashed potatoes began to take its toll. Elvis began to diet, and sometimes his mood reflected it. In the sixties his weight was like a seesaw. In *Paradise—Hawaiian Style* his bulk was embarrassingly noticeable.

In *It Happened at the World's Fair* Elvis was seen sporting a magnificent wardrobe. Exterior scenes for this film were filmed by MGM at the

Two legends, Elvis and his good friend Jackie Wilson.

magnificent World's Fair in Seattle. When the crew returned to Hollywood, Elvis was given Clark Gable's old dressing room at MGM.

For amusement, Elvis formed a football team and he and the boys would gather at the dusty schoolyard in Memphis. When the game started, his shirt and pants were spotless. Naturally, in less than five minutes he was covered in mud. Elvis was usually in the middle of every play and he spent half of the game at the bottom of the pile. The game usually began at 2 P.M. and lasted well past the dinner hour. He and the boys would then stop at Vanucci's Italian Restaurant, located a short distance from Graceland. They would order meat ball sandwiches to go. These sandwiches were so big that they would best be described as productions.

The games continued, and until late 1962 Elvis had it all his own way. Then in 1963 the Beatles arrived, bringing something fresh and different with them. The critics compared them with Elvis and forecast his immediate doom. The Liverpool explosion would send the careers of most of Elvis' contemporaries into a decline that many would never fully recover from.

61

Although Elvis' great talent hadn't deserted him, it was becoming increasingly difficult for him to produce anything of quality. This isn't hard to comprehend when one considers the material he was given to work with. A lesser talent would have drowned when faced with a script like *Kissin' Cousins*. This film was made on a slender budget by a "cheapie" producer. While the Beatles shouted "She Loves You," Elvis cried about "One Broken Heart for Sale." "One Broken Heart" was a failure by past Elvis standards—most fans single this record out when referring to the beginning of the lean years. "Bossa Nova Baby" was not good single material, and the sales figures reflected it, but "Devil in Disguise" managed to reach the top of the charts and remains an Elvis classic today.

The King went to Hollywood for his next feature, *Fun in Acapulco*. When the film was completed he returned to Memphis. The newspapers reported that he had been seen on his motorcycle along with a pretty passenger, Priscilla Beaulieu. She had recently come to Memphis and was Vernon and Dee's house guest at Graceland. Vernon told the press that she would be attending the Immaculate Conception High School in Memphis.

When Elvis wasn't motorcycling, he was riding amusement park Dodgem cars for hours on end, or entertaining fans and friends at the midnight movie shows. Two of his favorites were *To Kill a Mockingbird* and *Lawrence of Arabia*.

Most of Elvis' film soundtracks were recorded in Hollywood; unusually, *Kissin' Cousins* was recorded in Nashville. When Colonel Parker saw the script to *Kissin' Cousins,* he wanted Elvis to receive double salary. The producer asked why, and Parker replied, "You want my boy to play two characters and to run around in a silly blond wig—that's why!" The request was denied, and Elvis seemed pleased enough to have two leading ladies.

The names of Ann-Margret and Elvis were being linked by all the Hollywood columnists. Ann-Margret had been quoted as saying, "I want to be the female Elvis Presley." MGM decided to team the sexy couple in the film *Viva Las Vegas;* the film had a $3 million budget and was filmed on location. Elvis and Ann-Margret set sparks flying with their obvious attraction to each other. MGM kept the cameras rolling, and the result was the best Elvis Presley film since before the army days. The romance cooled when Ann-Margret talked too much to the Hollywood gossip columnists, although the two maintained a close friendship throughout Elvis' lifetime.

In 1963 an Elvis film was shown on TV for the first time; appropriately it was *Love Me Tender*.

Elvis had entered into a period that I refer to as the "lazy years." During the next few years he would make three films a year, release some of the most uncommercial singles ever, and make no TV or live appearances. Whether the decision was his or the narrow-minded Colonel Parker's, it worked. Instead of challenging the Beatles while they were at the peak of their popularity, he was content to ride out the storm in plush Hollywood luxury. He would ride to the studio in his $50,000 Rolls-Royce, sing to the guy he'd just beat up, get back in his car, and retreat to his Bel Air palace. All the while, he continued to gross $12 million a year.

Elvis and Dale Robertson.

In 1964 he drove his Rolls-Royce to the mayor's office in Memphis. He entered the courthouse wearing a black suit and a double-breasted topcoat that featured a velvet collar and white leather buttons. In an attempt to catch a glimpse of him, secretaries from different offices in the building fell all over themselves. Among the 150 people gathered in the mayor's office was old friend Anita Wood. Elvis and Vernon stepped from the corridor into the crowded office. As Elvis began to speak, he admitted that he was shaking all over. He told the crowd that he was happy to be in a position to help the charitable organizations and wished all of Memphis a merry Christmas and a happy New Year. It was announced that Elvis would pass out checks totaling $55,000.[1] Elvis smiled and said, "Elvis is going to pass out, period!" Elvis was presented with a six-foot trophy of walnut and brass by the fifty-eight organizations who would be benefiting from his charitable deed. He took one look at it and laughingly told them he would build a room around it.

In January 1965 Elvis celebrated his thirtieth birthday, and radio stations around the country paid tribute to the event by featuring his records. The TV show "Shindig" saluted him as he watched the show in Memphis. He completed work on two films, *Harum Scarum* and *Girl Happy*. It was reported at the time that he earned $1,000,000 per film, plus 50 per cent of the profits. Elvis continued to share his wealth when he gave the largest single donation of $50,000 to the Motion Picture Relief Fund. When he returned to Memphis for his summer vacation, he purchased nine Harley-Davidson cycles at a cost of $1,600 each. He and the boys would soon be known as "El's Angels." In July he went to Hawaii to work on the film *Paradise—Hawaiian Style*. He stayed at the Ilikai Hotel in Waikiki (the one

[1] Elvis continued to donate generously to charities. For example, at the 1966 Christmas season he donated $105,000 to various charities.

63

you see at the beginning of "Hawaii Five-O"). It was during this period that Elvis first heard Kui Lee's "I'll Remember You."

On August 27 Elvis played the host to John, Paul, George, and Ringo at his home located at Perugia Way in Bel Air. The Beatles were touring America and had expressed a desire to meet the King. Their chauffeur-driven limousine arrived at the Bel Air mansion at 10 P.M. The meeting of the giants lasted well into the night and the Beatles didn't leave until 2 A.M. I've had the opportunity to meet and speak with both John Lennon and Paul McCartney. Both have vivid memories of their historic meeting. John credits Elvis for his desire to be a musician. He has said, "Nothing really moved me until Elvis." You may recall that John wore an Elvis pin at the 1974 Grammy Awards Show. His office in New York has all five of Elvis' Sun recordings displayed along the main wall. John also has one of the finest Elvis record collections in the world. He recently gave me a gold record certifying one million sales of the Capitol LP *Abbey Road* in exchange for some super-rare Elvis discs. "We spent about four hours talking, listening to records, and jamming. During the jam session, Elvis played piano and drums. We ate a lot, shot some pool, and had a ball." Paul had this to say: "It was a real thrill sitting there with the King. I mean, he was always one of my favorites. I always knew that no matter how I felt, if I played an Elvis record it would make me happy. I've always dreamed of producing an album for Elvis. You know, the whole time we jammed with him, he had the tape machine running." I didn't know, but I'll tell you something: I'd give almost anything to hear those tapes.

Meanwhile, Elvis was remodeling Graceland for the umpteenth time. A fifty-by-eighty-foot room was added to one wing. He turned the room into an additional trophy room, covering the walls with gold records and plaques. He also added dozens of locked trophy cases. He had a full-sized soda bar installed and spent $40,000 enlarging the kitchen. Wrought-iron sculptured pieces were put on the windows for protection. Vernon and Dee moved into a house of their own; Priscilla and Elvis' grandmother (Minnie Presley) continued to live in the east wing at Graceland.

Priscilla had graduated from Immaculate Conception High School in Memphis, and Elvis then enrolled her in the Patricia Stevens Finishing and Career School, where she studied dance and modeling. She and Elvis continued to date, and they also continued to argue. The fiery relationship exploded, and Priscilla joined her parents at Travis Air Force Base, near San Francisco, where Major Beaulieu was now posted. Elvis was having weight problems and would spend days locked in his room. He neither spoke to nor saw anyone during these depressed periods. He sold his gold Cadillac to RCA for promotional purposes (they planned to tour it), replacing it with a brand-new 1966 Oldsmobile Toronado.

Elvis suffered a deep personal loss when Bill Black, at the age of thirty-nine, passed away. Bill had undergone surgery during the summer and on October 22, at the Memphis Baptist Hospital, he died of a brain tumor. His death meant that the fans would never have the opportunity of seeing the original trio of Elvis, Scotty, and Bill perform again.

Elvis formally presents the yacht *Potomac,* the former seagoing White House of President Roosevelt, to Danny Thomas, founder of St. Jude's Hospital in Memphis.

At that time, American teen-agers spent an estimated $1.5 billion a year on entertainment. Elvis Presley became the highest-paid entertainer in the world. Allied Artists producer Ben Schwalb offered this explanation of Elvis' worth: "The young people, not only of America, but of Japan, South Africa, Italy, and England, have made Elvis the biggest box office draw in the world today. For that reason alone, he's worth every penny he's getting." He was paid $25,000 a day by Allied Artists. For his six weeks' work on *Tickle Me* he received a total of $750,000. Metro paid him $1,000,000 for *Girl Happy* and Paramount gave him $1,000,000 for *Roustabout.* In addition, he received a hefty percentage of the profits from his two 1964 film releases *Kissin' Cousins* and *Viva Las Vegas,* which were Metro's biggest grossers of the year. Elvis' pictures seldom cost as much as $2 million and unfailingly returned somewhere between two and three times that amount after exhibition cuts. Producer Hal Wallis, to whom Elvis was under a nonexclusive contract, said, "A Presley picture is the only sure thing in show business."

Director Norman Taurog worked with Elvis in some of his most successful films, the most popular being *G.I. Blues* and *Blue Hawaii*. Norman had this to say: "Someday I want to direct him in a serious drama. No singing at all. I think he'd be great." But did Elvis want to attempt such a role? "Well, I've always wanted to do serious parts, and someday maybe I will. I don't want to push it. I'd rather just let it happen," said Elvis.

The screen colony had never been anything but vaguely conscious of Elvis, because he chose not to be a part of it. In all the years he spent in Hollywood, he had never been in a local restaurant or night club. He couldn't risk it—the fans would eat him up.

Hollywood stars like Audrey Hepburn and Elizabeth Taylor weren't thrilled when they heard that the Hillbilly Cat was earning more per film than they were. Elvis' earnings, however, made Uncle Sam very happy. Elvis never incorporated or availed himself of any other tax-reducing gimmick. Instead, he doggedly continued rendering unto Caesar in the highest bracket as a matter of principle. All the while, Colonel Parker stood on the sidelines twirling his cane and grinning to himself behind a big cigar. He owned 25 per cent of Elvis.

Jocelyn Lane, an English girl who may be described as looking like Brigitte Bardot with tawny hair and a golden tan, costarred in the film *Tickle Me*. She is a product of the exclusive Lady Eden's School, which was run by the sister-in-law of Britain's former Prime Minister Sir Anthony Eden (later the Earl of Avon). The lovely star became a princess in 1971 when she married a prince. She thanked me for calling her Elvis' prettiest costar in my book *Elvis in Hollywood*. Today, at the age of thirty-seven, she has lost none of the attributes that originally earned her my praise. She is five foot four and weighs 108 pounds. I asked Jocelyn (Jackie to her friends) what it was like working with Elvis. "It was a pleasure," she said. "He was one of the nicest, most considerate persons I ever met. Not at all what I expected." Such as what? "Well, you know—insufferably conceited. He was very modest. He's entirely unassuming, and he's very intelligent. I liked Elvis a lot."

By the time 1966 rolled around, Elvis had sixty-four gold records. He celebrated his thirty-first birthday with roman candles on the grounds at Graceland. His films were playing to less than packed houses. This wasn't surprising, as *Frankie and Johnny, Paradise—Hawaiian Style,* and *Spinout* were somewhat less than awe-inspiring. Priscilla had returned and was often seen with Elvis. The Hollywood columnists wrote of their secret engagement —the rumors were so widely spread that Vernon Presley had to issue a denial. Elvis went to Nashville and made his first non-film recording in years. For six days he was booked for recording sessions, from May 24 to May 29. Elvis forgot to bring the lyrics to any of the songs he was to record. He had

Hollywood cleaned him up, taking away much of his natural sex appeal.

one of the boys, Alan Fortas, call his wife in Memphis. Joey Fortas read the lyrics over the phone.

The fans were becoming more and more dissatisfied with Elvis' films. The Colonel's office even admitted that there had been a lot of complaints about *Harum Scarum*. The following singles were released: "Tell Me Why" (recorded in 1957)/"Blue River," "Joshua Fit the Battle," "Milky White Way," "Frankie and Johnny," "Love Letters," and "Spinout." All of these singles were flops by any commercial measure. He also recorded the beautiful "If Every Day Was Like Christmas," written by Red West. Although "Every Day" was a strong effort, the steady diet of poor films and weak recordings was indeed beginning to take its toll.

It is interesting to note that the soundtrack album from the film *Spinout* included three bonus songs that were recorded at the Nashville sessions. It is a shame that RCA chose to bury them on the *Spinout* LP, because they were certainly three of Elvis' strongest attempts of that period. "Tomorrow Is a Long Time" was written by Bob Dylan and had a running time of five minutes. In a *Rolling Stone* interview, Dylan stated that Elvis' version of this song was by far the best rendition that anyone had ever given of his work. "I'll Remember You," another bonus track, would play a major role in Elvis' life, and the classic R & B "Down in the Alley" was Elvis in the down-and-dirty style that made him famous in the first place.

The lazy years had taken hold, box office receipts started to dwindle, and what had become known as the Elvis Presley film was beginning to tire. It was obvious that a change would have to be made.

The Love Years

Elvis caught the "horse riding fever" early in 1967. He became so fanatical about riding he even lost interest in showing the midnight movies. He named his horse the Rising Sun, and he began riding at sunrise each day. The original owners of Graceland had kept their horses in a stable located in the rear of the house. Elvis remodeled the stable and equipped it with a stall for each horse—he owned seventeen fine thoroughbreds. Elvis, Vernon, and the boys would ride the horses on the grounds at Graceland. Fans would gather to watch and often caused traffic jams. Located at the rear of the grounds was a seven-room house that was used for storage. To solve the gaping problem Elvis drove a bulldozer through the center of the storehouse again and again until the walls came tumbling down. He and his friends began to ride there and, once again, the fans brought an end to it. It seems that they were jumping the fence and shouting at the boys. This made Elvis finally decide to buy a 160-acre cattle ranch, located at the Tennessee-Mississippi state line. He said, "I've wanted a place like this for a long time." He named the new ranch the Circle G.

Before leaving for Hollywood to begin work on his latest film, *Clambake*, he flew to Nashville aboard a private jet. When the recording session was over, he flew back and the private plane was used for a fifteen-minute tour over his ranch.

Elvis' name had been romantically linked with those of every Hollywood starlet, leading lady, and other member of the female species for over eleven years. Elvis himself once remarked, "If I slept with every woman they [the movie magazines] say I have, I would have been dead a long time ago." In 1967 America's favorite bachelor would temporarily silence the gossip mag-

azines. On Sunday, April 30, the Colonel sent telegrams to his friends and associates. Among them were Abe Lastfogel, president of the William Morris Agency (Elvis' booking agency); the president of RCA; and the head of publicity at Metro, Stan Brossette. Elvis and Priscilla, Vernon and Dee, and the other members of the wedding party flew from Palm Springs to Las Vegas. No one other than the members of this wedding party knew that on May 1, 1967, the King would take his Queen. The one hundred invited guests met in the lobby of the Aladdin Hotel. They were led to the private suite of Milton Prell, the owner of the Aladdin. They were told of the wedding and were instructed not to leave the suite until the time of the ceremony. Colonel Parker wasn't taking any chances. Rona Barrett, the famous gossipmonger, had said on TV that Elvis was getting married in Palm Springs. The media was off and running at the bit. By this time, reporters began to arrive at the Vegas resort hotel, but the Colonel wasn't talking.

At 9:41 A.M., the beautiful double-ring ceremony was performed by Nevada Supreme Court Justice David Zenoff. Elvis wore black tuxedo pants

and a black-on-black paisley jacket. Priscilla was stunning in her floor-length gown of white chiffon. The ceremony lasted eight minutes, and Elvis gave Priscilla a ring that featured a three-carat diamond as the center stone, with twenty smaller diamonds around it. Joe Esposito was Elvis' best man; Michelle Beaulieu, Priscilla's sister, was the maid of honor.

The invited guests and the bridal party were led by guards to the Aladdin Room. They drank champagne as Elvis and Priscilla danced to the strains of "Love Me Tender." Priscilla would later recall "Love Me Tender" as being the first song of Elvis' that she ever heard. "It has always been my favorite," she exclaimed.

The wedding cake was five feet high and had six tiers. It reportedly cost $3,500. There were eight round tables for the guests, and seated at the head table were the bride and groom with their families. The menu included chicken, roast suckling pig, lobsters, clams casino, smoked salmon, and oysters Rockefeller. Following the party, a brief press conference was held and the couple answered the reporters' questions. Elvis looked happier than I've

ever seen him. The Colonel called a halt to the conference and the reporters fled quickly. Each tried to beat the others with his coverage of the wedding of the decade. At 2:50 P.M. the happy couple flew to Palm Springs, and two days later they flew to Hollywood, where Elvis would complete work on *Clambake*.

On May 4 they flew via commercial airline to Memphis. Elvis wasn't allowing any photos or interviews with the press. Immediately afterward he and Priscilla were settled at Graceland. Elvis then drove to the Circle G ranch to see the new colt that had been born while he was away. Priscilla gave Elvis a Cadillac Eldorado as a wedding gift. They would watch films like *The Sand Pebbles* and *A Shot in the Dark*. Their time was divided between Graceland and the Circle G. They had a quiet honeymoon and seemed to love every moment of it. One evening, they bowled from midnight till 4 A.M. at the Whitehaven Bowling Lanes. On another occasion they

rented the fairgrounds, and both Priscilla and Elvis behaved like children as they rode the Pippin, Tilt-A-Whirl, and, of course, the Dodgems.

On May 29 a second wedding reception was held at Graceland. The 125 invited guests included friends and relatives who had not been able to attend the wedding in Vegas. The reception was held in the huge enclosed patio. An attendant parked the guests' cars and as they entered the reception area their wedding gifts were placed on the round oak table. The large bridal arch was covered with red and white carnations. Directly in front of the arch a table covered in white satin held the beautiful four-tier wedding cake. Located in the center of the room were eight tables covered in white satin, each with its own floral arrangement surrounded by lighted candles. The menu resembled a smorgasbord. It included ham, turkey, a variety of cheeses, stuffed lobster, shrimp, meat balls, sausages, hot dogs, potato salad, and coleslaw. There was also plenty of champagne.

At 8:30 Elvis' grandmother, Minnie, was ushered in and seated at the head table. She was followed by Vernon, Dee, and Dee's children. At 8:45 P.M. Joe Esposito came into the room and signaled accordionist Tony Barasso to begin playing "Love Me Tender." Elvis and Priscilla entered and stood in front of the bridal arch as their guests applauded. Joe Esposito announced, "In case no one here knows it, that's Mr. and Mrs. Elvis Presley." Priscilla wore her beautiful wedding gown with its six-foot train. Elvis was wearing his black brocaded formal suit with vest, formal white shirt, black bow tie, and a white carnation in his lapel. The receiving line formed and the bride and groom were kissed and congratulated by everyone. Elvis and Priscilla mixed with all of their guests and really seemed to be enjoying themselves. As they cut the wedding cake, Elvis teased his bride. Finally he took her in his arms and they danced to the music of "Let Me Call You Sweetheart." After stepping on her train, he lifted it and wrapped it around her shoulders. The reception ended at midnight and Elvis invited everyone to the Memphian Theatre, where he would show a Kirk Douglas film.

On June 8 Priscilla was given a bridal shower. There were thirty guests in attendance. The newlyweds then left for Hollywood, where Elvis was scheduled to begin work on his next film, Metro-Goldwyn-Mayer's *Speedway*.

A problem soon arose when Priscilla revealed her feelings regarding the Memphis Mafia. She didn't want to share her man with the boys, no matter how loyal they were. Many of the men were also jealous of her. They were hurt because only Joe Esposito and Marty Lacker had been invited to the wedding.

The Mafia had always used their position with Elvis to help them get girls, and Priscilla didn't want this footloose entourage around her. She also didn't approve of the idea of Elvis paying so many salaries. The couple had quarreled over this, and in the end all of the boys with the exception of Joe Esposito and Richard Davis were fired. Mr. Davis was his valet, and Joe Esposito was Elvis' bookkeeper and adviser. Charlie Hodge continued to serve him and also remained a close friend.

The Presleys purchased the Trousdale Estate at 1174 Hillcrest Road. The house had a huge pool, four large bedrooms, a circular living room with adjoining recreation room, and six bathrooms. The house was hidden behind an electrically operated gate.

In 1960 Elvis had recorded "Crying in the Chapel," which, released in 1965, had been his last million-seller. His next film, *Speedway*, costarring Nancy Sinatra, could have easily been called *Viva Las Vegas, Part 2*. In retrospect, I think that acknowledgment should be made to the fact that all of Elvis' films have been good, clean, family entertainment; but by 1967 the lack of originality in the scripts, the tired, cliché-ridden dialogue, and the seeming outdatedness of Elvis were threatening to destroy his career. Elvis' movies were boring him out of his mind. He could no longer stand the routine, and he'd become so insulated by the people around him and his own fame that the situation looked hopeless.

After completing work on *Speedway*, the King and his Queen, accompanied by Joe Esposito and wife Joanie, traveled via commercial airline to

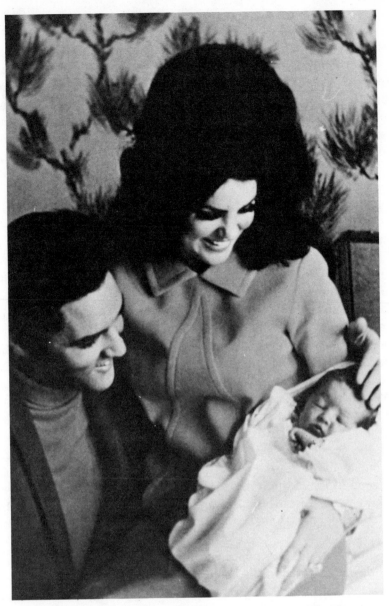

Elvis, Priscilla, and their four-day-old daughter, Lisa Marie.

Memphis. Once inside the walls of Graceland, Elvis announced, "Priscilla is going to . . . uh . . . uh . . . have . . . uh . . . Priscilla is going to have a baby." He was congratulated by everyone. He smiled and said, "Yeah, we're going to have another rock 'n' roll singer."

In October, Elvis flew to Arizona to begin work on the film *Stay Away, Joe.* Priscilla, who was expecting their baby in February, remained home at Graceland. *Stay Away* presented a different kind of Presley. Elvis looked great in this wonderful free-for-all comedy, and the film deserved a better fate than empty seats. He returned to Memphis for the holiday season. His annual New Year's Eve party was held at the plush Thunderbird Lounge, located in the exclusive part of Memphis. (Usually the party was held at the Manhattan Club, but there had been some difficulties there the year before.) The festivities began at 9 P.M. and didn't break up until 4 A.M. Elvis arrived in blue jeans and a light blue turtleneck sweater. Priscilla wore a black chiffon maternity dress. They were entertained by three bands; one of the performers was an old friend from the Sun days, Billy Riley. The midnight hour arrived and everyone went bananas. Elvis gave Priscilla a long, passionate kiss. The entertainment continued, and at 4 A.M. Priscilla and Elvis said their good-nights. Elvis was thinner than he'd been in years, and it was obvious that family life was agreeing with him. He remained at Graceland for the last months of Priscilla's pregnancy.

The newspapers across the country were giving daily coverage to the event. It's ironic how the boy they once called a threat to the nation's young, an out-and-out sex maniac, was now being praised for this charitable deeds, his humanity, and the shining example he set for American youth. It was always Colonel Parker's goal to clean up his image. He made sure we knew that Elvis loved his mother, his country, God, and his pregnant wife. The Colonel undoubtedly didn't want the fans to think Elvis was Jesus Christ, but that's exactly the image he created. Elvis had become a fine example of the American establishment.

On the night before Priscilla gave birth, she was asked when the baby was due. She answered, "In the week. . . . I'm so excited—we're both so nervous; every time I move, he's there to catch me." On February 1, at 8:30 A.M., Mr. and Mrs. Presley were driven by Charlie Hodge to the Baptist Memorial Hospital. Joe Esposito followed them in case of an auto emergency. The hospital's entrance was crowded with reporters. Two hospital guards ushered the Presley party inside. Priscilla was admitted immediately, and Elvis went to the doctors' lounge to await the blessed event. Joe, Charlie, Vernon and Dee, Marty Lacker, friend Lamar Fike, and George Klein joined him there. Lisa Marie Presley was born at 5:01 P.M., weighing six pounds fifteen ounces, nine months to the day after Elvis and Priscilla's wedding.

Elvis hired two off-duty policemen to remain outside Priscilla's room for the four days she stayed in the hospital. The switchboard there received over ten thousand calls from all over the world. Gifts by the truckload were delivered to Graceland.

Sadly, Elvis heard tragic news on the day after he brought Priscilla home. Nick Adams, who had starred in the TV series "The Rebel," was dead. Nick and Elvis had been friends ever since Elvis' early days in Hollywood.

After Lisa's birth, Elvis went to Hollywood to begin work on *Live a Little, Love a Little*. The film actually showed Elvis in bed with a woman (a board had been placed between them). Could it be that they were actually letting our actor mature? Vernon had a bit part in the film, but no lines. Elvis made three other films in 1968. They were the excellent *Charro!*, the above-average *Change of Habit*, and *The Trouble with Girls*, which was only fair (and I'm being generous). Unfortunately the movie houses were either booking Elvis pictures as a second feature or not showing them at all. The lazy years had certainly had their influence. In *Charro!* Elvis appeared unshaven and disheveled—yet he looked great as he added a new dimension to his screen career. He also did quite well with his role as a young ghetto doctor in *Change of Habit*. *The Trouble with Girls* gave us a sideburned Elvis. The story line in this film was so weak that the film was not shown in most of the major cities.

The biggest news as far as the fans were concerned came when it was announced that Elvis would do his first TV special for NBC. Today this show is referred to as the " '68 Comeback." Not that Elvis had ever been away, but the boy who dared to rock had been sleeping for some time.

Jerry Hopkins, a contributing editor to *Rolling Stone* magazine, has written many fine books, among them the biography *Elvis*. Today Jerry and his family are living in Hawaii, where Jerry is putting the finishing touches to his latest work, a Raquel Welch biography. I am happy to be able to say that this gifted journalist is a friend of mine. In my trophy room sits the original manuscript for his Elvis biography. In his book Jerry relates the following story: Steve Binder, the musical producer of the '68 TV special, was having plenty of trouble with the Colonel. It seems Parker wanted Elvis to come out on stage, "say 'Good evening, ladies and gentlemen,' sing twenty-six Christmas songs, say 'Merry Christmas and good night.' . . . 'The way I felt about it,' says Steve today, 'was I felt very, very strongly that the television special was Elvis's moment of truth.' "

Elvis had lived in the fantasy world of stardom for so long that it was cheating him out of his life. To feel, to touch, to create, one has to be able to relate to the people. His business advisers, bodyguards, and servants had kept him isolated for twelve long years and he had lost contact with reality. It was under these circumstances, Steve Binder says, that "he asked Elvis what would happen if they walked out on the [Hollywood] Strip. Elvis seemed apprehensive, but he said he was willing to find out. 'So we did it,' says Steve. 'Four o'clock in the afternoon and there we were, standing outside the Classic Cat [a topless bar]—Elvis, Joe Esposito and me. We stood there to the point of embarrassment. Kids were bumping into us and saying "excuse me" or not even saying that. Elvis started talking louder than normal, trying to be recognized or noticed or something. But nothing happened. Nothing. Zero.' "

Reality! Elvis learned that it wasn't 1956 any longer and that the King must serve his subjects. From this disillusionment emerged the peak of his artistic career.

King of the Jungle

The TV special was to be taped during the last week in June, 1968, and a press conference was held at the NBC studios on the twenty-seventh. Elvis wore black pants, a midnight-blue shirt, and a neck scarf at the conference. Forty-five TV reporters fired questions at him, but he was ready for them and fielded each one, displaying a quick wit and a truly remarkable sense of humor.

The two hundred that were fortunate enough to get tickets to the taping stood outside the NBC studios in Burbank for nearly two hours, waiting for the rehearsal to end. Upon entering the studio, they gazed upon a fifteen-foot-square platform with three steps leading up to it. The stage was surrounded on three sides by bleachers that ascended about seven rows, the fourth side being occupied by the orchestra. After the audience was seated, Priscilla and three friends were ushered to their seats. Backstage, the Colonel was instructing Bob Finkel, the executive producer of the show, to move the prettiest girls in the audience closer to the stage, which was covered by four cameras. Bob Finkel came out and said, "Ladies and gentlemen . . . Mr. Elvis Presley."

It had been a long time—eight years—since Elvis had sung to a live audience. He was worried. "What am I gonna do if they don't like me? What if they laugh at me?" The King approached the square white platform and reached for the guitar that Charlie was holding. He was dressed from head to toe in black leather. His thick coal-black hair was combed back away from his face. He was leaner than he'd been in any of his recent films. His half-closed eyes smoldered and one could feel his inborn sexuality. He raised

"Guitar Man."

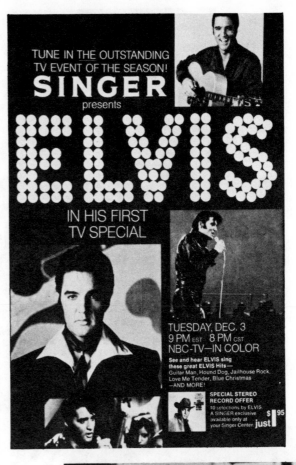

"This leather suit's hot,
I'll tell you."

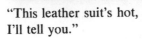

"Trouble."

"Memories."

his arms, the band struck a note, he spread his legs and began to move his left leg in the famous corkscrew motion. The old magic still worked. They were panting and screaming, and he smiled, feeling reborn. The boy from Tupelo had come back. They felt it, and he knew it. He was on fire, burning up the passion of the long, wasted years. He was almost godlike. The emotion between the performer and the audience was an example of the love that the Beatles sang about. At the conclusion of the first number, "Hound Dog," he remarked, "It's been a long time, baby."

"King of the Jungle."

He continued through "Blue Suede Shoes," "Don't Be Cruel," "Heartbreak Hotel," and "Jailhouse Rock." He was cooking! The sweat poured from inside his leathers. He strutted back and forth across the stage, every bit the champion of the world. He was peaking, and so were his subjects. This would be the first time an orgy of this magnitude would escape the network censors. You could feel the energy when he screamed, "I'm the king of the jungle—they call me the tiger man." The presence he commanded was incredible. He returned to his roots, to his first days at Sun. He curled his lip, moaned and grunted through a rocking version of "That's All Right, Mama." He snarled and sizzled as he shouted the lyrics to "Lawdy, Miss Clawdy." I couldn't help thinking that Elvis defied all logic, all reason. Certainly the Lord had included flesh and bone, but in Elvis' case these mortal ingredients were mixed with plenty of magic. He sang a few more of the old greats like "Love Me Tender" and "Can't Help Falling in Love," his voice smoother and more beautiful than ever. As he held the mike in his hand, I imagine every element in his body was pulsating as he began to sing a number that was especially for the show. From his heart he wailed, "If I Can Dream." At that moment, he was truly sublime. He transcended all human attributes. As he left the stage, he collapsed. Vernon, Joe, and Charlie carried him to his dressing room. He asked to be alone. They retreated, closing the door behind them. Through the door, you could hear him crying. He was speaking, but to whom? Perhaps somewhere Gladys Presley was listening. She must have been very proud.

NBC would edit the four hours of tape to fifty minutes, and on December 3, 1968, this edited version would make television history. RCA released "If I Can Dream" as Elvis' next single. This song became his first million-seller in nearly four years. The soundtrack LP went into the top ten and was a consistent seller for more than a year.

For the first time in his fifteen-year career, the critics were praising him. Suddenly Elvis Presley had become everyone's favorite. "There is something magical about watching a man who has lost himself find his way back home," said Jon Landau in *Eye* magazine. "He sang with the kind of power people no longer expect from a rock and roll singer. He moved his body with a lack of pretension and effort that must have made Jim Morrison green with envy. And while most of the songs were ten or twelve years old, he performed them as freshly as though they were written yesterday."

The Myth,
the Legend, The Man

In September, while vacationing at Graceland, Elvis lost another loved one. When learning of Dewey Phillips' death, he said, "I am awfully hurt and feel very sorry about Dewey's death. We were very good friends and I have always appreciated everything he did for me in helping me in my career in the early days."

While at home, he and Priscilla continued to ride bareback at the ranch. On Sundays he would spend his time relaxing, watching football on TV.

But changes were coming at a fast pace. Tom Diskin told a reporter that Elvis' movie income was dropping rapidly. "For the time that goes into making a film, it's more profitable for him to appear in public. It took Elvis fifteen weeks to make a film. If he tours for ten weeks, doing one concert a week at $100,000 each, he can do much better." Elvis said, "I'm planning a lot of changes. You can't go on doing the same thing year after year. It's been a long time since I've done anything professional, except make movies and cut albums. From now on, I don't think I'd like to do as many pictures as I've done. Before too long I'm going to make some personal appearance tours. I'll probably start out here in this country and, after that, play some concerts abroad, probably starting in Europe. I want to see some places I've never seen before. I miss the personal contact with audiences."

The records he was releasing in 1968 all showed a marked improvement. Jerry Reed's rocking "Guitar Man" recaptured the primitive rocking Elvis sound. "U.S. Male" received plenty of air play and reached the number 28 position on the charts. His Easter release was his classic rendition of "You'll Never Walk Alone." The song was a commercial failure, but it showed his tremendous range and incredible vocal abilities.

Elvis at the gates of Graceland.

The TV special, sponsored by Singer, was broadcast on Tuesday evening, December 3, and became the highest-rated special of the year. Elvis, Priscilla, and Lisa Marie, who was now almost one year old, spent the holiday season at Graceland. Elvis had blue lights installed on the curbs lining the winding driveway, to shine all the way to the front gate. The nativity scene on the front lawn took over four thousand bulbs. The Presley grounds were the most outstanding Christmas display in the city. By now the midnight movies had become a regular habit for both Priscilla and Elvis. Christmas Eve was devoted to Lisa Marie, who was fussed over by her parents, Dee and Vernon, and Minnie Presley. The Presleys had a ball and Elvis filmed the entire evening's happenings.

The New Year's party was again held at Fred Alfanso's Thunderbird Lounge. Many of the same performers, including Billy Riley, provided the entertainment. Elvis looked very relaxed in his black velvet Edwardian suit. He and his wife left the party at 1:30 A.M.

In January of 1969 Elvis went to the American Recording Studios in Memphis. This was the first time since he had left Sun (nearly fourteen years earlier) that he had recorded in Memphis. He booked the studio for eleven days, but suffered throat problems through four of them. The sessions began at 7:30 in the evening and continued till sunrise. The twenty-one songs he put on tape were possibly the strongest recordings of his entire career. Among those he recorded were the monster hits "In the Ghetto" and "Don't Cry, Daddy."

Mac Davis was an unknown songwriter at the time. He recalls seeing Elvis perform in Lubbock, Texas, in 1954. "After seeing Elvis perform, I wrote my first tune. It's funny how things work out; I mean, Elvis is now recording my songs. When Elvis finished recording 'In the Ghetto,' the

Colonel called me over and said, 'Boy, I understand you want to be a singer.' He smiled and put his hand on my head, said, 'You tell them the Colonel touched you and you'll be a big star.'"

Elvis, Priscilla, and his entourage (by this time he had rehired many of the boys) left Memphis by plane on January 25 for a skiing vacation in Aspen, Colorado. He took skiing lessons and had a great time on the slopes. From Aspen the Elvis entourage moved to Hollywood, where he would film *Change of Habit*. When the film was completed, they flew to Honolulu for a two-week vacation. On May 28 they arrived back in Memphis. During Elvis' vacation Vernon had sold the Circle G for his son, to L. McClellan. McClellan paid $440,100 for the ranch and said he planned to turn it into a country club. The horses were moved back to the stables at Graceland.

After a night at the midnight movies, Elvis and Priscilla would return to Graceland around 5:30 A.M. They slept until late afternoon and upon waking would go for a swim. This was followed by breakfast, and by the time they had finished eating, their horses were saddled up and ready to ride. Elvis and Priscilla took off, riding their horses all over the grounds.

In no time, a crowd of over five hundred fans gathered at the fence, throwing shoes and other items over the gates. Elvis picked them up, autographed them, and tossed them back. He then rode to the front gate and instructed Uncle Vester to open the gates. He sat on his horse and signed autographs for over two hours. Priscilla was right by his side, also giving out her autograph. In all, over four thousand people had come through the gates. Elvis and Priscilla repeated this gesture every day for the next week.

On June 10 Elvis flew to Las Vegas to tie up some loose ends concerning his first live appearance in almost eight years. It had been announced that Elvis would be appearing at the International Hotel there, opening on July 26.

Priscilla flew to New York for a shopping spree. Dee and Vernon babysat for Lisa while Elvis and Priscilla were out of town. Mrs. Presley returned from New York on June 17, and two days later her parents and sister arrived. Elvis returned to Graceland on June 21.

Glen Campbell was a friend of Elvis' for many years and had played guitar on many of the film soundtracks. When his film *True Grit* opened on Memphis, his parents made a personal appearance at the theater. When their son's film ended, they were driven to Graceland. The Campbells and the Presleys spent an enjoyable evening together.

Although Elvis was nervous, he was looking forward to his Vegas engagement. He would earn $1 million for his four-week stint at the International Hotel. On July 5 he left Graceland to begin rehearsals for the show.

The Vegas performances were a major triumph. They were a continuation of the spectacular TV special. Every seat for the month-long engagement was filled; fans from all over the world flew in for the historic happening. Barbra Streisand had opened the Showroom on July 2 and was not able to fill the 2,000-seat room. The talk was that if Streisand couldn't fill the room, nobody could. To this day, Elvis is the only star in the world to fill the giant

In July 1969 Elvis gives his famous "I'm Back" press conference at the International Hotel in Las Vegas.

Showroom, which has twice the capacity of any other in town. During his strenuous rehearsals, Elvis had lost fifteen pounds. The tiger man never looked better.

On August 17, the halfway mark of the engagement, the TV special was repeated. Because of the seasonal difference, "Blue Christmas" was replaced with "Tiger Man." The show once again drew record ratings. Reporters from the New York *Times* as well as *Rolling Stone* were flown to Vegas in hotel owner Kirk Kerkorian's private jet. The opening-night audience was there by invitation. Elvis performed songs that had made him famous. By the time he introduced the song that would be his next single, "Suspicious Minds," the audience was in a frenzy. He turned the stage into a karate exhibition. He kicked, crouched, and punched like a man who was dosed with LSD. He left the stage to a wild standing ovation. The critics were unanimous in their praise. "Elvis Retains Touch in Return" was the headline on *Billboard* magazine. *Rolling Stone* said: "Elvis Is Supernatural." *Variety* called him "Superstar." The Colonel couldn't have written better reviews.

Immediately following the opening show, a press conference was held:

Q: How do you like being a father?

A: I like it.

Q: Are you and Priscilla planning on adding to your family?

87

A: You'll be the first to know.

Q: What kind of scripts do you like?

A: Something with meaning. I couldn't dig always playing the guy who'd get into a fight, beat the guy up, and in the next shot sing to him.

Q: What do you think of the Hollywood social scene?

A: I just don't go for it. I have nothing against it, but I just don't enjoy it.

Q: How long did you rehearse for these shows?

A: I practiced for nearly three months. Today I went through three complete dress rehearsals. This was the fourth time I did that show today.

Q: Do you want to do more live shows?

A: I want to. I would like to play all over the world. I chose Las Vegas to play first, because it is a place people come to from all over.

Q: Are you trying to change your image with songs like "In the Ghetto"?

A: No, "Ghetto" was such a great song, I just couldn't pass it up after I heard it.

Q: Why have you led such a secluded life all these years?

A: It's not secluded. I'm just sneaky.

Q: It is true you dye your hair?

A: Sure, I've always done it for the movies.

Slowly, a new pattern was taking shape. He would appear in Vegas twice a year and tour the United States on the average of six months a year. As soon as it was announced that Elvis was coming to town, the auditorium was sold out. In many instances, a second or third show had to be added to accommodate the faithful thousands. After all the years of living with only an image of him, the fans couldn't get enough of the real thing. The more tours he embarked upon, the more they wanted to see him. It was as if they were afraid he'd never come their way again.

The night after he closed his first engagement at the hotel, he went to Nancy Sinatra's opening. He and Priscilla then flew to Palm Springs for a three-week vacation before returning to Graceland on September 23. Priscilla had pleaded with him to take her somewhere they could be alone. In October he took her to Hawaii, but Elvis' idea of alone included twelve of the boys and their wives.

On the professional front, his career was reaching a peak. "Suspicious Minds" had gone to the top of the charts and sold over one million copies. "Don't Cry, Daddy," a song he recorded because it reminded him of his mother, became his next million-seller.

The annual New Year's party was held at a supper club called T.J.'s. On January 6, 1970, he flew to Los Angeles to begin rehearsals for his second Vegas stint. RCA released an LP from this appearance entitled *On Stage, February, 1970*. The album contained his smashing single "The Wonder of You."

Elvis, Priscilla, and Vernon attend Nancy Sinatra's opening in Vegas.

The Presleys' first family portrait.

Rehearsing for his Vegas engagement.

After his Las Vegas triumph, Elvis announced that he would begin touring. This photo shows Elvis arriving in Houston. He gave two shows a night for three evenings at Houston's Astrodome, drawing over 300,000 paid admissions.

By now the air was rife with rumors of a Presley separation. The Vegas parties did nothing to dispel the gossip. Located in the center of the lobby at the International Hilton (Kirk Kerkorian had sold the hotel to the Conrad Hilton chain) is a huge circular couch. It is constantly occupied by redheads, blondes, and brunettes. These girls all have two things in common: large breasts and a desire to meet Elvis. I've been asked thousands of times, "How do you meet Elvis?" Continue to read and you will discover one method I learned during my interviews on the circular couch.

They come from every state in the union, with only one purpose in mind —to sleep with Elvis. They sit on the couch and wait, and if they're good-looking or lucky enough, they are soon approached by either the guys in the band or one of Elvis' boys. After a few polite formalities, such as "My name is . . ." they are asked if they would like to attend an Elvis Presley party. They are then escorted to the Imperial Suite, located on the thirtieth floor. As they step from the elevator, they are met by an armed guard. The boys

Elvis arriving at the "Top Ten Young Men of America" awards ceremony. Red West, as ever, present.

show their passes and they are then permitted to enter the party. Once inside, the girls are instructed to approach Charlie Hodge and say, "Mr. Hodge, what would you like to drink?" They have already been told what is expected of them. If they co-operate, they will attend Elvis' shows for free, and when the show ends, they will be ushered through the kitchen entrance and onto a rear elevator that leads to the Presley suite.

I asked a young lady what Elvis was doing all this time. She replied, "Sometimes after a show he doesn't come up from his dressing room for hours. When he arrives, we wait until he's seated, then we gather around him. The real reason for the parties is to take care of the boys. And if you won't make them, you don't get invited back. It's that simple." I asked if there was any chance that I might attend one of the parties. She smiled and said, "You're nuts! You're a guy and none of them go *that* way."

The second Vegas engagement was a giant success, and when it ended, the boys went home to their wives and Elvis returned to Priscilla. They

91

rested and enjoyed the sun at their Palm Springs home. In May, Elvis signed a three-picture deal with MGM. It was announced at that time that MGM would film his August engagement at the International. Elvis and Priscilla went to Vegas to catch the Tom Jones show and then on May 21 flew to Memphis, where they would remain until July 5. Elvis bought four snowmobiles at a cost of $900 each. He and the boys raced them around the grounds in spite of the lack of snow. He continued the autograph sessions at the main gate, although not as often as in the past. He went to Nashville for a few days of recording and, on July 5, to Los Angeles to begin rehearsals for his August Vegas shows. MGM filmed the rehearsals and the entire month-long Vegas engagement. Elvis' thirty-second movie stands out as a monument to him and his music. *That's the Way It Is* was something special: at last an Elvis film that Elvis could be proud of.

The rumors of trouble in Elvis' marriage spread, but were brushed aside. The tours continued, and each one was more successful then the previous one. Critics coast to coast joined the fans in proclaiming him King. In Memphis the city named a street after him. Graceland was located on Highway 51, which would now be called ELVIS PRESLEY BOULEVARD. In 1971 Memphis gave its favorite son another honor. The Jaycees elected him as one of the "Top Ten Young Men of the Year." The Jaycees are a very conservative group. They're very prudish at times, much like the Optimist Club that had tried to have Elvis arrested in Jacksonville, Florida, in 1956. The Jaycees announced the following names as their nationwide winners on January 9:

Elvis Presley   "Unlike many performers, past and present, Elvis can't be categorized as eccentric or snobbish. He has not forgotten his birthplace, Tupelo, Mississippi, to which he recently donated funds for a youth development program."

Ronald L. Ziegler   "A vital link between the President and the nation. He is known to the White House press corps as being accurate, informed, and loyal to the chief executive."

Thomas I. Atkins   "The first Negro councilman in Boston's history."

Dr. Mario R. Capecchi   "A biophysicist at the Harvard Medical School."

Walter J. Humann   "One of the developers of the United States Postal System."

Wendell Cherry   "A self-made millionaire, part owner of the Kentucky Colonels, a professional basketball team."

Thomas Edward Coll   "Who is the founder of the 'Revitalization Corps,' a private version of the Government's VISTA program."

Jim Goetz   "Owner of a chain of radio stations and formerly the youngest Lieutenant-Governor in the state of Minnesota."

Dr. George J. Todaro   "A National Cancer Institute scientist."

Captain William Bucha   "A West Point professor and Medal of Honor winner in Vietnam."

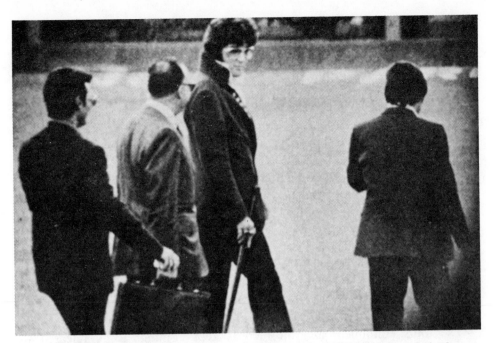

Elvis arriving at the White House complete with walking stick and shades.

Elvis with President Nixon.

The ten awards were given equally, none placed above the others. On January 16 Elvis had a special breakfast meeting with Ronald Ziegler. Microphones with nameplates were set in front of them. The United States ambassador to the United Nations, George Bush, addressed an estimated 1,100 people at the Holiday Inn. He complimented the Jaycees on their Top Ten selections and said, "You Memphis politicians had better watch out if Elvis Presley ever decides to enter politics." That evening, Ambassador Bush commented, "Elvis held his own with his more learned colleagues." George Cajoleas, President of the Brandenton, Florida, Jaycees said, "Elvis was forthright in his answers and didn't stumble. The guy came off looking very good, although he seemed very impressed with the other men around him in terms of their contributions to social advancement."

The other nine award winners were dressed rather conservatively at the Jaycee's luncheon, while Elvis was resplendent in long hair, a black fox fur suit, and yellow sunglasses. The award winners were asked if they made a religious commitment before undertaking their life's work. Elvis answered, "God is a living presence in all of us." In his acceptance speech, he also commented, "I've always been a dreamer. When I was young, I used to read comic books and go to the movies. I was the hero. My dreams have come true a hundred times over. These men here [motioning toward the other nine award winners], they care! You stop to think—and they are building the kingdom of heaven." Elvis ended by saying that, "without a song, the day never ends."

The tours continued, and hit records kept coming. RCA released the beautiful classic "American Trilogy" and a song that contained all of the rocking power that the kid from Tupelo ever possessed—"Burning Love." It was announced that Elvis would be giving four concerts at New York's famous Madison Square Garden. These would be his first New York concerts ever. In all, they would be witnessed by over 80,000. The city was bursting with Presley fever. A billboard welcoming him to New York hung in Times Square. Record stores displayed his LPs in their windows. Then on Friday, June 9, the afternoon of the first concert, a bulletin flashed through the city's three top TV stations' offices. One would have thought that the President of the United States was about to address the nation. Instead, live from the New York Hilton, the King of rock and roll would be giving his landmark New York press conference.

Elvis had arrived in the city only hours earlier. He'd been met by his friend and personal barber, Gil, for it seems that the hair composing those famous sideburns had turned red. Gil had flown in from Memphis to give his client an emergency touch-up. Once this was taken care of, Elvis, Vernon, and the Colonel went to the Hilton Hotel. Gathered there were reporters from every New York newspaper and rock publication. Geraldo Rivera, a nice guy and a great Elvis fan, was the emcee. Geraldo said, "Ladies and gentlemen, I have the pleasure in presenting Mr. Vernon Presley, Elvis Presley's father. Mr. Presley has a friend coming out!" That was how Elvis was introduced to New York's press. The conference was recorded by Buddah Records and was available to the record-buying public for a short time. The following is a complete transcript of the questions and answers that made world-wide news:

ELVIS: Do you mind if I sit down? First of all I plead innocent of all charges. [One of the lady reporters yells, "I love you, Elvis"—and he replies, "Thank you, dear, I love you too!"]

PRESS: Why have you waited so long to appear in New York at Madison Square Garden?

The King displays his latest gold disc (Vernon in the background).

COLONEL PARKER: Will you gentlemen get down in front, and get your pictures later?

ELVIS: I think it was a matter of getting the building, the right building. We had to wait our turn.

PRESS: How do you feel about appearing here?

ELVIS: I like it. I enjoy it. I hope we put on a good show.

PRESS: Why do you think you've outlasted every other entertainer?

ELVIS: I take vitamin E. I'm only kidding. I don't know, dear. I enjoy the business. I just enjoy what I'm doing.

PRESS: Over the years, everyone has said you're very shy. What do you think about that?

ELVIS: I don't know what makes them think that. I'm wearing this belt [his diamond-encrusted solid gold belt, given to him by the International Hotel for breaking all of Las Vegas' attendance records], ain't I?

PRESS: I'm reminded of "The Ed Sullivan Show."

ELVIS: So am I, that's why I'm sitting down.

PRESS: Do you still grease your hair?

ELVIS: I stopped using that greasy kids' stuff, just like everyone else.

PRESS: You used to be fond of long hair and doing all those gyrations on stage. How do you feel about it now?

ELVIS: Man, I was tame compared to what they're doing now. Are you kidding? I didn't do anything but just jiggle.

PRESS: Would you give us a jiggle now? [Elvis jiggles.]

PRESS: How do you feel about entertainment today? How do you feel about the way today's entertainers perform?

ELVIS: Oh, I don't know. I really can't criticize anybody in the entertainment field. I think there's room for everybody. I hate to criticize another performer.

95

PRESS: Are you satisfied with the image that you've established?

ELVIS: Er, well, the image is one thing, and the human being is another.

PRESS: How close does the image come to the man himself?

ELVIS: It's very hard to live up to an image. I'll put it that way.

PRESS: Elvis, you're thirty-seven now. Do you disagree that everyone over thirty is finished?

ELVIS: I'd like to believe they're wrong.

PRESS: What kind of audiences do you attract now?

ELVIS: The audience we have is mixed. It's older people, younger people, and the very young.

PRESS: After this tour, what comes next?

ELVIS: I just made a film of the last tour I did, the first tour we've ever filmed. That's the next project that's coming out.

PRESS: Elvis, what made you return to live shows?

ELVIS: I just missed it. . . . I missed the closeness of an audience, of a live audience, so just as soon as I got out of my movie contract, I started to do live performances again.

PRESS: Will you be doing more tours?

ELVIS: I hope so. There are so many places I haven't been yet. I've never played New York until now, I've never been to Britain either.

PRESS: Are you going there?

ELVIS: I'd like to, yes, sir. I'd like to very much. I'd like to go to Europe. I'd like to go to Japan. I've never been out of this country except in the service.

PRESS: What are your views on compulsory national service?

ELVIS: Er, honey, I'd like to keep my personal views to myself. I'm just an entertainer, and that's that.

PRESS: Will you perform again in New York?

ELVIS: I might.

PRESS: Why did MGM film the concert earlier in Boston for *Elvis—Standing Room Only* [title was later changed to *Elvis on Tour*] when they could have filmed it here?

ELVIS: I don't know, that's a good question. Why is that, Colonel?

COLONEL PARKER: I didn't hear the question.

ELVIS: She said, why did they film the concert in Boston when they could've filmed it here?

COLONEL PARKER: We wanted to spread it around.

PRESS: Why don't you write a biography of yourself?

ELVIS: I don't think it's the right time. . . . I will someday, but not right now.

PRESS: What about politics?

ELVIS: No, sir, I don't have any aspirations in politics or anything of that nature.

PRESS: How about acting?

ELVIS: I'd like to do a dramatic film. If I can find the right property. In fact, we're looking for it now. I'd sure like to do a non-singing film.

PRESS: Why don't you do more of the hard rock and roll that you used to do?

ELVIS: It's pretty difficult to find that kind of song. It's tough to find good material, nowadays, for everybody—for all of us. It's very difficult to find hard rock songs. If I could find them, I would do them.

PRESS: Who do you find sexy?

ELVIS: There's a lot of people. . . .

PRESS: Are you currently campaigning for any political personality or political party?

ELVIS: No, sir, I'm not. No political party. I'm just an entertainer.

PRESS: Elvis, what do you miss most about the fifties?

ELVIS: I really don't miss much about it. I just enjoyed it, and enjoy it just as much now, if not more. I'd like to think that we've improved ourselves over the past fifteen years.

PRESS: How about musically?

ELVIS: I mean musically and vocally. I'd like to think that I've improved.

PRESS: Do you get fed up with people asking for your autograph?

ELVIS: No, I'm used to it. I'd kinda miss it if it didn't happen. To me, it's part of the business, and I accept it.

PRESS: Will there be a recording of this concert?

ELVIS: It's possible. They have RCA Victor officials here, so I don't know.

PRESS: What is your favorite recording of your own?

ELVIS: "It's Now or Never."

PRESS: Which was the largest seller?

ELVIS: "It's Now or Never" was the largest, with "Don't Be Cruel" next and "Hound Dog," then "Heartbreak Hotel" or whatever.

PRESS: Is your wife with you?

ELVIS: No, she's not.

PRESS: Elvis, why don't you form a company of songwriters so you can get the best songs?

ELVIS: Er, I don't think so. I think there are too many companies. The people that write the songs are recording them. That's why it's difficult to get good material. Yes, I'm in a publishing firm, but I take songs from everywhere, if they're good.

COLONEL PARKER: Wouldn't it be a nice gesture if some of you people who have taken all those pictures would kindly step aside and let some others take some?

PRESS: Elvis, what is that belt you're wearing?

ELVIS: The belt is an award from the International Hotel for the championship attendance record. It's like a trophy, but I wear it around here to show it off. Do you want to talk to my father?

PRESS: At what point did you know your son was more than just an ordinary son?

VERNON: Well, it's kind of hard to say. It happened so fast, it's hard to keep up with it, you know. Just "boom," overnight, and there it was. So I'd say probably 1956, and the first TV shows.

ELVIS: I tried to tell him sooner, but he wouldn't listen.

PRESS: Do you have any regrets?

VERNON: No no, I haven't! In fact, I have enjoyed it, really.

ELVIS: All kidding aside, it happened very fast. My mother and my father, all of us—everything happened overnight. We just had to adjust very quickly. A lot of good things, I might add.

PRESS: With all of this, did Elvis change much?

VERNON: No, not really; I can't say that he's changed much.

ELVIS: I sweat more.

PRESS: Elvis, what kind of songs do you enjoy doing?

ELVIS: It's a conscious sort of thing. I like to mix 'em up, in other words; I like to do a song like "Bridge over Troubled Waters" or "American Trilogy" and do some rock and roll.

PRESS: Are you tired of the old stuff?

ELVIS: I'm not the least bit ashamed of "Hound Dog" or "Heartbreak Hotel."

PRESS: Elvis, can you see yourself retiring?

ELVIS: No, not really. I've got too much to do.

PRESS: Elvis, are there any new pop groups you particularly like?

ELVIS: I can't think of any one. I like a lot of them.

COLONEL PARKER: I'd like to live up to my reputation of being a nice guy. This is it, folks!

The press conference had lasted twenty minutes. Immediately following the New York concerts, RCA released a live recording of the Saturday night performance. Actually, the Saturday matinee was much better, featuring a live version of the 1960 classic "Reconsider, Baby." The matinee captured the emotions of Elvis far better than the other three New York performances; RCA chose to ignore this, however. *Elvis As Recorded at Madison Square Garden* earned our hero another gold record.

In July, shortly before he began another stint in Vegas, it was announced that Elvis' marriage was over. There were no denials when it was reported that Priscilla was living with her karate instructor, Mike Stone. Mike had been a close friend of Elvis', and the King himself had brought him into their home to instruct Priscilla in the art. In August, Elvis began divorce proceed-

Lisa looking more like Mommy every day.

ings on the grounds of irreconcilable differences. Priscilla told the press that the basic problem had been Elvis' long absences. Elvis' lawyers declared, "I'm sad to say the reason for the divorce is that Elvis has been spending six months a year on the road, which puts a tremendous strain on the marriage." Elvis confirmed this, but admitted there were other problems. "The problems," he said, "have been building a long time. They probably started to brew when I was in Las Vegas." When Elvis was on tour, Priscilla was bored. She was tired of the role of the good, faithful little wife. Elvis was the superstar, and her own identity was drowning in his fame. She wanted to be special, to be recognized, to be a vital part of her own world and not just someone's trimming on the cake.

The fans were shocked. They asked each other how any woman could leave Elvis Presley.

In the fall of 1972 Elvis' thirty-third (and last) film, MGM's *Elvis on Tour,* was released. With a national concert tour as a musical and visual backdrop, much of Presley's life crosses the screen, punctuated by the star's own recollections of how it all happened. The movie gave us Elvis as the shy country boy during a flashback showing him rocking on "The Ed Sullivan Show." It depicts the mature Elvis, with his custom-made clothing, his eyes shaded by lavender sunglasses with his initials engraved in the center of the frame. The southern accent has all but vanished. He is very much aware of his own being. When he comes on stage, he sizzles. There, on his private throne, he is superhuman. Typically, the Academy of Motion Picture Arts and Sciences failed to nominate *Elvis on Tour* in any category. The film did, however, win the Golden Globe Award as the best documentary of the year. The tragic thing about Elvis' being left out of the nomination category is that politics means more than effort. If the Presley organization had been a bit more courteous to the members of the academy, he could have been nominated. To top that off, the fact that not one of the songs in the film was nominated is a disgrace. I found one scene particularly touching. It showed Elvis recording the song "Separate Ways." The lyrics were most certainly autobiographical, and I'm sure that everyone in the audience realized that Elvis was singing about Priscilla.

Elvis on Tour didn't play in the metropolis. I attended a private screening of the film at MGM in New York. At the movie's conclusion, I asked an MGM executive why the film wasn't getting a nationwide release. "The theatre owners are refusing to book it. We won't spend a nickel on promoting it because we feel we won't earn a penny." It is apparent to me that the only way an Elvis film could ever have reached success would be to have ignored his name and cast him in a dramatic first-rate film where he could have used his creative skills. I'm sure a challenge like this would certainly have helped to break up the monotony of his never-ending personal appearances for him. Elvis needed a good script in order to abolish the "Elvis Presley movie." Elvis was a fine actor and, given the proper role, he could have proved this to many nonbelievers.

In 1973 the Presleys were granted a divorce. The newspapers had tried to drag Elvis through the mud, claiming that he tried to cheat Priscilla in the divorce settlement. In his original suit he had told the court that Priscilla had agreed to receive $100,000 in cash, plus $1,000 a month alimony and $500 a month for the support of Lisa. Elvis had loved Priscilla for almost nine years before their marriage. He sent her to dancing school, art classes, and finishing school. He had promised Gladys that the girl he married would be forever. It isn't hard to understand how Elvis, in the emotional state he was in, would consider the above settlement fair. Of course, Priscilla had always lived with the fact that her husband was a sex god to millions of women. She had seen his name linked with every Hollywood starlet for the last fifteen years. She stayed at home while her famous husband worked and played.

Priscilla told of how she had not been informed of her husband's earnings throughout their marriage and claimed the settlement was not enough for her and Lisa to live on. Elvis was accused of extrinsic fraud—keeping his wife deliberately in ignorance of her entitlement. Since Elvis still cared for her, a new deal was quickly worked out. This time, Priscilla received $1,445,000 in cash, $4,200 a month in alimony for one year, half of the sale price of their $750,000 Bel Air home and 5 per cent of two of Elvis' music publishing companies. After the divorce, she and Elvis showered each other with expensive gifts. Lisa, who lived with her mother, visited with Elvis often. Priscilla has had several business ventures and, of course, will never have to worry about money.

In a career made up of triumph after triumph, Elvis probably peaked in January of 1973 when his "Aloha from Hawaii" special was beamed via satellite throughout the world. This show was seen by over one and a half billion people. In February, RCA shipped over one million copies of the *Elvis: Aloha from Hawaii* double album.

Elvis arriving in Hawaii.

As one watched the TV screen, a globe slowly came into focus, bouncing beams of sound. The name ELVIS, written in almost every language, flashes from the tube. In the background you hear Elvis' voice singing "Hawaii, U.S.A." A helicopter lands, and from it emerges Elvis, clad in a white corduroy suit and bright red shirt. Thousands are lined against the mesh fence as he walks by. He stops to shake hands, kiss girls, and tenderly embrace a baby. He gets into a red Jeep, accompanied by Vernon Presley and Red West. As the Jeep prepares to depart, he waves to the screaming throngs. The cameras switch to the entrance of the Hawaiian International Center. As the *2001* theme reaches its finale, the words ELVIS IN PERSON are superimposed over a view of the crowd entering the center. The drums roll, and Elvis, the man and the magic, appears.

The white jumpsuit he was wearing was a sight to see, complete with an American eagle design. It featured three eagles on each pant leg. Across the front was a spread-winged eagle, and another across the back, done in gorgeous red and blue stones. The belt, as if not large enough, had chains hanging from the bottom borders. Elvis was so resplendent that the monster diamond on his left hand was nothing compared to his presence. Although I've heard Elvis comment about the quantity of carats in the diamond-encrusted ring, the exact amount escapes my memory. It should suffice to say that you could pay your mortgage with it. He would often point to the ring during a performance, saying, "The reason I'm showing this to you is that you paid for it."

101

The historic "Aloha from Hawaii" concert seen via satellite around the world. In the United States thirty minutes was added to the show, and NBC aired it as a ninety-minute special. RCA released a double album from the show and this LP sold over $2 million worth of records. The show itself was seen by more people than man's first walk on the moon!

He grabs his guitar and goes right into "See See Rider." In the background are neon lights flashing Elvis' name in every tongue. He begins to sing "Burning Love," and we're treated to four close-up shots of "his highness" looking mean, mighty, sexy, and impish, all rolled into one. (During these close-ups, I realized how a dentist must feel as he peers into a patient's mouth. Only Adonis or Elvis could have survived these intense inspections!) He approaches the long walkway located at center stage. The audience is screaming requests, and Elvis tells them to be still and he'll sing all 429 of them (his hits). He sings "Johnny B. Good," "Love Me," and possibly the best live version of "Blue Suede Shoes" he's ever sung. If he was the tiger man in the 1968 special, then most certainly he has left the realm of the mere mortal during this performance. He tells the audience he'd like to sing the saddest song he's ever heard, and it went something like this: ". . . Hear that lonesome whippoorwill, he sounds too blue to fly." The notes catch in his throat and tears tug at your heart. When he sang "Lord, This Time You Gave Me a Mountain," he made me feel his pain.

With each verse, the agony Elvis is feeling becomes more intense. With the emotion creasing his face, tears begin to flow. Over one and a half billion people witnessed a man not only feeling his pain but displaying it.

The special was a benefit for the Kuiokalani Lee Cancer Fund. Kuiokalani Lee was the composer of "I'll Remember You"—which Elvis also sang. Elvis said, "We expected to get $25,000, and we raised $75,000—thank you!" He performed a rocking version of "Long Tall Sally" and "Whole Lotta Shakin'." He had the audience at a fever pitch when he suddenly switched gears. The boy they called a hood, a sex maniac, and an illiterate proceeded to honor his country when he sang the hauntingly beautiful "American Trilogy." By the time he reached the "glory halleluyahs," the audience was standing with their hands over their hearts. He drastically changed the tempo with "A Big Hunk o' Love." As this song reached its climax, he threw his belt into the audience. He then announced, "Thank you, you really are a fantastic audience. This is a song we did in *Blue Hawaii* about ten years ago, and I'd like to do it for you." Charlie Hodge fastened Elvis' cape, which had a blue lining and featured an enormous spreadeagle across the entire back. As he reached the final note of "Can't Help Falling in Love," he tore the cape off, spun it above his head, and tossed it to the crowd. The closing vamp began and Elvis strutted from one end of the stage to the other. He was handed a symbolic king's crown, a fitting memento of this historic occasion.

Following the giant success of the "Aloha" special, Elvis began to withdraw even deeper into his private world of servants, hangers-on, and bodyguards. Immediately following his divorce, it had become apparent that he was suffering from acute depression. It seemed that the once virile superstud was falling apart. Almost daily the nation's newspapers reported another malady that had befallen him.

Elvis' constant companion since his divorce was a former Miss Tennessee, Linda Thompson. Although he dated others, it was always Linda who was

Recording the song "Separate Ways." This song told the sad story of Elvis' divorce.

there when he needed someone. He had been hospitalized on at least five occasions in recent years, and each time it was Linda who was there to love and care for him. In August of 1974 he was forced to miss two Las Vegas shows because of influenza. He returned full of fever and apologies, telling the audience that he had missed only five shows in eighteen years. Later that year he was hospitalized again, suffering from pneumonia. In January, shortly before his fortieth birthday, he was again admitted to the hospital. To avoid publicity, he was smuggled into a $400-a-day suite for a routine examination. It was discovered that he was suffering from a stomach condition. He was put on a special diet and was given cortisone and injections of medicine that caused his body to retain fluids and add an excess of seventy pounds to his once-lean frame. It was reported that Elvis was suffering from glaucoma, a disease that causes blindness. In reality, Elvis was extremely nearsighted and, like countless millions, wore eyeglasses. The fan magazines and scandal sheets were having a field day. Some typical headlines read:

Linda Decorates Nursery in New Presley Home

Elvis Presley Still Secretly Married to Priscilla

Elvis' Girlfriend Reveals Baby News

Elvis Reveals: "I'm Going to Marry Liz"

Elvis Near Death in Nashville Car Crash

These are but a few of the headlines that appeared on various magazine covers. As editor of the *Memphis Flash,* I've been deluged with letters inquiring about the truth of these stories. Elvis Presley was such a big-name entertainer that these so-called fan magazines will print anything that may catch the Elvis fan's eye. In reading such stories, I find that there is a unique play on words used for the sole purpose of shocking the public into spending its money to buy this rubbish. Every story has a simple and seemingly innocent explanation that makes one feel foolish when one realizes that one has

105

Priscilla and Lisa today.

been ripped off. In the final analysis, I say believe what you read in the newspapers two thirds of the time, believe only 5 per cent of what you see in the fan mags, and believe 99 per cent of what appears in the pages of the *Flash* (to err is human).

On January 8, 1975, Elvis celebrated his fortieth birthday. Once again the critics had a fiesta. They wrote of the "Aging Rock Star" and that "time is passing him by." They indicated that the King of Rock was too old. This assertion was ridiculous when one carefully examines the ages of other superstars. For example, Sammy Davis, Jr., is fifty-two years old and is as popular and successful as ever. Frank Sinatra was in his mid-forties when he hit his vocal peak with Capitol records in 1958. Two of the biggest sex symbols of the seventies are Steve McQueen, age forty-eight, and Paul Newman at age fifty-three. In pop music, Ray Charles, Chuck Berry, and James Brown are still successful, and yet they are past forty. So while others are approaching fifty, Elvis was severely criticized for turning forty. I believe Elvis was attacked for his age for the very same reasons that his great vocal abilities have never been recognized. A phenomenon common to all geniuses has been the

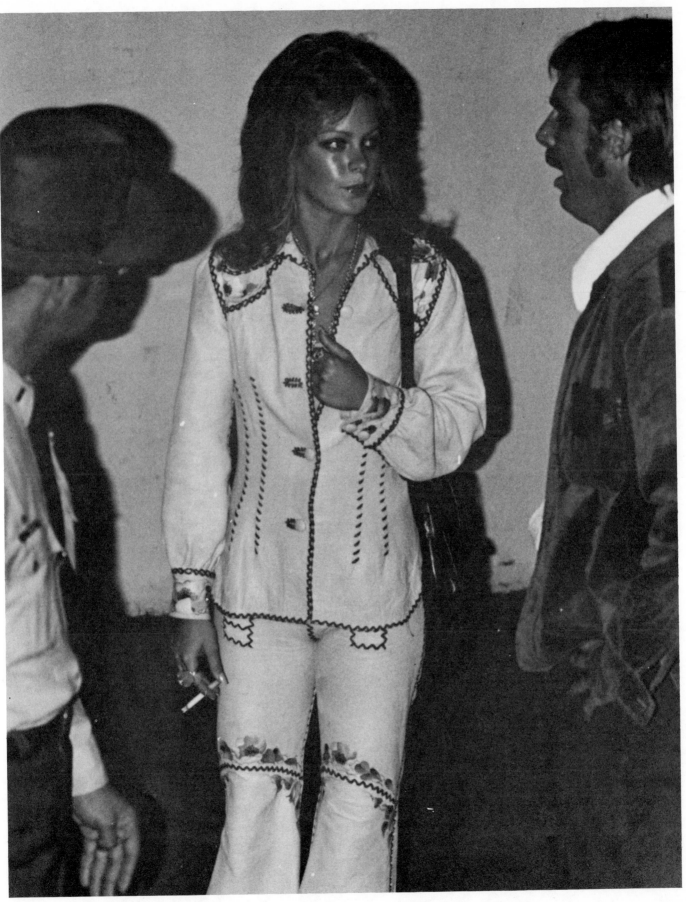

Sheila Ryan backstage at College Park, Maryland. After a brief fling with Elvis, Sheila married actor James Caan.

animosity they have aroused. The critics roasted Jolson and laughed at the abilities of Crosby and Sinatra. But no one has ever been the victim of a loathing press to the extent that Elvis Presley has. I'm quite sure his art is too close to us today to be fully appreciated. In his book *The Great American Popular Singers* Henry Pleasants describes Elvis' vocal abilities:

The voice covers about two octaves and a third, from the baritone's low G to the tenor's high B, with an upward extension in falsetto to at least a D flat. His best octave is in the middle, from about D flat to D flat, granting an extra full step either up or down. . . . He has always been able to duplicate the open, hoarse, ecstatic, screaming, shouting, wailing, reckless sound of the black rhythm-and-blues and gospel singers. But he has not been confined to that one type of vocal production. In ballads and country songs he belts out full-voiced high Gs and As that an opera baritone might envy. . . . [No other single artist has] influenced the course of popular music so profoundly.

The tours continued and the critics ripped him apart for being fat, slow, and forty. Didn't these critics ever gain a few pounds, slow down once in a while if they were under pressure, or age? As for aging, there is no man alive, of course, who can prevent this from happening. Knowing Elvis, I'm sure that his ego suffered greatly every time he went out on stage, but because of his love and devotion to his profession and to his fans he continued his tours; and in every town he tore his heart out to please.

In August of 1975 he opened another festival in Vegas. He'd been dieting and exercising, against his doctor's advice—the critics' heartless references to his weight had hit home. Elvis was advised by both his doctor and his father not to go on stage. The man was desperately ill, and only his great determination and loyalty to his fans kept him going. The fact that he performed for three nights was a miracle. After Elvis canceled, he went directly to Memphis and was immediately admitted to the Baptist Hospital. I flew straight to Memphis, and during my week's stay there I learned that Elvis was ordered not to work again until the first of the year.

In 1976 Elvis marked his forty-first birthday, and America celebrated. Radio stations played Presley hits and featured interviews with myself. Signs hung in store windows offered birthday greetings and travelers at Memphis International Airport heard announcements throughout the day that Elvis was born on January 8. As usual, crowds of tourists and residents gathered outside Graceland's white guitar-studded gates. Gifts and cards from passers-by were placed in boxes for delivery to Elvis. There were guest books for people to sign. "You can live ten lifetimes and you'll never find another like him. He's got a heart of gold. He'll give you the shirt off his back," said his long-time friend Richard Davis.

Apparently Mrs. Jerry Kennedy of Denver, Colorado, agreed with Davis. "He's a very generous person," she said. And she should know, because on January 14, six days after Elvis' forty-first birthday, Mrs. Kennedy was talking on the phone to her husband, Captain Jerry Kennedy, who heads the Denver Police Vice Squad, when the conversation was suddenly interrupted

Elvis and Vernon.

by another voice on the line. It was Elvis. Kennedy had met Elvis in 1970 and since had served as a security guard for the performer on his trips to Colorado. "We had a nice chat of about forty minutes, and then he asked what kind of car I drive," said a joyous Mrs. Kennedy. "I told him, and he asked about our other car. I said we didn't have one." "You will tonight," said Elvis. That night, Elvis bought two Lincoln Mark IVs. One was for the Kennedys and one for a police doctor, Dr. Gerald Starkey. He also purchased an ice-blue Cadillac with a sun roof for a Denver detective and two luxury cars for two people who were vacationing with him. The total cost of the cars came to $70,000.

Backstage in Vegas.

Buying such expensive gifts was nothing new for Elvis. In 1975 he purchased over fifty new cars for friends and strangers. One Memphis lady was presented with a new Eldorado, along with enough money for a new wardrobe and a vacation with her husband. When Elvis was in the hospital he gave new automobiles to three nurses. For years he'd been giving away cars as most people give flowers. In 1975, also, the proceeds from a Jackson, Mississippi, concert went to the victims of a killer tornado. "Money's meant to be spread around," observed the $250,000-a-week entertainer. "The more happiness it helps to create, the more it's worth. It's worthless as an old cut-up paper if it just lays in a bank and grows there without ever having been used to help a body." Sure, a car or any gift from Elvis was expensive, but they are presented without obligation. Only trust, loyalty, and his desire to give were involved. His life and career were based on giving. Even his fans received all he could give. Considering the magnitude of change the world has experienced because of Elvis, it can be said that his generosity was more than we deserve.

It's about time we put Elvis Presley where he belongs—on a pedestal with the other originals like Caruso and Jolson. Elvis Presley was the single most influential artist in the history of rock. He was the driving impulse behind the success of both Bob Dylan and the Beatles. I still have fantasies of Elvis fronting a tough young band, singing "One Night" the way it should be sung. I dream of Elvis recording an album produced by one of our contemporary artists, such as Elton John, Paul Simon, or Paul McCartney. All expressed a desire to work with the King.

Elvis, like Beethoven, Bach, and the Beatles, will be appreciated for many lifetimes.

Aloha

AUTHOR'S NOTE: It is with great sorrow that I add this final chapter to a book that was written as a tribute to a Living Legend!
"That Legend Will Live Forever."

On August 16, 1977, at 5 P.M. E.D.T., my office phone rang. It was Lois Quinn of RCA calling. She asked if I was sitting down. I had been expecting a call from RCA about a statement that I was going to issue to the public. The statement was in the form of a letter expressing love and devotion to Elvis and urging him not to worry, because we all cared. I told Lois that I was sitting down, but in fact I was standing at my desk. She then said, "Paul, Elvis is dead." I couldn't believe what I'd heard. I was sure it was just another Elvis story like the recent wedding hoax that the nation's newspapers had reported. Elvis was bigger than life, and although he was a friend and a human being, it's hard to imagine his actually dying.

In less than ten minutes, ABC, CBS, and NBC local and national news representatives began arriving at my home. The phones had started ringing faster than my wife, Janice, or my friend and photographer Glen Griffin could answer them. Radio stations from all over the country were asking me to give their listeners an on-the-air interview. *Playboy* magazine, the *National Enquirer, Crawdaddy, Rolling Stone,* and just about every newspaper in the country were waiting their turn on the phone lines. There were seventy-five to a hundred photographers in my music room fighting among themselves and shouting for me to look in their direction. This scene was repeated for some sixteen hours. As the reality of Elvis' death and the pressure began to crush me, I wondered how Elvis' heart had been able to last for forty-two years.

The sea of mourners began to gather at the gate of Elvis' beloved Graceland. I found myself thinking of Elvis' father, Vernon, and his beautiful Lisa Marie. A telephone operator called and asked Glen why there were 5,800 calls backed up on my phone lines. She told him we were knocking the phone service of the entire Northeastern Region of Pennsylvania out of whack. He explained I was a friend of Elvis Presley's, and the operator said she understood.

It was amazing. Elvis' wonderful fans, in their moment of supreme grief, calling me to offer their condolences. Flowers and cards began to arrive by the hundreds.

Wednesday, August 17, 1977

Countless thousands had descended upon Memphis. Literally miles of humanity lined Elvis Presley Boulevard. It was announced that Vernon Presley would let the mourners file past Elvis' open casket from 3 to 5 P.M. The family finally closed the gates at 6:30 P.M. In all, more than 20,000 people had seen their fallen idol. They had witnessed a handsome young man dressed in a pure white suit accented by his blue-black hair.

Thursday, August 18, 1977

The crowds of friends and fans remained outside the gates of Graceland and at 4 A.M. tragedy struck again when an automobile driven by a young man struck three young girls. Alice Hovatar and Juanita Johnson were killed instantly. A third young lady, Tammy Baiter, was seriously injured.

The Presley family had requested a plain and private funeral. Jackie Kahane, the comedian who opened Elvis' shows, gave the eulogy. Kathy Westmoreland, who sang the high notes at Elvis' concerts, sang two of his favorite gospel songs. Pallbearers were Elvis' long-time friends Charlie Hodge, Joe Esposito, George Klein, Lamar Fike, Felton Jarvis, and Elvis' physician, Dr. George Nichopoulos. Police officers saluted as the funeral procession, led by a silver Cadillac followed by a white Cadillac hearse carrying Elvis' body and seventeen white Cadillac limousines, drove by the crowds to Elvis' final resting place, Forest Hill Cemetery. Elvis was entombed in a white marble mausoleum at 4:24 P.M.

Vernon spent about twenty minutes alone with his son, and, ironically, Elvis and Vernon were only fifteen feet from the gravesite of Gladys Presley. Elvis and his beloved mother would be together again at last.

Because of crowds estimated to be in the millions, Vernon Presley petitioned the courts of Tennessee explaining that the security to protect his son's body was costing $200 an hour and his mental anguish was unbearable. A favorable ruling was handed down, and both Elvis and his mother, Gladys Presley, were to be moved and laid to rest in the grounds of Graceland.

BOOK 2

STANDING ROOM ONLY

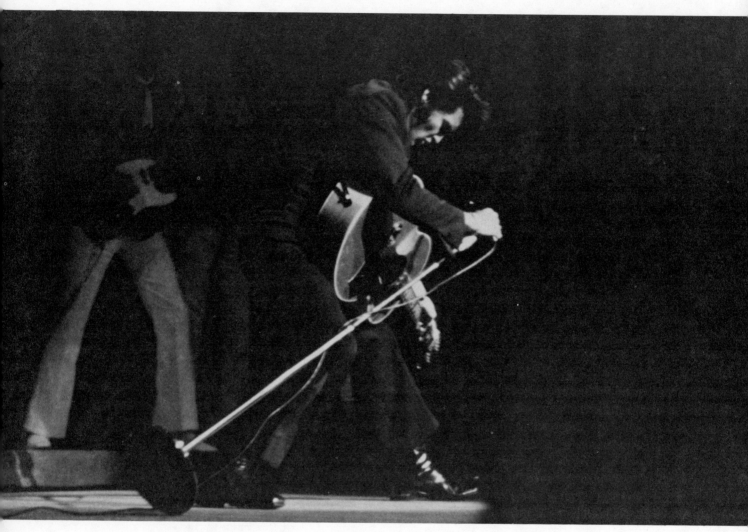

July 26, 1969. Elvis gave his first live show in almost eight years at the Las Vegas International Hotel. During his one-month stand, Elvis broke all existing Vegas records of attendance. Critics from every newspaper in the country shouted that Elvis was certainly the King of entertainment.

That's the Way It Was

Our audience was brief. He signed autographs, exchanged a few words with my wife, Janice, and then thanked us politely for coming to see him. We withdrew into a rising tidal wave of sound.

The word quickly spread around the immediate area as we came through the hall. From the stalls swept a covey of devotees, Presley skirts swishing, ponytails bobbing. They surrounded Janice ten deep, pressing her against the low rail that bordered the floor. There were gasps, unbelievable sighs, looks of sheer wonder. "You saw him!" Janice looked up, her eyes starry: "That's not all—I kissed him!" There was a startled shriek.

Elvis' show carried a half-dozen vaudeville acts that were used to torture the audience into a frenzy of anticipation. Finally he made his appearance, shooting onstage like a young stallion.

He is on the stage of the Arena. Elvis—1957—his first time in Philly. *Live!!* From the thousands of healthy young female throats rises a sound that is difficult to describe. It can be felt rather than heard. For the first few moments he merely stands there. If the sound threatens to subside, he turns on a slow, sleepy smile. He would toss his knee—retract—move a shoulder—retract—gyrate the pelvis—retract. Scream!

He is wearing white shoes and socks, black pants, and a black velvet shirt opened halfway down a hairy bare chest. A three-inch pendant hangs from his neck. Elvis passionately clutches the microphone and brings it close to his pouting lips. He moans a few tender lines from "That's When Your Heartaches Begin." The screams wash toward the stage in a relentless surf. The fans don't have to hear him, as they have memorized the words to every record he has made.

In the Arena aisles the vendors are doing a brisk business hawking their Elvis scarves, "I Like Elvis" buttons, "Elvis Is a Jerk" buttons, and twenty-five-cent field glasses for one dollar.

The girls scream because he belongs to them. A pretty young girl rushes to the stage, arms outstretched to Elvis. Presumably she is screaming, for her mouth is open. Whatever sound she emits blends into the other shrieks. Her friends and two policemen lead her away.

Girls press their palms to the side of their heads in sweet, painful ecstasy. Some jump, some are still, all eyes starry, and all heads tilted in reverie.

Seconds before his final number, a cordon of special police locks arms around the stage. Elvis is concluding his concert, singing "Hound Dog. . . ." He is gone in a flash. He jumps into a waiting car, there is a snarl of tires, and "Elvis has left the building."

The sudden quiet is deafening. Inside the Arena a somber parade of bobby-soxers moves past the stage, each rubbing the floor with a tissue or a handkerchief and hurrying away with their precious memento.

That's the Way It Is

The story you've just read took place some twenty years ago. Sound familiar? It should!

Janice and I were escorted down a long corridor by a special security officer. He was cordial, but he never seemed to move his hand from the pistol that hung menacingly from his hip. At the end of the hall we were met by yet another security officer stationed in front of the door to Elvis' dressing room.

We learned that we were directly below the enormous stage of the beautiful Showroom International at the Hilton Hotel. The door to Elvis' dressing room was locked from the outside. When it was opened, we were greeted by Joe Esposito and Red West. They advised us that Elvis was busy entertaining some friends who were in Vegas to catch his show. I recognized the Checkmates, and a very pregnant Nancy Sinatra. Elvis spotted us in the gathering and smiled. He approached us, shaking my hand and kissing Janice. We spoke for a few minutes, after which I gave Elvis a red belt with huge silver thunderbirds. He in turn presented me with a beautiful multicolored shirt. Elvis then invited us to stay and enjoy ourselves, but we declined; Janice reminded him that he had another show to do and would have to be onstage in about forty minutes. We thanked him for being so considerate in taking the time to be with us. He thanked us for stopping in and kissed Janice good-by.

As we made our way out of the maze of corridors, I held the shirt tightly, appreciating Elvis' act of love and generosity. I had idolized the boy, and I loved the man.

The lights dim, the huge gold curtain slowly begins to rise, and the screaming begins. It starts spontaneously and builds into a crescendo as trumpets, electric guitars, and drums blast the rocking opening bars of "Blue Suede Shoes." As he approaches the stage, a strobe light begins flickering and he struts slowly from one end of the platform to the other. They scream! It is July of 1969 and Elvis is LIVE onstage for the first time in almost eight years.

He is wearing a black jumpsuit with bright red satin vents on the pant legs. A red scarf drapes his bare chest, and tassels hang from the red belt. His appearance is anything you choose to call it—gaudy, vulgar, or magnificent. He looks like a king from another dimension with his glaring eyes and sexy mouth. His high cheekbones and bronzed face seem to be untouched by the years that have passed.

Before he had opened his mouth, the audience was out of its seats, screaming and giving him a standing ovation. He smiled and without warning broke into "Blue Suede Shoes." He sang "I Got a Woman" and "That's All Right, Mama," the first song he ever released. He had already lifted the audience beyond belief. Exhaling a nervous sigh, he spoke. "Hi! I'm Elvis Presley." There was utter pandemonium throughout the Showroom, and the screams grew louder.

For over an hour he flogged himself to near-exhaustion. He was like a wild man! He moved with both grace and animal sexuality. His voice never missed a note when he was doing flips and cartwheels.

While he concentrated mainly on his own hits, he also did some other contemporary songs made popular by other artists. When Elvis finished his renditions there could be no denying the Presley magic! He began to sing the beautiful "Can't Help Falling in Love." He held the final note for what seemed like an eternity, and the gold curtain slowly descended. Once again the audience stood, screamed, and shouted, "Bravo!!" He stood dripping perspiration, his arms outstretched like a modern-day Christ.

Displaying more confidence than would seem possible for any performer, Elvis made believers out of all who had ever doubted his talents and abilities. It was a memorable night—a night when Elvis, the founder of modern pop music, proved that he was still King.

It was announced that Elvis would have another month-long engagement at the International Hotel, beginning on January 26, 1970. Many people feared that his return to Vegas after only five months had passed was too soon. Elvis quickly dispelled that theory when he sold out the huge Showroom night after night, breaking his own August 1969 attendance record.

On opening night he wore a white jumpsuit (this suit is shown on the RCA *On Stage* LP, which was recorded during this engagement) and was looking exceptionally well and quite thin. The King was more at ease at this show. There were many celebrities in attendance, including Juliet Prowse, George Chakiris, Zsa Zsa Gabor, and Dean Martin.

Killing them at
Houston's Astrodome in
1970.

Elvis sang "All Shook Up" and then introduced a few new songs that were hits for fellow artists, on which he made his own indelible mark. The King's show-stopper of the season was his version of "Polk Salad Annie." Elvis staged an incredible karate exhibition during this tune.

Closing night (February 23, 1970) was an extra-long show. When Elvis sang "Love Me Tender," Priscilla ran up to the stage and they embraced as the audience applauded. For his month's work he picked up a cool $1,000,000. Also in the audience at shows during his four-week stint were Liberace, Lana Turner, James Brown, and Joe Namath (who visited backstage). Elvis then flew to Houston in a private jet furnished by Kirk Kerkorian, owner of the International Hotel.

"The Eighth Wonder of the World" is the term applied to Houston's Astrodome, where the King would now do six shows. He was met by the press at the airport. Elvis told the reporters that it was good to be back in Texas, because in his early career he had played many cities there and he had fond memories of those days. He also explained that the Astrodome frightened him because of its size. Not only did the size concern him, but so did performing in the round, which he felt would affect his contact with the audience. He also wondered about the acoustics in such a huge arena. The first

119

matinee did have sound trouble, so Elvis had his own engineers flown in to remedy the situation.

At the start of each show our hero was driven around the Astrodome in a convertible. The crowd went wild as he waved to them while circling the arena. The circular rotating stage was located in the center of the arena. It was here that Elvis performed for forty-five minutes each night. Once again he broke all existing records by drawing standing-room-only crowds at all six shows—over 200,000 people witnessed the King.

Elvis and Priscilla stayed at the Astroworld Hotel. After the final show on Sunday evening there was an awards presentation back at the hotel, when RCA presented Elvis with five gold records. They were for "Don't Cry, Daddy," "In the Ghetto," and "Suspicious Minds" (45s) and the albums *Elvis in Person* and *From Elvis in Memphis*. The promoters of the shows gave him a $2,000 gold watch.

On August 10, 1970, Elvis opened his third season at the Las Vegas International. He was acknowledged as the King of Las Vegas. Metro-Goldwyn-Mayer announced that it would be filming Elvis' shows for the documentary *That's the Way It Is*. This Vegas appearance was the first to be designated the "Elvis Summer Festival."

The entire hotel was plastered with pictures of Elvis. Every employee of the hotel wore a white Styrofoam hat with a colorful band that once again proclaimed the month an "Elvis Summer Festival." Adding a final unusual touch was the presence of a forty-man camera crew from MGM. Denis Sanders, the director, said, "We are going to capture Elvis the entertainer, from the point of view of the fans, the hotel, and the audience."

Elvis was in fine form on opening night, as he was throughout the entire engagement. First-night guests (many of whom were filmed as they entered the Showroom) included Sammy Davis, Jr. (who owns a 157-carat black sapphire ring given to him by the King), Cary Grant, Sonny Liston, Jack Benny, and Nancy Sinatra. These celebrities, as well as everyone else attending the show, were given a bag of Elvis souvenirs.

The Elvis Summer Festival concluded on September 7, 1970. He then began his first tour in nearly fourteen years on September 9. The tour began in Phoenix and finished in Mobile. All in all, he would appear in six cities, doing seven shows in six days. In Phoenix a bomb scare delayed the performance. Elvis' grandmother, Minnie Presley, was in the audience in Tampa. In every city Elvis played to standing-room-only crowds. In both Tampa and Mobile, he set all-time records for attendance.

On November 14, 1970, Elvis gave two performances at the Los Angeles Forum. He wore a special jumpsuit with caped, fringed sleeves. He made the crowd laugh by telling them not to read the crap they read in the movie magazines. He also mentioned his disc sales. The box office revealed that Elvis had set yet another record by grossing $313,000 for the two shows. The Los Angeles *Free Press* called his show the show business event of the year. It said Elvis the performer was bigger than even the legend.

The "sold out" sign was displayed in every city Elvis appeared in. He said that it was most heartwarming the way the West Coast fans welcomed him.

Loving them tender in
Phoenix, 1970.

Detroit, 1970.

Meet me in St. Louis,
1970.

On January 26, 1971, Elvis began his fourth engagement at Las Vegas, at the Hilton. Again every seat for every performance was sold out. In July–August of 1971 another two-week Elvis Summer Festival took place at the Sahara at Lake Tahoe. Two days after the closing at the Sahara, Elvis began his fifth season at Las Vegas, again at the Hilton. He opened on August 9, 1971, and closed on September 6. This engagement had been another triumph for the King.

It was announced that Elvis would be embarking on his first major tour in almost fourteen years. His first stop would be Minneapolis on November 5, where he played to a capacity crowd of 17,600 people. Tickets sold out in less than twenty-four hours (which was the case at every stop along the way).

In Cleveland the demand for tickets was so great that Elvis did a matinee and an evening show. His shows grossed $146,000. His outfits were becoming more and more outlandish. At his Cleveland performance he wore a black jumpsuit with a red-lined cape, and the papers described him as looking like a black-studded tornado. In Louisville he played to an audience of 18,550, the largest crowd in the history of Louisville's Freedom Hall.

Giving a karate
demonstration in
Philly's Spectrum, 1971.

"That's All Right
Mama," Boston, 1971.

Next it was on to Philadelphia, where on November 8 he played to 20,000 people—the gross for this show: a rousing $150,000. He wore a white jumpsuit with a black-lined cape. Local TV personalities and Mayor Frank Rizzo were denied admission because they didn't have tickets. Elvis strutted onto the stage and thousands of flashbulbs lit the Spectrum. It looked like an explosion! The King worked the audience into such madness that it took twenty-five special police and fifty Philadelphia police officers to keep the crowd from rushing the stage.

Baltimore was the next city to witness the Elvis magic. In Boston he performed for 15,509 people; the gross for the show was a whopping $150,000. He rolled into Cincinnati, and the morning newspaper review read: "He gave them hell and they melted in his flame." The next stop was Houston's Hofenheinz Pavilion, and then on to Dallas, where the sell-out crowd would be crying, screaming, and spellbound. The Elvis show flew to Tuscaloosa, where he again drew the largest crowds ever to fill the Memorial Coliseum. He played before packed houses in both Kansas City, Missouri, and the final stop of the tour, Salt Lake City.

Elvis would open his sixth one-month stand at Las Vegas, at the Hilton, on January 26, 1972. He wore many new outfits during this engagement. On opening night he wore black bellbottoms with a black sleeveless jacket. The Spanish-styled outfit came complete with silver conchas ascending the sides of his slacks and giving a starburst effect on the back of his jacket. His red shirt had puffed sleeves gathered above the elbow; a black scarf adorned his bare chest. He sang many requests, including "Memphis." People began shouting for their favorites from every corner of the huge Showroom. Closing night, February 23, 1972, Elvis performed for nearly two hours. Richard Egan, Elvis' costar in his first film, *Love Me Tender,* began a rousing five-minute standing ovation when midway through "Can't Help Falling in Love" the veteran actor stood and applauded. There were tears of joy in the King's eyes as the curtain began to fall.

In April of 1972 Elvis began a fifteen-city tour. It had become apparent to the crafty Colonel Parker that his boy was capable of bringing millions of people to pay ten dollars to see him perform. The Colonel didn't need a calculator to figure how much Elvis was earning for his hour on the stage. This, coupled with the thought of what the concessionaires were making at every stop, made Parker feel as if it were 1957 all over again. Meanwhile, MGM was filming most of the shows, to be utilized in what would later be the award-winning documentary *Elvis on Tour*.

The tour opened in Buffalo, and a crowd of 17,340 was on hand. The audience didn't seem to care if Elvis sang or just smiled. They were mesmerized by his presence. At Detroit's Olympia Stadium he performed before 16,216 people, the largest crowd ever to witness a concert in the stadium's forty-four years. The Elvis charisma moved on to Dayton, where he drew 14,000 people and reaped a record gross of $157,000. In Knoxville the ticket demand was again so overwhelming that he did a matinee and an evening performance. Needless to say, both were sold out. Elvis rocked 22,000 people during his next shows in Hampton Roads, Virginia. The

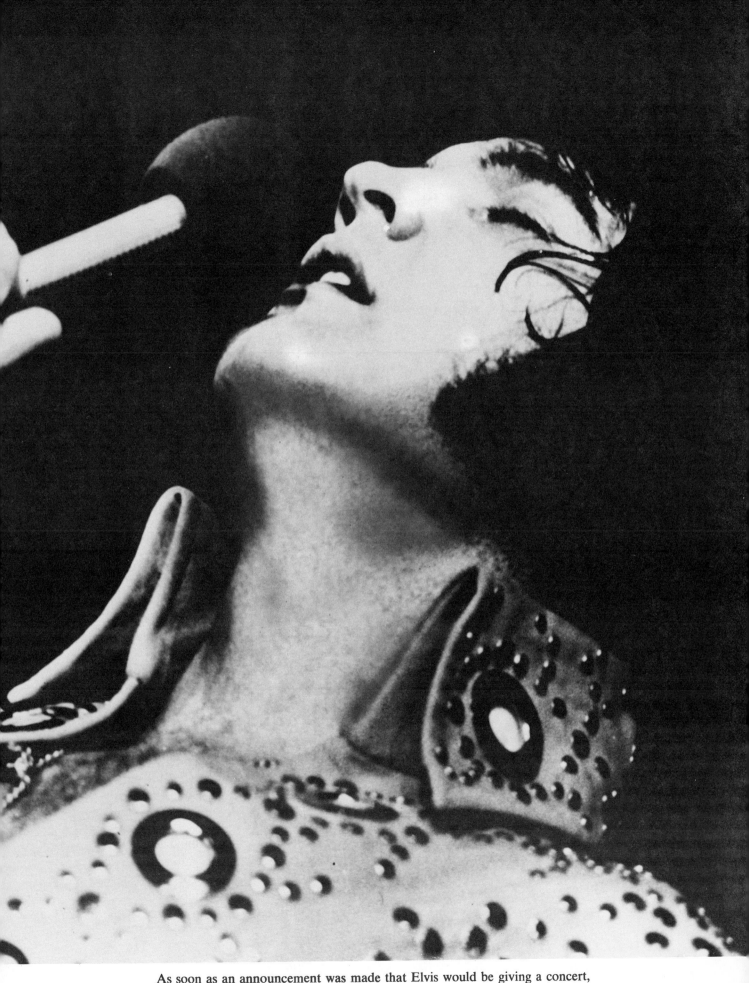

As soon as an announcement was made that Elvis would be giving a concert, tickets sold out in a matter of hours in every city. This photo shows Elvis in a tender mood.

Elvis in Buffalo, 1972.

Richmond Coliseum was the next stop. The following day Elvis gave his wildest performance at the Roanoke Coliseum. At the conclusion of an extremely sensual version of "Polk Salad Annie" all hell broke loose. Fans began rushing the stage from both sides. Charlie Hodge, Red West, Sonny West, and a host of others fought to hold the masses back. Elvis continued to sing as he retreated toward the rear of the stage. The attendance census was a Coliseum record of 10,481, the gross $90,000.

The next tour stops were Indianapolis and Charlotte, North Carolina. The King shattered the existing attendance figures in both cities. In Greensboro, North Carolina, he performed before 16,300 people and grossed $150,000. He gave two sold-out performances in Macon and grossed better than $200,000. Then he was off to Jacksonville, where he did an afternoon and evening show; when he left town he had another $200,000. From Little Rock he moved on to San Antonio. He appeared before 11,000 folks and grossed $100,000. The tour ended before another standing-room-only crowd in Albuquerque.

In June 1972 Elvis began another eight-city tour. The demand for tickets was so great that he was forced to add an extra show in Milwaukee and two more in Chicago. Having had New York hold its red carpet for seventeen years, Elvis Presley finally came to the Big Apple for another sold-out appearance for four nights. He drew more than 80,000 during his stay at the

Three views of Elvis'
legendary Madison
Square Garden
performance in 1972.

Vegas, August 1972.

famous Madison Square Garden. There were no complimentary tickets, no special guests, and no tickets for the mayor. Both John Lennon and Bob Dylan sat in the rear of the giant arena. George Harrison sat high in the balcony. From the stage you could hear big Al Devoure, the emcee, barking, "Get your super-special Elvis souvenirs, the Elvis poster, the souvenir program, and the eleven-by-fourteen photos, especially designed for this tour only. . . ."

At the first show, comedian Jackie Kahane ran into an extremely rude New York audience. They hissed, booed, and shouted, "We want the King." Jackie, however, bravely continued, but the crowd became even more disrespectful. With the words "There are 20,000 of you, and only one of me," he surrendered. The Sweet Inspirations followed, and were greeted by the predominantly white audience with polite yawns. Next, intermission and another chance to buy one's Elvis goodies.

The lights dimmed, the orchestra and choir broke into the opening bars of *2001,* Elvis materialized in a white suit of lights, sparkling with gold studs. Around his shoulders was a gold-lined cape, and his $10,000 gold-and-diamond-encrusted belt graced his waist. He started working with the

128

Elvis in his now classic red "Burning Love" jumpsuit.

mike, his right hand extended, his left leg moving in a corkscrew motion. Time stopped and everyone was innocent. He dominated the mortals who filled the Garden. He used the stage and played to the people. He strutted, shook, and was quite simply brilliant! The girls moaned and stood in their seats. One young lass took a giant leap from the balcony and barely missed the stage. We had to hope that she had not broken her back in this vain but glorious attempt. Friday night, June 9, 1972, Elvis demonstrated his sexual attraction by standing, arms spread, with the great gold cape appearing to give him wings. He was the greatest sex symbol of our times, the champion of the world. He repeated this amazing spectacle three more times and at each performance he turned the Garden inside out and upside down. The gross for Elvis' Madison Square Garden appearances was $730,000!

He grossed better than $100,000 in Fort Wayne, Evansville, and Milwaukee. He rocked Chicago for three sold-out performances and left town with a gross of $500,000. When he departed from Fort Worth, $120,000 went with him. Elvis closed out this tour with successful stops in Wichita and Tulsa. Now it was time to return to the ever-faithful Las Vegas Hilton for the month-long Summer Festival in his honor. Elvis' show on August 4,

1972 (opening night), lasted for forty minutes. This opening night audience boasted stars like Paul Anka, Telly Savalas, Richard Harris, and Sammy Davis, Jr. Elvis' variety of two-piece outfits were breathtaking. I visited him in his dressing room and found myself dazzled by the collection of various belts, jackets, and multicolored shirts that were lining the wall, which Elvis referred to as his wardrobe wall.

Priscilla and Elvis' little girl, Lisa, attended the dinner show on August 27, 1972. Despite his recent separation from his wife, he seemed happy onstage. On more than one occasion he shouted back at the screaming girls, "Don't worry, honey, I'm free now."

The Summer Festival ended on September 4, 1972.

Lubbock, Texas, was the starting point of the next seven-city tour, which commenced on November 8, 1972. The following day he really tore 'em up in Tucson. In fact, the police had a hard time controlling the crowd. In El Paso he wore the famous red "Burning Love" jumpsuit (which now hangs in my music room).

His Oakland show grossed him $147,000. The King then moved on to San Bernadino for two days and to Long Beach for two shows. Lisa was seated in the first row during the second show. Elvis dedicated "Lord, This Time You Gave Me a Mountain" to his daughter.

The final stop of this tour was Honolulu, Hawaii. He wore three specially designed outfits for his three concerts there. The first show lasted an hour and five minutes. And what a show! He sang a total of twenty-six songs. He was dressed in a beautiful white jumpsuit that featured a gold-sequined phoenix on the back. The cape also had a phoenix and had a bright blue lining. On the following day Elvis performed twenty-three songs during his one-hour show. He wore a black jumpsuit with sparkling gold ornaments. At his third performance he crooned through twenty-five tunes and pleased the crowd for a total of one hour and twenty-five minutes. He wore a shocking-blue jumpsuit with a belt that he tossed into the audience at the end of the concert.

Elvis returned there on January 12, 1973, at which time he would perform for a packed house. The show was a full dress rehearsal for his satellite special "Aloha from Hawaii." The following night he did his historic "Aloha" show, which was viewed via satellite by people in twenty countries.

At the end of January it was back to the Hilton in Las Vegas. Once again, all shows were sell-outs. However, Elvis was forced to cancel three of the performances, owing to illness. Some of his shows reflected the fact that the King was not in the best of health. As April approached, he embarked on an eight-city western states tour, which began in Phoenix and closed in Denver. Some 15,000 fans were present to see him in Phoenix, where Elvis received three standing ovations and $110,000. He performed for two packed houses in Anaheim. Next the King of Rock rolled Fresno into a frenzy during two sold-out performances. The legend then moved on to San Diego, where he thrilled the capacity crowd. He sang for 13,000 people in Portland, Oregon, and gave two standing-room-only performances in Spokane, Washington,

Giving out a precious scarf in Providence, 1974.

where he grossed better than $100,000. The final stops on this tour were Seattle and Denver, where 13,000 tickets were sold in less than two hours.

In May, Elvis returned to Lake Tahoe and as usual all shows were sold out. He was forced, however, to cut short this engagement because of illness. June found the King opening another tour, his first stop being Mobile, Alabama. His appearances in Long Island, New York, were a smashing success. People actually stood in line for one week prior to the time that tickets were to go on sale. He gave four concerts in the Nassau Coliseum for a gross of $600,000! This figure broke all previous records for this particular building. The folks in Pittsburgh were elated to hear that the King would be coming to their city—finally! Naturally, he broke all attendance records, and he grossed $250,000. Elvis' show met with the same success in Cincinnati and St. Louis. He played to a capacity audience of 17,200 during his five shows

131

in Atlanta. The performances were mind-boggling and record-shattering. In all, about 85,000 people had come to see the King. He grossed $850,000, which is a record for any single performer in any indoor arena in America.

He visited Nashville next, where his two shows brought him another $180,000. In Oklahoma City it took seventy-five extra police officers to keep the fans from mobbing the stage.

It was back to the Hilton for the Summer Festival. The Las Vegas press did not publicize the August 8, 1973, return as widely as previous Vegas engagements. Regardless of this fact, our hero once again broke his own Vegas attendance record. While he was here in January–February of 1974 (starting January 26), each show was somewhat better than the one that preceded it. For two weeks he was greeted with cheers and excitement. He moved about the stage and really got into the music. His wardrobe during the stay was predominantly a white jumpsuit. On several occasions, though, he wore a black jumpsuit. At one performance, while stalking the stage, he stopped to toss a sweat-soaked scarf into the audience. Much to the audience's surprise, he did this two more times. At one point he bent down and mumbled, "I hope this suit doesn't tear." Here was a performer who made the stage his own from the very minute he stepped onto it.

His first tour of 1974 consisted of twenty-seven shows in twenty days. The tour began with two sold-out shows in Tulsa. From there it was back to the scene of an earlier triumph: the Houston Astrodome. He worked his heart out for about fifty minutes during his afternoon and evening performances. At the evening concert he humbly thanked the crowd and announced that over 89,000 Texans had packed the Astrodome for his two concerts. This figure shattered all other attendance records for a solo performer.

In Alabama Governor George Wallace proclaimed "Elvis Presley Week" when the King appeared for the first time ever in Auburn. He completely awed the capacity crowd. He wore a white outfit with gold braids, his shirt was open at the front, and a giant diamond cross dangled from his neck. He drew an overwhelming ovation when he said, "I'm a big fan of Auburn's football team." When he sang "American Trilogy" everyone stood. In Montgomery Governor Wallace took his wife to see Elvis.

The show moved to Monroe, Louisiana, and then to Charlotte, North Carolina, where he drove the crowd into wave upon wave of screaming adulation. He shifted from the heavy fifties backbeat of "Don't Be Cruel" to the country gospel of "Why Me, Lord." In Roanoke, Elvis sang and shook his way to a new attendance record for the Civic Center. Next he appeared in Hampton Roads, where he once again proved his versatility. At his concert in Greensboro he spotted a little boy dressed in a white sequined jumpsuit. He asked that the spotlight be placed upon the child and joked that the little boy was dressed better than he was. The "greatest show on earth" moved to Murfreesboro, Tennessee, where the audience was the largest in the center's history. When Elvis sang "American Trilogy," I believe everyone was feeling patriotic. He played to two standing-room-only crowds in Knoxville.

The man who said "You can't go home again" obviously didn't have Elvis

The King in Dayton, 1974.

Playing the fool,
1974.

Presley in mind. Elvis performed before six sold-out audiences in Memphis' Mid-South Coliseum—his first Memphis appearances in over thirteen years.

Like a streak of white lightning, he mounts the stage. He nods approval to the overwhelming hometown audience. He is clad in all-white, sparkling with jewels, his slit shirt threatening to reveal his navel. Fans move in clusters down the aisles leading to the stage. They shout his name, forever keeping their arms outstretched in hopes to catching a precious scarf thrown by their King. Elvis' girl friend Linda Thompson is sitting with his family; his

133

love ballads are directed toward where Linda is seated. In one hour he sings just the songs the audience wants to hear. He croons, bumps, wiggles, and leaves the crowd howling for more. "The President lives in the White House, but the King lives in Memphis," one man yells.

He rested for two months and then began a three-city West Coast tour. He then returned to Lake Tahoe, where he played before twenty-two packed show rooms at the beautiful Sahara. The following month he kicked off another cross-country tour. He started on June 15, 1974, in Fort Worth, Texas, where he did four shows and broke the attendance records again. A screaming mob of 20,000 watched the King do his thing in Baton Rouge. He wiggled, snarled, wagged, and pouted to the crowd, bringing thousands of women to their knees by merely shaking one foot in the air. Eleven thousand people in Des Moines cheered just as loudly as the 14,500 in Amarillo who came to see their man. He thrilled 15,000 fans in Cleveland, and in Providence he broke the Civic Center's attendance record.

Elvis was a sight to see at the Spectrum in Philadelphia. We heard the momentous strains of *2001* as the King appeared, glittering in a white outfit highlighted by blue peacock motifs. From every section of the hall, cameras flashed in a strobe-like wave. He never stopped playing up to the audience, handing out one perspiration-soaked scarf after another. All too soon a voice announces that Elvis has left the building—the vision has dematerialized.

In Niagara Falls, New York, he gave one of his greatest performances, and in Columbus, Ohio, he told the crowd, "This is the best audience we've had on this tour." The King went on to Louisville, where he blew everybody away. He gave the audience just enough to make them come back for another sell-out performance. He left the stage to a chorus of cries, "Please don't go!"

He brought his show to Bloomington, Indiana, where he helped the audience relive a bit of their youth. His two concerts in Kansas City, Missouri, were almost as holy to his fans as the Second Coming would be to Christendom. He performed for sold-out audiences in Omaha. He keeps proving that he is one superstar whose flame keeps growing to greater heights of brightness. The tour ended in Salt Lake City, where Elvis performed for over ninety minutes.

From August 19 to September 2 the King returned to his domain at the Las Vegas Hilton. He discarded most of his jumpsuits for the majority of these performances. He wore two-piece leather outfits featuring famous paintings as an alternative. During this Vegas engagement, Elvis earned his eighth-degree Black Belt in karate. He was rightfully proud to reach this goal; now the King was considered a "Master of the Arts." A cast of stars attended his shows; among them were Tom Jones, Telly Savalas, and Vicki Carr. On closing night, Priscilla brought six-year-old Lisa to see her daddy.

In September he began yet another tour, with College Park, Maryland, being the first sold-out crowd to see the King. In most cities he wore his famous peacock jumpsuit. He played another show in College Park before moving on to Detroit, where he wore a rainbow jumpsuit. In Indianapolis,

Philadelphia,
June 1974.

LEFT TO RIGHT: Joe
Esposito, Elvis, Sonny
West, Red West, and
Jerry Schilling.

Like a "Prince
from Another Planet."

he was clad in a dragon jumpsuit and also wore a stunning tiger outfit. The popular *Playboy* jet was used for transportation during this tour. He appeared in ten cities and, as usual, all concerts were sold out in advance. No one left disappointed. On October 10, 1974, Elvis began a brief engagement at the Sahara in Lake Tahoe. The seating arrangements were handled in a similar way as for concerts. This Tahoe appearance was a reimbursement for the previous year's when Elvis was forced to cancel because of illness.

The Hilton, Las Vegas, was once again the scene of obsessive dedication as the Hillbilly Cat began a two-week engagement there on March 18, 1975. Banners were strung on the walls and Elvis souvenirs were on sale in the lobby. Over 2,000 people poured into the Showroom each night. Not one quivering female (or her date for that matter) seemed to care that the Memphis phenomenon had put on some weight, even though he lost it quickly during his two-week stay. His fans showered him with gifts of love and generous sighs. He tossed silk scarves to his many admirers, men and women. Gals struggled to get closer to the stage—to Elvis; in many cases they would return to their seats disappointed. On special occasions he shared the spotlight with Sherril Nielson of· Voice and Bill Baize of the

Making them feel it in Columbus, June 1974.

Stamps. The shows left everyone wanting more. The King had never been in better voice.

Closing night was an experience! Elvis sang just about everyone's favorite song. He was congenial and gracious. Everybody onstage was having a good time, and the feeling (you might call it vibes) spread to the eager audience. There was a three-way water pistol fight among Elvis, Charlie Hodge, and Duke Bardwell. He hit notes that sent chills up one's spine. There were more standing ovations on this evening than any previous night. He turned the entire Showroom on to what was Elvis at his best. A memorable night was shared by all, a night that none of us who were lucky enough to witness it are ever likely to forget.

The first tour of 1975 concentrated on the South. Before the band could complete even the first note of *2001,* which had become Elvis' theme for his arrival on stage, the 11,000 fans in the Mobile auditorium screamed in anticipation. When he completed his set, he waved to the crowd, walked off the stage, and stepped into the limousine waiting just behind the stage. The audience was still standing and cheering. In Jacksonville there was utter chaos over the King. In Tampa 10,000 eager fans greeted Elvis and his people. The Civic Center at Lakeland, Florida, found the Presley show to be the smoothest-running, most professional ever to grace their arena. Shortly thereafter he thrilled 30,000 folks during the three sold-out shows in Murfreesboro, Tennessee.

The singer and his entourage stormed Atlanta, where he gave three more standing-room-only concerts. A bright green bra sailed onto the Omni Stadium stage. He picked up the intimate souvenir: Who did this, he wanted to know. The culprit stood and brazenly admitted her guilt. And so it went all evening. Flashbulbs pop by the thousands, simulating daylight in the huge auditorium. He struts across the stage. More shrieks. He plucks his guitar.

137

The President lives in the White House, but the King lives in Memphis, 1971.

More pandemonium. Twisting his leg, he begins to sing. Surely the walls of the Omni will tumble at any moment. He has the crowd wrapped around his finger. Elvis is in Atlanta, and the Omni is the only place to be.

The next stop was Monroe, Louisiana, where he racked up another gross of over $100,000. On the final leg of the tour he performed in Jackson, Mississippi. Elvis donated all of the money from this performance to aid the victims of the horrendous tornado. (Jackson is not too far from Elvis' birthplace, Tupelo.)

On May 31, 1975, only twenty-three days after completing his southern tour, he took to the road once again. He arrived in Huntsville, Alabama, where he performed four sold-out concerts. More than 10,000 greeted his show in Houston. He completed this tour by giving Memphis, his home town, a chance to catch his show. The crowd of 12,367 screaming fans, friends, and fanatics shouted "We love you" at Memphis' most famous son. He wore a tight-fitting white jumpsuit laced with Indian-style embroidery. A favorite with the audience was Elvis' stirring version of "How Great Thou Art." The crowd applauded wildly when he introduced his father, Vernon, who was recovering from a heart problem. He also informed the audience that after a brief rest he would be starting another tour, mainly in the North.

The tour he mentioned began on July 8, 1975, in Oklahoma City. Shimmering and sparkling in his outrageous black and baby-blue sequined outfit, rings flashing, Elvis belted out the songs and burlesqued his own sexy image. In Terre Haute, Indiana, he wiggled his hips, shook a leg, paused while the girls went bonkers, grinned, and wiggled some more. For 10,000 Cleveland area fans, he proved he is still King. The Civic Center was the setting as Presley conquered the hearts of his audience. He next shook Charleston, West Virginia. His one concert on Friday and two on Saturday were, natu-

"I need your body,
baby."

rally, sold out weeks in advance. Together they grossed $253,000 and officials said that $38,000 of that was left in state and local taxes, labor, and lease of the center. Fans came in all sizes, in all sorts of dress, and from all places. An estimated 23,000 streamed into Niagara Falls, New York, from as far away as Columbus, Ohio, and as close as Buffalo to give Elvis one standing ovation after another during his two appearances here.

The next stop was Springfield, Massachusetts, where he turned 18,000 people on to the magic that was his alone. "Elvis, I love you" read the sign hanging from the railing in back of the stage in New Haven's Veterans Memorial Coliseum. Singing into the microphone, swaying like the Elvis of the fifties and singing at least as well, he more than satisfied the faithful. He asked the throngs to sit down as a few people almost managed to get on the stage. The show was a huge success. He brought his show to Long Island's Nassau Coliseum, where he performed for two sold-out audiences. When he sang "You'll Never Walk Alone," he let his voice loose, reaching the same power and emotion that established him as the King of Rock. He was magnificent, so superb that it was hard to comprehend that any human could possibly hit and hold the notes that I had just heard. They held a religious service in Norfolk's Scope Auditorium, where Elvis performed before his grateful fans. He's wearing a suit that appears so white and sparkling that it makes his shock of shoe-polish-black hair gleam like black coal.

He still makes them scream with "Hound Dog," "All Shook Up," and "Teddy Bear." Even on the newer songs like "Promised Land" and "T-R-O-U-B-L-E" he really rocks. At the end of the day he is $200,000 richer than when the day began.

The tour came to an end in Asheville, North Carolina, where the King gave three concerts. He had lost none of his magic, as the audience witnessed with great pleasure. He wore a shirt open to the waist and ran through two decades of hits. His Asheville shows were sold out three months in advance.

Following the success of this tour, Elvis opened at the Las Vegas Hilton on August 18, 1975. The band played *2001* as drummer Ronnie Tutt gave a long roll. The packed house counted the seconds to Elvis' entrance. Finally he came running onstage. He sang "See See Rider" to a great reaction from the audience. He then joked, "You'll never guess where I just came from"; the audience roared with laughter as Elvis confessed that he had been delayed in the bathroom. He then told a story in connection with this. Here is how it basically went: He attended a football game with a friend. A fan was talking to his friend and eventually found out that Elvis was at the game. Upon hearing that he was in the bathroom, she said, "I didn't know he did that." The story brought much laughter.

Now Elvis did something different. He had a Hilton ice bucket passed around for requests. He sang for nearly an hour. When the curtain began to fall he was looking very ill. Elvis' Summer Festival 1975 grew cold after only three days when he was hospitalized for exhaustion.

The Hilton announced that Elvis would be returning to Vegas on December 2, 1975. This engagement would be different from his earlier Vegas ap-

Joe Esposito helps Elvis from the stage after an exhausting show.

pearances in that he would be doing only one show a night because of doctor's orders. The hotel was filled with the same banners, posters, and billboards that were used during the Summer Festival. The Hilton was jammed with people lining up across the lobby, the souvenir stand packed with people buying Elvis photo albums, records, and pictures. The King, sporting a sleeveless white and silver embroidered jumpsuit with a V-neck shirt, ran on stage and quickly began. He was smiling. The audience sensed that he was in an extraordinary mood. The reason became obvious when he introduced seven-year-old Lisa. She stood, hammed it up, and waved to the crowd until her beaming father said, "Whoa there, honey, that's enough, now." He sang new as well as old songs. Everyone applauded wildly at the

Las Vegas,
August 1974.

conclusion of each tune. He broke all Vegas winter house records, as he drew 32,000 people and racked up a healthy $800,000 for the hotel, not including drinks, room rates, or gambling losses.

New York City can keep Guy Lombardo and Times Square. It was announced that Elvis would appear at Pontiac Stadium in Pontiac, Michigan. His special New Year's Eve show would be seen by 60,000 fans.

December 28, 1975

Along with my wife, Janice, I arrived at Detroit's Metro Airport on Sunday evening, December 28. The first thing that caught my eye was a not unpleasing giant window display for *Elvis in Hollywood*. We picked up our rented car and drove to the hotel.

December 29, 1975

My day began at 5 A.M. and, before it would end, I would do seven TV shows, one radio show, and one newspaper interview. The purpose of my appearances was to plug *Elvis in Hollywood* and Elvis' historical New Year's Eve concert.

THE BIG DAY ARRIVES!

December 31, 1975

In the center of the huge football field was a round stage, some thirty-six feet high. Attached to the stage was a seventy-yard walkway with the words "Happy New Year" displayed on the side. Elvis would use this to get to the stage. The thought of playing to 60,000 people apparently had Elvis nervous. While preparing for the show, he learned of a bomb scare and an assassination threat. At 11 P.M. this courageous man made his way down the long runway, pausing to take a deep breath, and then bolted onto the stage like a great tiger that had been freed from his cage. Sixty thousand people, including his beautiful daughter and his father, were going wild. Elvis stated that he was nervous, but didn't mention the threats. The lights reflected off of his stunning white studded jumpsuit as he sang and wildly danced around the stage. He sang "See See Rider," "I Got a Woman," "Tryin' to Get to You," "Lord, This Time You Gave Me a Mountain," "Don't Be Cruel," "All Shook Up," "Teddy Bear," "Heartbreak Hotel," and "One Night." The audience was going insane when Elvis went into "Polk Salad Annie." This

143

"How Great Thou Art,"
May 1975.

was positively the best I've ever seen him perform this number. He was moving like the wind when the pants on his jumpsuit split. He finished the song and then went to change his suit. He returned in what seemed like seconds and told the audience that he was a quick-change artist. After introducing the band, he sang "It's Now or Never," "My Way," and "How Great Thou Art." It was now three minutes until twelve, and Elvis began to sing his first movie song, "Love Me Tender." The clock on the stadium's scoreboard stood at ten seconds to the New Year. He began the countdown, 10—9—8 . . . "Happy New Year!" Balloons began to fall from the sky and Elvis asked everyone to join him in singing "Auld Lang Syne." The spotlight swirled and the cheers were deafening. He then sang an unbelievable version of "America." At the song's end he received an ovation. He sang "Wooden Heart" next, then thanked the audience for setting a new indoor attendance record for the largest crowd ever to witness a solo performer. He closed the show with the beautiful "Can't Help Falling in Love." This great man had just given the performance of his life and given us something to be thankful for, for years to come. "Happy New Year!"

"Bridge over Troubled
Water," 1976.

"You got a lot of nerve, baby."

I've been fortunate enough to witness over eight hundred of Elvis' shows. I also had the opportunity to meet with and have a closer look at the man behind the image. Despite the fact that Elvis no longer needed the money that his personal appearances brought, he continued his back-breaking tours and Vegas appearances. He unselfishly stripped his soul bare time after time in an attempt to share his love for his friends and fans.

ELVIS! The name creates a gallery of images: Coal-black hair, surly mouth, long sideburns, and blue suede shoes. Even after his death, Elvis continues to be the "King" of entertainment.

Rock on,

Paul

P.S. The following pages reveal a chronological listing of all Elvis' concerts.

Live Appearances

1969		Shows
7/26/69–8/28/69	Las Vegas—International	57

1970		
1/26/70–2/23/70	Las Vegas—International	57
2/27/70–3/1/70	Houston—Astrodome	6
8/10/70–9/7/70	Las Vegas—International	58
9/9/70	Phoenix	1
9/10/70	St. Louis	1
9/11/70	Detroit	1
9/12/70	Miami	1
9/13/70	Tampa (aft. & eve.)	2
9/14/70	Mobile	1
11/10/70	Oakland	1
11/11/70	Portland, Oreg.	1
11/12/70	Seattle	1
11/13/70	San Francisco	1
11/14/70	Los Angeles—Forum (aft. & eve.)	2
11/15/70	San Diego	1
11/16/70	Oklahoma City	1
11/17/70	Denver	1
	TOTAL FOR 1970	137

1971		
1/26/71–2/23/71	Las Vegas—Hilton	57
7/20/71–8/2/71	Lake Tahoe, Nev.—Sahara	28
8/9/71–9/6/71	Las Vegas—Hilton	57
11/5/71	Minneapolis	1
11/6/71	Cleveland (2 shows)	2
11/7/71	Louisville	1
11/8/71	Philadelphia	1
11/9/71	Baltimore	1
11/10/71	Boston	1
11/11/71	Cincinnati	1
11/12/71	Houston	1
11/13/71	Dallas (2 shows)	2
11/14/71	Tuscaloosa	1
11/15/71	Kansas City, Mo.	1
11/16/71	Salt Lake City	1
	TOTAL FOR 1971	156

1972		
1/26/72–2/23/72	Las Vegas—Hilton	57
4/5/72	Buffalo	1
4/6/72	Detroit	1
4/7/72	Dayton	1

LIVE APPEARANCES

1972		Shows
4/8/72	Knoxville (aft. & eve.)	2
4/9/72	Hampton Roads (aft. & eve.)	2
4/10/72	Richmond	1
4/11/72	Roanoke	1
4/12/72	Indianapolis	1
4/13/72	Charlotte	1
4/14/72	Greensboro	1
4/15/72	Macon (aft. & eve.)	2
4/16/72	Jacksonville (aft. & eve.)	2
4/17/72	Little Rock	1
4/18/72	San Antonio	1
4/19/72	Albuquerque	1
6/9/72	New York, Madison Square Garden	1
6/10/72	" " " " " (aft. & eve.)	2
6/11/72	" " " " "	1
6/12/72	Fort Wayne	1
6/13/72	Evansville	1
6/14/72–6/15/72	Milwaukee	2
6/16/72	Chicago (aft. & eve.)	2
6/17/72	"	1
6/18/72	Fort Worth	1
6/19/72	Wichita	1
6/20/72	Tulsa	1
8/4/72–9/4/72	Las Vegas—Hilton	63
11/8/72	Lubbock	1
11/9/72	Tucson	1
11/10/72	El Paso	1
11/11/72	Oakland	1
11/12/72–11/13/72	San Bernardino	2
11/14/72–11/15/72	Long Beach	2
11/17/72	Honolulu	1
11/18/72	" (aft. & eve.)	2
	TOTAL FOR 1972	164

1973		
1/12/73	H.I.C. Arena, Hawaii—rehearsal for "Aloha from Hawaii via Satellite" show	1
1/14/73	H.I.C. Arena, Hawaii—"Aloha from Hawaii" show	1
1/26/73–2/23/73	Las Vegas—Hilton (sick for 3 shows)	54
4/22/73	Phoenix	1
4/23/73–4/24/73	Anaheim	2
4/25/73	Fresno (aft. & eve.)	2
4/26/73	San Diego	1
4/27/73	Portland, Oreg.	1
4/28/73	Spokane (aft. & eve.)	2
4/29/73	Seattle (aft. & eve.)	2
4/30/73	Denver	1
5/5/73–5/20/73	Lake Tahoe, Nev.—Sahara (finished on 5/16/73, sick)	25

149

1973   Shows

Date	Location	Shows
6/20/73	Mobile	1
6/21/73	Atlanta	1
6/22/73	Uniondale, N.Y.—Nassau Coliseum	1
6/23/73	" " " (aft. & eve.)	2
6/24/73	" " "	1
6/25/73–6/26/73	Pittsburgh	2
6/27/73	Cincinnati	1
6/28/73	St. Louis	1
6/29/73	Atlanta (aft. & eve.)	2
6/30/73	" (aft. & eve.)	2
7/1/73	Nashville	1
7/2/73	Oklahoma City	1
8/6/73–9/3/73	Las Vegas—Hilton	59

TOTAL FOR 1973   168

1974

Date	Location	Shows
1/26/74–2/9/74	Las Vegas—Hilton	29
3/1/74–3/2/74	Tulsa	2
3/3/74	Houston—Astrodome (aft. & eve.)	2
3/4/74	Monroe, La.	1
3/5/74	Auburn, Ala.	1
3/6/74	Montgomery	1
3/7/74–3/8/74	Monroe, La.	2
3/9/74	Charlotte	1
3/10/74	Roanoke	1
3/11/74	Hampton Roads	1
3/12/74	Richmond	1
3/13/74	Greensboro	1
3/14/74	Murfreesboro, Tenn.	1
3/15/74	Knoxville (aft. & eve.)	2
3/16/74	Memphis (aft. & eve.)	2
3/17/74	"	1
3/18/74	Richmond	1
3/19/74	Murfreesboro, Tenn.	1
3/20/74	Memphis (aft. & eve.)	2
3/21/74	"	1
5/10/74	San Bernardino	1
5/11/74	Los Angeles—Forum (aft. & eve.)	2
5/12/74	Fresno	1
5/16/74–5/26/74	Lake Tahoe, Nev.—Sahara	22
6/15/74	Fort Worth (aft. & eve.)	2
6/16/74	" " " "	2
6/17/74–6/18/74	Baton Rouge	2
6/19/74	Amarillo	1
6/20/74	Des Moines	1
6/21/74	Cleveland	1
6/22/74	Providence (aft. & eve.)	2
6/23/74	Philadelphia (aft. & eve.)	2
6/24/74	Niagara Falls, N.Y.	1
6/25/74	Columbus, Ohio	1

LIVE APPEARANCES

1974   **Shows**

6/26/74	Louisville	1
6/27/74	Bloomington, Ind.	1
6/28/74	Milwaukee	1
6/29/74	Kansas City, Mo. (aft. & eve.)	2
6/30/74	Omaha (aft. & eve.)	2
7/1/74	"	1
7/2/74	Salt Lake City	1
8/19/74–9/2/74	Las Vegas—Hilton (2 canceled)	27
9/27/74–9/28/74	College Park, Md.	2
9/29/74	Detroit	1
9/30/74–10/1/74	South Bend	2
10/2/74–10/3/74	St. Paul	2
10/4/74	Detroit	1
10/5/74	Indianapolis	1
10/6/74	Dayton	1
10/7/74	Wichita	1
10/8/74	San Antonio	1
10/9/74	Abilene, Tex.	1
10/10/74–10/14/74	Lake Tahoe, Nev.—Sahara	8

TOTAL FOR 1974   152

1975

3/18/75–4/1/75	Las Vegas—Hilton	29
4/23/75	Mobile	1
4/24/75	Macon	1
4/25/75	Jacksonville	1
4/26/75	Tampa (aft. & eve.)	2
4/27/75	Lakeland, Fla. (aft. & eve.)	2
4/28/75	"	1
4/29/75	Murfreesboro, Tenn.	1
4/30/75–5/2/75	Atlanta	3
5/3/75	Monroe, La.	1
5/4/75	Lake Charles	1
5/5/75	Jackson, Miss.	1
5/6/75–5/7/75	Murfreesboro, Tenn.	2
5/30/75	Huntsville	1
5/31/75	" (aft. & eve.).	2
6/1/75	"	1
6/2/75	Mobile (aft. & eve.)	2
6/3/75	Tuscaloosa	1
6/4/75–6/5/75	Houston	2
6/6/75	Dallas	1
6/7/75	Shreveport (aft. & eve.)	2
6/8/75	Jackson, Miss. (aft. & eve.)	2
6/9/75	"	1
6/10/75	Memphis	1
7/8/75	Oklahoma City	1
7/9/75	Terre Haute	1
7/10/75	Cleveland	1
7/11/75	Charleston, W.Va.	1
7/12/75	" (aft. & eve.)	2

1975 Shows

7/13/75	Niagara Falls, N.Y. (aft. & eve.)	2
7/14/75–7/15/75	Springfield, Mass.	2
7/16/75–7/17/75	New Haven	2
7/18/75	Cleveland	1
7/19/75	Uniondale, N.Y.—Nassau Coliseum (aft. & eve.)	2
7/20/75	Norfolk (aft. & eve.)	2
7/21/75	Greensboro	1
7/22/75–7/24/75	Asheville	3
8/18/75–8/20/75	Las Vegas—Hilton (closed through illness)	5
12/2/75–12/15/75	Las Vegas—Hilton	17
12/31/75	Pontiac, Mich.	1

TOTAL FOR 1975 106

1976

3/17/76–3/19/76	Johnson City, Tenn.	3
3/20/76	Charlotte	1
3/21/76	Cincinnati	1
3/22/76	St. Louis	1
4/22/76	Omaha	1
4/23/76	Denver	1
4/24/76	San Diego	1
4/25/76	Long Beach	1
4/26/76	Seattle	1
4/27/76	Spokane	1
5/27/76	Bloomington, Ind.	1
5/28/76	Ames, Iowa	1
5/29/76	Oklahoma City	1
5/30/76	Odessa, Tex.	1
5/31/76	Lubbock	1
6/1/76	Tucson	1
6/2/76	El Paso	1
6/3/76	Fort Worth	1
6/4/76–6/6/76	Atlanta	3
6/25/76	Buffalo	1
6/26/76	Providence	1
6/27/76	Largo, Md. (aft. & eve.)	2
6/28/76	Philadelphia	1
6/29/76	Richmond	1
6/30/76	Greensboro	1
7/1/76	Baton Rouge	1
7/2/76	Fort Worth	1
7/3/76	Tucson	1
7/4/76	Tulsa	1
7/5/76	Memphis	1
7/23/76	Louisville	1
7/24/76	Charleston, W.Va. (aft. & eve.)	2
7/25/76	Syracuse	1
7/26/76	Rochester	1
7/27/76	Syracuse	1

LIVE APPEARANCES

1976   **Shows**

Date	City	Shows
7/28/76	Hartford	1
7/29/76	Springfield, Mass.	1
7/30/76	New Haven	1
8/1/76	Hampton Roads	1
8/2/76	Charlottesville	1
8/27/76	San Antonio	1
8/28/76	Houston	1
8/29/76	Mobile	1
8/30/76	Tuscaloosa	1
8/31/76	Macon	1
9/1/76	Jackson, Miss.	1
9/2/76	Tampa	1
9/3/76	St. Petersburg	1
9/4/76	Lakeland, Fla.	1
9/5/76	Jacksonville	1
9/6/76	Huntsville	1
9/7/76–9/8/76	Pine Bluff	2
10/14/76–10/15/76	Chicago	2
10/16/76	Duluth	1
10/17/76	Minneapolis	1
10/18/76	Sioux Falls, S.Dak.	1
10/19/76	Madison	1
10/20/76	South Bend	1
10/21/76	Kalamazoo	1
10/22/76	Champaign	1
10/23/76	Cleveland	1
10/24/76	Evansville	1
10/25/76	Fort Wayne	1
10/26/76	Dayton	1
10/27/76	Carbondale, Ill.	1
11/24/76	Reno	1
11/25/76	Eugene	1
11/26/76	Portland, Oreg.	1
11/27/76	Eugene	1
11/28/76–11/29/76	San Francisco	2
11/30/76	Anaheim	1
12/2/76–12/12/76	Las Vegas—Hilton	15
12/27/76	Wichita	1
12/28/76	Dallas	1
12/29/76	Birmingham	1
12/30/76	Atlanta	1
12/31/76	Pittsburgh	1

TOTAL FOR 1976   100

1977

Date	City	Shows
2/12/77	Miami	1
2/13/77	St. Petersburg	1
2/14/77	West Palm Beach	1
2/15/77	Orlando	1
2/16/77	Montgomery	1
2/17/77	Augusta	1
2/18/77	Columbia, S.C.	1

153

1977   **Shows**

2/19/77	Johnson City, Tenn.	1
2/20/77	Charlotte	1
3/23/77	Phoenix	1
3/24/77	Amarillo	1
3/25/77–3/26/77	Norman, Okla.	2
3/27/77	Abilene, Tex.	1
3/28/77	Austin	1
3/29/77–3/30/77	Alexandria, La.	2
4/21/77	Greensboro	1
4/22/77	Detroit	1
4/23/77	Toledo	1
4/24/77	Ann Arbor	1
4/25/77	Saginaw	1
4/26/77	Kalamazoo	1
4/27/77	Milwaukee	1
4/28/77	Green Bay	1
4/29/77	Duluth	1
4/30/77	St. Paul	1
5/1/77–5/2/77	Chicago	2
5/3/77	Saginaw	1
5/20/77	Knoxville	1
5/21/77	Louisville	1
5/22/77	Largo, Md.	1
5/23/77	Providence	1
5/24/77	Augusta, Maine	1
5/25/77	Rochester, N.Y.	1
5/26/77–5/27/77	Binghamton, N.Y.	2
5/28/77	Philadelphia	1
5/29/77	Baltimore	1
5/30/77	Jacksonville	1
5/31/77	Baton Rouge	1
6/1/77	Macon	1
6/2/77	Mobile	1
6/17/77	Springfield, Mo.	1
6/18/77	Kansas City, Mo.	1
6/19/77	Omaha	1
6/20/77	Lincoln, Nebr.	1
6/21/77	Rapid City, S. Dak.	1
6/22/77	Sioux Falls, S. Dak.	1
6/23/77	Des Moines	1
6/24/77	Madison, Wisc.	1
6/25/77	Cincinnati	1
6/26/77	Indianapolis	1

TOTAL FOR 1977   54

BOOK 3

RECORDING SESSIONS

When an artist walks into a recording studio to make a record, it is referred to as a recording session. The session involves Elvis, his backup musicians, vocalists, the engineer, and the producer. During the Sun days, Sam Phillips was the producer. The Beatles are given credit by music buffs as the first artists to produce themselves. As you know, the Beatles explosion really began in 1964. Elvis had been producing his own records from 1956 to 1964. This fact is not generally known because RCA gave official production credit to Steve Sholes and Chet Atkins.

Felton Jarvis began acting as the official producer of all Presley recordings in 1966. Together with Elvis, he did the mixing, overdubbing of horns, strings, voices, and so on. A matrix number is given to every recording by RCA. These numbers serve as archive numbers enabling RCA to locate the recording in the easiest manner. The matrix number also gives information on what year the recording took place. (In some cases, particularly with film recordings, the matrix number is unavailable.)

A. RCA matrix numbers were in two parts. The last four figures are serial numbers. The first four can be subdivided into two sets.

B. The first two figures denote the year of the recording (purchase date).

C. The next two denote the manufacturer of the original recording (company).

D. RCA's numbering system has changed several times through the years.

RCA used a system of prefixes to denote the year: i.e., F = 1955, G = 1956, H = 1957, J = 1958, and so on. In 1963 the prefix changed to RP, and then to DP in 1976.

Also indicated were the following:
From 1956 to 1958 all recordings owned by RCA were WB.

Any purchase tapes were prefixed as PB.

In 1961 RCA changed WB to WW.

Starting in 1963, all recordings owned by RCA were A4, while tapes delivered by the movie companies were A3, or in some cases A1.

Studio or live recordings not owned by RCA were A5.

When a song is recorded, it is seldom acceptable on the first take. When the artist and the producer are satisfied, a master tape is made. It is this master tape that the public hears as the finished product. In many cases various takes are spliced together to create the master tape.

The matrix numbers used in connection with film recordings are also the release numbers. The film company generally handed the original masters ,over when the film was completed. Elvis' film songs were usually recorded at the movie company's sound studio. In the fifties and sixties, these recordings followed the usual pattern. In the mid-sixties, however, L.A. studio musicians gathered and recorded the backing tracks on one particular day. Elvis would cut the vocal tracks at a later date.

The musicians who backed Elvis during the movie years were:

James Burton—guitar   Joe Osbourne—bass
Glen Campbell—guitar   Hal Blaine—drums
Charlie McCoy—harmonica   Leon Russell—piano

If no other information is given, these were the musicians for the movie recordings.

Sometimes the songs in the films differed from the soundtrack recordings.

I did not include the following recordings because they were talking records (but see listings in the "Rare Records" section):

1. *The Truth About Me*
2. *Elvis Sails*
   J2PB 7302 *Press Interviews with Elvis Presley*
   J2PB 7303 *Elvis Presley News Interview*
   J2PB 7304 *Pat Henry Interviews Elvis* (Producer: B. P. McCuen)
3. *Buddah Press Conference* (*Buddah Records Current Audio Magazine, Volume 1*)
4. *Having Fun with Elvis on Stage*

A most popular question among fans is "When will RCA release the unreleased Sun songs?" The answer is never. Why? Simply because RCA used all the tapes that Sam Phillips turned over to them. It is true that Elvis recorded many songs in the Sun studios that have never been released. Sam Phillips, however, still has these treasures in his possession, but can never release them, as RCA owns all rights to any Elvis recordings.

I have included every studio and film recording Elvis has made, along with the facts surrounding them.

When talking about Elvis' recording sessions, one has to begin in 1953, when he made his first private record. This took place in a converted garage in Memphis. The name of the company was Memphis Recording Service; it was a sideline of the Sun Record Company, located at 706 Union Avenue. Sam Phillips owned both companies.

In July of 1953 Elvis walked into the studio. He wanted to make a record for his mother's birthday. He recorded an old Ink Spots hit, *My Happiness*, and *That's When Your Heartaches Begin*. The songs were put directly onto the wax and Elvis owned the only copy. Some nine months later, on January 4, 1954, Elvis returned to make another private record. This time he recorded *Casual Love Affair* and *I'll Never Stand in Your Way*. Once again Elvis left the studio with the only existing copy.

1954

July 1954   **Sun studio, Memphis**
        I Love You Because   G2WB 1086
U-128 *That's All Right* [*Mama*] F2WB 8040
U-129 *Blue Moon of Kentucky*   F2WB 8041
        Blue Moon   F2WB 8117

Elvis' first commercial recording session took place on July 5, 1954, and lasted four days. There are several unreleased songs from this session.

September 1954		Sun studio, Memphis
U-130	*I Don't Care if the Sun Don't Shine*	F2WB 8042
U-131	*Good Rockin' Tonight*	F2WB 8043
	Just Because[1]	F2WB 8118

December 1954		Sun studio, Memphis
U-140	*Milkcow Blues Boogie*	F2WB 8044
U-141	*You're a Heartbreaker*	F2WB 8045

[1] *Just Because* could be from the former session.

1955

January 1955		Sun studio, Memphis
	I'll Never Let You Go	F2WB 8116

February 1955		
U-143	*Baby, Let's Play House*	F2WB 8046
U-156	*Mystery Train*	F2WB 8001

July 1955		
U-142	*I'm Left, You're Right, She's Gone*	F2WB 8047
U-157	*I Forgot to Remember to Forget*	F2WB 8000
U-131	*Tryin' to Get to You*	F2WB 8039

This was the first and only Elvis Sun session where drums were used. Joining Scotty Moore (lead guitar), Bill Black (bass), and Elvis (rhythm guitar) was D. J. Fontana.

	Tomorrow Night	SPA4 2331

RCA included additional music and released this song in July 1965 (*Elvis for Everyone*, LP).

Sun had no system for its master serial numbers. In recent years, RCA has released alternate takes from the Sun sessions. An alternate version of *I Love You Because* can be found on the 1974 *A Legendary Performer, Volume 1* LP. Steve Sholes spliced takes numbers 2 and 4 together on January 20, 1956. On Volume 2 of the album of the same name (1976) you will find *Harbor Lights*.

Elvis recorded the following unreleased songs for Sun:

1. *Uncle Penn*—Elvis sang this on the "Louisiana Hayride" TV show, as well as in concert. This song appeared on a bootleg single in 1956.

2. *Tennessee, Saturday Night*—performed on "Louisiana Hayride."

3. *Oakie Boogie*

4. *Down the Line*

5. *Blue Guitar*

159

6. *Always Late with Your Kisses*

7. *Night Train to Memphis*

8. *Gone*

9. *Crying Heart Blues*

10. *Sunshine*

11. *Satisfied*

The most amazing thing about Elvis' Sun recordings is the fact that by using only guitar, bass, and (on later recordings) drums Sam Phillips was able to get such a full sound. Elvis' Sun recordings have withstood the test of time. Some twenty years have passed and Elvis' Sun records still remain definitive rock and roll recordings.

1956

Elvis signed with RCA and added a new style to music. His early RCA recordings featured piano, vocal backings, and a much more electrified lead guitar. Country and blues songs were replaced by rock and rollers.

January 10–11, 1956   **RCA Nashville studio**

G2WB 0208	*I Got a Woman*	January 10, 1956
G2WB 0209	*Heartbreak Hotel*	January 10, 1956
G2WB 0210	*Money Honey*	January 10, 1956
G2WB 0211	*I'm Counting on You*	January 11, 1956
G2WB 0218	*I Was the One*	January 11, 1956

MUSICIANS:

Lead guitar—Scotty Moore   Drums—D. J. Fontana
Guitar—Chet Atkins   Piano—Floyd Cramer
Guitar—Elvis   Vocal—Gordon Stoker
Bass—Bill Black   Vocal—Ben and Brock Speer

This is Elvis' first session in an RCA studio. As can be seen here, *Heartbreak Hotel* was not his first RCA recording. The numbers between 0211 and 0218 were not recorded by Elvis.

January 30–31 and February 3, 1956   **RCA New York studio**

G2WB 1230	*Blue Suede Shoes*	January 30, 1956
G2WB 1231	*My Baby Left Me*	January 30, 1956
G2WB 1232	*One-sided Love Affair*	January 30, 1956
G2WB 1233	*So Glad You're Mine*	January 30, 1956
G2WB 1254	*I'm Gonna Sit Right Down and Cry*	January 31, 1956
G2WB 1255	*Tutti Frutti*	January 31, 1956
G2WB 1293	*Lawdy, Miss Clawdy*	February 3, 1956
G2WB 1294	*Shake, Rattle and Roll*	February 3, 1956

MUSICIANS:

Lead guitar—Scotty Moore   Drums—D. J. Fontana
Guitar—Elvis   Piano—Shorty Long

Bass—Bill Black

Elvis recorded mainly older "black" material at this session.

April 11, 1956   **RCA Nashville studio**

G2WB 0271   *I Want You, I Need*   April 11, 1956
                 You, I Love You

MUSICIANS:

Lead guitar—Scotty Moore   Drums—D. J. Fontana
Guitar—Chet Atkins   Piano—Marvin Hughes
Guitar—Elvis   Vocal—Gordon Stoker
Bass—Bill Black   Vocal—Ben and Brock Speer

July 2, 1956   **RCA New York studio**

G2WB 5935   *Hound Dog*   July 2, 1956
G2WB 5936   *Don't Be Cruel*   July 2, 1956
G2WB 5937   *Any Way You Want*   July 2, 1956
                 Me

MUSICIANS:

Lead guitar—Scotty Moore   Drums—D. J. Fontana
Guitar—Elvis   Piano—Shorty Long
Bass—Bill Black   Vocal—The Jordanaires

This was the first session to feature the Jordanaires: Gordon Stoker, Neal Matthews, Jr., Hoyt Hawkins, and Hugh Jarrett. It was the beginning of a very long and successful association.

August 1956   **Hollywood**

G2WB 4767   *Love Me Tender*
G2WB 7260   *We're Gonna Move*
G2WB 7223   *Poor Boy*
G2WB 7225   *Let Me*

BACKING: Ken Darby's Trio

Love Me Tender was handed over by 20th Century-Fox on August 2, which indicates that the song may have been recorded in July. The other three tunes were handed over on September 24. *Love Me Tender* had one extra verse in the film.

September 1–3, 1956   **Radio Recorders, Hollywood**

G2WB 4920   *Playing for Keeps*   September 1, 1956
G2WB 4921   *Love Me*   September 1, 1956
G2WB 4922   *Paralyzed*   September 1, 1956
G2WB 4923   *How Do You Think I*   September 1, 1956
                 Feel
G2WB 4924   *How's the World*   September 1, 1956
                 Treating You
G2WB 4925   *When My Blue Moon*   September 2, 1956
                 Turns to Gold Again
G2WB 4926   *Long Tall Sally*   September 2, 1956
G2WB 4927   *Old Shep*   September 2, 1956
G2WB 4928   *Too Much*   September 2, 1956
G2WB 4929   *Anyplace Is Paradise*   September 3, 1956
G2WB 4930   *Ready Teddy*   September 3, 1956
G2WB 4931   *First in Line*   September 3, 1956

161

G2WB 4932 *Rip It Up*   September 3, 1956

MUSICIANS:
Lead guitar—Scotty Moore   Drums—D. J. Fontana
Guitar—Elvis   Piano—Unknown
Bass—Bill Black   Vocal—Jordanaires
   Elvis played piano on *Old Shep.*

December 9, 1956   **Sun studio, Memphis**

Unreleased *Big Boss Man*   December 9, 1956
Unreleased *Blueberry Hill*   December 9, 1956
Unreleased *I Won't Have to Cross* December 9, 1956
            the Jordan Alone
Unreleased *Island of Golden Dreams* December 9, 1956
Unreleased *That Old Rugged Cross* December 9, 1956
Unreleased *Peace in the Valley*   December 9, 1956

MUSICIANS:
Guitar and vocal—Carl Perkins   Piano and vocal—Elvis
Guitar and vocal—Johnny Cash   Piano and vocal—Jerry Lee Lewis
   This recording session is now known as the *Million-Dollar Session.* Sam
Phillips turned the tape recorder on and has three tapes in his possession to
this very day.

1957

January 12–13 and 19, 1957   **Radio Recorders, Hollywood**
H2WB 0253 *I Believe*   January 12, 1957
H2WB 0254 *Tell Me Why*   January 12, 1957
H2WB 0255 *Got a Lot o' Livin' to* January 12, 1957
           Do
H2WB 0256 *All Shook Up*   January 12, 1957
H2WB 0257 *Mean Woman Blues*   January 13, 1957
H2WB 0258 *Peace in the Valley*   January 13, 1957
H2WB 0259 *I Beg of You*   January 13, 1957
H2WB 0260 *That's When Your*   January 13, 1957
           Heartaches Begin
H2WB 0261 *Take My Hand,*   January 13, 1957
           Precious Lord
H2WB 0282 *It Is No Secret*   January 19, 1957
H2WB 0283 *Blueberry Hill*   January 19, 1957
H2WB 0284 *Have I Told You*   January 19, 1957
           Lately That I Love
           You?
H2WB 0285 *Is It So Strange*   January 19, 1957

MUSICIANS:
Lead guitar—Scotty Moore   Drums—D. J. Fontana
Guitar—Elvis   Piano—Dudley Brooks
Bass—Bill Black   Vocal—Jordanaires
   Elvis recorded his first religious songs at this session. After twenty-seven
takes, *I Beg of You* still was unsatisfactory.

162

February 23–24, 1957 | **Radio Recorders, Hollywood**

H2WB 0259   *i Beg of You*   February 23, 1957
H2WB 0414   *Don't Leave Me Now*   February 23, 1957
H2WB 0415   *One Night*   February 23, 1957
H2WB 0416   *True Love*   February 23, 1957
H2WB 0417   *I Need You So*   February 23, 1957
H2WB 0418   *Loving You*   February 24, 1957
H2WB 0419   *When It Rains, It*   February 24, 1957
          Really Pours

MUSICIANS:
Lead guitar—Scotty Moore   Drums—D. J. Fontana
Guitar—Elvis   Piano—Dudley Brooks
Bass—Bill Black   Vocal—Jordanaires

    I Beg of You is finally completed. There was a total of thirty-four takes.

February–March 1957 | **Hollywood**

H2WB 2193   *Teddy Bear*
H2WB 2194   *Lonesome Cowboy*
H2WB 2195   *Party*
H2WB 2196   *Hot Dog*
H2WB 2197   *Loving You*
H2WB 2198   *Got a Lot o' Livin' to*
          Do

MUSICIANS:
Lead guitar—Scotty Moore   Drums—D. J. Fontana
Guitar—Elvis   Vocal—Jordanaires
Bass—Bill Black

    These are soundtrack recordings for *Loving You.*

May 2, 1957 | **MGM studios, Culver City, California**

H2WB 6777   *Young and Beautiful*   May 2, 1957
H2WB 6778   *Treat Me Nice*   May 2, 1957
H2WB 6779   *Jailhouse Rock*   May 2, 1957
H2WB 6780   *Jailhouse Rock*   May 2, 1957
H2WB 6781   *I Want to Be Free*   May 2, 1957
H2WB 6782   *Baby, I Don't Care*   May 2, 1957
H2WB 6783   *Don't Leave Me Now*   May 2, 1957

MUSICIANS
Lead guitar—Scotty Moore   Drums—D. J. Fontana
Guitar—Elvis   Piano—Mike Stoller
Bass—Bill Black   Vocal—Jordanaires

    Number 6779 is the record version, and 6780 is the film version. MGM gave the tapes to RCA on June 14, 1957.

September 5–7, 1957 | **Radio Recorders, Hollywood**

H2PB 5523   *Treat Me Nice*   September 5, 1957
H2PB 5524   *My Wish Came True*   September 5, 1957
H2PB 5525   *Blue Christmas*   September 5, 1957
H2PB 5526   *White Christmas*   September 6, 1957
H2PB 5527   *Here Comes Santa*   September 6, 1957
          Claus
H2PB 5528   *Silent Night*   September 6, 1957

H2PB 5529	*Don't*	September 6, 1957
H2PB 5530	*O Little Town of Bethlehem*	September 7, 1957
H2PB 5531	*Santa, Bring My Baby Back*	September 7, 1957
H2PB 5532	*Santa Claus Is Back in Town*	September 7, 1957
H2PB 5533	*I'll Be Home for Christmas*	September 7, 1957

MUSICIANS:

Lead guitar—Scotty Moore
Guitar—Elvis
Bass—Bill Black
Piano—Dudley Brooks

Vocal—Millie Kirkham,
Jordanaires
Drums—D. J. Fontana

Elvis made several attempts at *My Wish Came True* on September 5, but the acceptable take was completed on the sixth.

1958

January 1958   **Hollywood**

J2PB 3603	*Hard-headed Woman*
J2PB 3604	*T-R-O-U-B-L-E*
J2PB 3605	*New Orleans*
J2PB 3606	*King Creole*
J2PB 3607	*Crawfish*
J2PB 3608	*Dixieland Rock*
J2PB 3609	*Lover Doll*
J2PB 3610	*Don't Ask Me Why*
J2PB 3611	*As Long As I Have You*
J2PB 3612	*King Creole*
J2PB 3613	*Young Dreams*
J2PB 4228	*Steadfast, Loyal and True*

MUSICIANS:

Lead guitar—Scotty Moore
Guitar—Elvis
Bass—Bill Black

Drums—D. J. Fontana
Vocal—Jordanaires

Kitty White was the female voice heard on *Crawfish*. The horns were overdubbed at a later date. The alternate take of *King Creole* is 3606. Numbers 3603 through 3613 were handed over by Paramount Pictures on May 12, 1958; 4228 was delivered on June 3, 1958.

J2WB 3261	*Steadfast, Loyal and True*
J2WB 3262	*Lover Doll*

Chet Atkins produced the above session on June 14, 1958, at which time the songs received new matrix numbers.

164

RECORDING SESSIONS

January 23, 1958   **Radio Recorders, Hollywood**

J2WB 0178 *My Wish Came True*   January 23, 1958
J2WB 0179 *Doncha' Think It's*   January 23, 1958
            Time

MUSICIANS:
Lead guitar—Scotty Moore   Drums—D. J. Fontana
Guitar—Elvis   Piano—Dudley Brooks
Bass—Bill Black   Vocal—Jordanaires

Elvis had a difficult time completing a satisfactory take on either of these songs.

February 1, 1958   **Radio Recorders, Hollywood**

J2WB 0178 *My Wish Came True*   February 1, 1958
J2WB 0179 *Doncha' Think It's*   February 1, 1958
            Time
J2WB 0180 *Your Cheatin' Heart*   February 1, 1958
J2WB 0181 *Wear My Ring Around*   February 1, 1958
            Your Neck

MUSICIANS:
Lead guitar—Scotty Moore   Piano—Dudley Brooks
Guitar—Elvis   Drums—D. J. Fontana
Bass—Bill Black   Vocal—Jordanaires
Guitar—H. J. Timbrell

Once again, 0178 was not satisfactory. Two versions of 0179 were released. There is no master for 0180; the released version consisted of takes 9 and 10.

June 10–11, 1958   **RCA Nashville studio**

J2WB 3253 *I Need Your Love*   June 10, 1958
            Tonight
J2WB 3254 *A Big Hunk o' Love*   June 10, 1958
J2WB 3255 *Ain't That Loving You,*   June 10, 1958
            Baby
J2WB 3256 *A Fool Such as I*   June 10, 1958
J2WB 3257 *I Got Stung*   June 11, 1958

MUSICIANS:
Lead guitar—Hank Garland   Drums—D. J. Fontana
Guitar—Chet Atkins   Bongos—Murrey Harman
Guitar—Elvis   Vocal—Jordanaires
Bass—Bob Moore   Piano—Floyd Cramer
(The Jordanaires: Gorden Stoker, Neil Matthews, Hoyt Hawkins, Ray Walker)

For this session Elvis used new musicians. This crew would stick with him (with a few changes) until 1966. At this session Elvis recorded all night long. In the future, almost all sessions would take place in the evening.

1960

Elvis returns from the Army and for the first four years his recording sessions would follow a strict pattern. He would use the Nashville recording studio and all sessions would take place in the evening. Elvis didn't record as much rock and roll during this period, but he produced some of the strongest ballads of his career.

March 20–21, 1960 **RCA Nashville studio**

L2WB 0081	*Make Me Know It*	March 20, 1960
L2WB 0082	*Soldier Boy*	March 20, 1960
L2WB 0083	*Stuck on You*	March 21, 1960
L2WB 0084	*Fame and Fortune*	March 21, 1960
L2WB 0085	*A Mess of Blues*	March 21, 1960
L2WB 0086	*It Feels So Right*	March 21, 1960

MUSICIANS:

Lead guitar—Scotty Moore
Guitar—Elvis
Bass—Bob Moore
Bass—Hank Garland

Drums—D. J. Fontana
Drums—Murrey Harman
Piano—Floyd Cramer
Vocal—Jordanaires

Elvis' first stereo recordings came from this session.

April 3–4, 1960 **RCA Nashville studio**

L2WB 0098	*Fever*	April 3, 1960
L2WB 0099	*Like a Baby*	April 3, 1960
L2WB 0100	*It's Now or Never*	April 3, 1960
L2WB 0101	*The Girl of My Best Friend*	April 4, 1960
L2WB 0102	*Dirty, Dirty Feeling*	April 4, 1960
L2WB 0103	*Thrill of Your Love*	April 4, 1960
L2WB 0104	*I Gotta Know*	April 4, 1960
L2WB 0105	*Such a Night*	April 4, 1960
L2WB 0106	*Are You Lonesome Tonight?*	April 4, 1960
L2WB 0107	*The Girl Next Door Went Awalking*	April 4, 1960
L2WB 0108	*I Will Be Home Again*	April 4, 1960
L2WB 0109	*Reconsider, Baby*	April 4, 1960

MUSICIANS:

Lead guitar—Hank Garland
Guitar—Scotty Moore
Guitar—Elvis
Bass—Bob Moore
Drums—D. J. Fontana

Drums—Murrey Harman
Piano—Floyd Cramer
Tenor sax—Homer (Boots) Randolph
Vocal—Jordanaires

April–June 1960 **Hollywood**

L2PW 3678	*Tonight Is So Right for Love*
	What's She Really Like
	Frankfort Special
L2PW 3681	*Wooden Heart*
	G.I. Blues

             Pocketful of Rainbows
             Shoppin' Around
             Big Boots
             Didja Ever
             Blue Suede Shoes
             Doin' the Best I Can

WPA1 8124 *Tonight's All Right for Love*

Vocal—Jordanaires

Paramount gave RCA the tapes on July 19, 1960, with the exception of WPA1 8124, which it delivered on September 19, 1960.

August 12, 1960   **Hollywood**

M2PB 1986 *Summer Kisses, Winter Tears*
M2PB 1987 *Flaming Star*
M2PB 1988 *A Cane and a High Starched Collar*

Vocal—Jordanaires

20th Century-Fox gave RCA the tapes on September 18, 1960. *M* indicates that RCA released these songs in 1961 (with the exception of 1988).

October 30–31, 1960   **RCA Nashville studio**

L2WB 0373	*Milky White Way*	October 30, 1960
L2WB 0374	*His Hand in Mine*	October 30, 1960
L2WB 0375	*I Believe in the Man in the Sky*	October 30, 1960
L2WB 0376	*He Knows Just What I Need*	October 30, 1960
L2WB 0377	*Surrender*	October 30, 1960
L2WB 0378	*Mansion over the Hilltop*	October 31, 1960
L2WB 0379	*In My Father's House*	October 31, 1960
L2WB 0380	*Joshua Fit the Battle*	October 31, 1960
L2WB 0381	*Swing Down, Sweet Chariot*	October 31, 1960
L2WB 0382	*I'm Gonna Walk Dem Golden Stairs*	October 31, 1960
L2WB 0383	*If We Never Meet Again*	October 31, 1960
L2WB 0384	*Known Only to Him*	October 31, 1960
L2WB 0385	*Crying in the Chapel*	October 31, 1960
L2WB 5001	*Working on the Building*	October 31, 1960

In spite of the odd matrix number, 5001 was recorded at this session.

November 1960   **Hollywood**

L2PB 5381 *Lonely Man*
L2PB 5382 *I Slipped, I Stumbled, I Fell*
L2PB 5383 *Wild in the Country*
L2PB 5384 *In My Way*
L2PB 5385 *Forget Me Never*

On January 9, 1961, 20th Century-Fox gave these tapes to RCA.

1961

March 12–13, 1961		**RCA Nashville studio**
M2WW 0567	*I'm Comin' Home*	March 12, 1961
M2WW 0568	*Gently*	March 12, 1961
M2WW 0569	*In Your Arms*	March 12, 1961
M2WW 0570	*Give Me the Right*	March 12, 1961
M2WW 0571	*I Feel So Bad*	March 12, 1961
M2WW 0572	*It's a Sin*	March 13, 1961
M2WW 0573	*I Want You with Me*	March 13, 1961
M2WW 0574	*There's Always Me*	March 13, 1961
M2WW 0575	*Starting Today*	March 13, 1961
M2WW 0576	*Sentimental Me*	March 13, 1961
M2WW 0577	*Judy*	March 13, 1961
M2WW 0578	*Put the Blame on Me*	March 13, 1961

MUSICIANS:

Lead guitar—Hank Garland
Piano—Floyd Cramer

Tenor sax—Homer (Boots)
Randolph
Vocal—Jordanaires

June 25–26, 1961		**RCA Nashville studio**
M2WW 8854	*Kiss Me Quick*	June 25, 1961
M2WW 8858	*That's Someone You Never Forget*	June 25, 1961
M2WW 8859	*I'm Yours*	June 26, 1961
M2WW 8860	*His Latest Flame*	June 26, 1961
M2WW 8861	*Little Sister*	June 26, 1961

Vocal—Jordanaires

April 1961		**Hollywood**
M2PB 2984	*Blue Hawaii*	
M2PB 2985	*Almost Always True*	
M2PB 2986	*Aloha Oe*	
M2PB 2987	*No More*	
M2PB 2988	*Can't Help Falling in Love*	
M2PB 2989	*Rock-a-hula Baby*	
M2PB 2990	*Moonlight Swim*	
M2PB 2991	*Ku-u-i-po*	
M2PB 2992	*Ito Eats*	
M2PB 2993	*Slicin' Sand*	
M2PB 2994	*Hawaiian Sunset*	
M2PB 2995	*Beach Boy Blues*	
M2PB 2996	*Island of Love*	
M2PB 2997	*Hawaiian Wedding Song*	
M2PB 3038	*Steppin' Out of Line*	

Vocal—Jordanaires

Paramount gave RCA the tapes on September 25, 1961. Number 3038 was given this matrix number because it would not be on the soundtrack LP.

July 5, 1961		RCA Nashville studio
M2WW 0878	*Sound Advice*	July 5, 1961
	Follow That Dream	July 5, 1961
	Angel	July 5, 1961
	What a Wonderful Life	July 5, 1961
	I'm Not the Marrying Kind	July 5, 1961

MUSICIANS:

Lead guitar—Hank Garland
Piano—Floyd Cramer

Tenor sax—Homer (Boots) Randolph
Vocal—Jordanaires

In spite of the fact that these songs could be found on the film soundtrack, they were recorded as a regular session. *On Top of Old Smokey* appears in the film, but was not issued as a record.

October 15–16, 1961		RCA Nashville studio
M2WW 1002	*For the Millionth and the Last Time*	October 15, 1961
M2WW 1003	*Good Luck Charm*	October 15, 1961
M2WW 1004	*Anything That's Part of You*	October 15, 1961
M2WW 1005	*I Met Her Today*	October 16, 1961

Vocal—Jordanaires

October–November, 1961		Hollywood
N2PB 3131	*King of the Whole Wide World*	
	This Is Living	
	Riding the Rainbow	
N2PB 3134	*Home Is Where the Heart Is*	
	I Got Lucky	
	A Whistling Tune	

Vocal—Jordanaires

The Mirish Company gave RCA these tapes in 1962.

1962

March 18–19, 1962		RCA Nashville studio
N2WW 0685	*Something Blue*	March 18, 1962
N2WW 0686	*Gonna Get Back Home Somehow*	March 18, 1962
N2WW 0687	*Easy Question*	March 18, 1962
N2WW 0688	*Fountain of Love*	March 18, 1962
N2WW 0689	*Just for Old Time Sake*	March 18, 1962
N2WW 0690	*Night Rider*	March 18, 1962

N2WW 0691	*You'll Be Gone*	March 18, 1962
N2WW 0692	*I Feel That I've*	March 19, 1962
	Known You Forever	
N2WW 0693	*Just Tell Her Jim Said*	March 19, 1962
	Hello	
N2WW 0694	*Suspicion*	March 19, 1962
N2WW 0695	*She's Not You*	March 19, 1962

Vocal—Jordanaires

March 1962   **Hollywood**

N2PB 3272	*Girls! Girls! Girls!*
N2PB 3273	*I Don't Wanna Be Tied*
N2PB 3274	*Where Do You Come*
	From
N2PB 3275	*I Don't Want To*
N2PB 3276	*We'll Be Together*
N2PB 3277	*A Boy Like Me, a Girl*
	Like You
N2PB 3278	*Earth Boy*
N2PB 3279	*Return to Sender*
N2PB 3280	*Because of Love*
N2PB 3281	*Thanks to the Rolling*
	Sea
N2PB 3282	*Son of the Shrimp*
N2PB 3283	*The Walls Have Ears*
N2PB 3288	*We're Comin' In*
	Loaded
WPA1 8122	*Mama*

Vocal—Jordanaires   Vocal—Amigos

All songs with the exception of 8122 were delivered by Paramount Pictures on September 24, 1962; 8122 wasn't turned over until 1968.

October 1962   **Hollywood**

PPA3 2717	*Happy Ending*
PPA3 2722	*How Would You Like*
	to Be
PPA3 2724	*One Broken Heart for*
	Sale
PPA3 2725	*They Remind Me Too*
	Much of You
PPA3 2726	*Relax*
PPA3 2719	*Beyond the Bend*
PPA3 2718	*I'm Falling in Love*
	Tonight
PPA3 2721	*Take Me to the Fair*
PPA3 2720	*Cotton Candy Land*
PPA3 2723	*A World of Our Own*

Vocal—Mello Men

MGM gave RCA the tapes on January 11, 1963. Number 2724 had an extra verse in the movie.

1963

January 20, 1963		**Hollywood**
PPA3 4423	*Fun in Acapulco*	January 20, 1963
PPA3 4424	*Vino, Dinero y Amor*	January 20, 1963
PPA3 4425	*Mexico*	January 20, 1963
PPA3 4426	*El Toro*	January 20, 1963
PPA3 4427	*Marguerita*	January 20, 1963
PPA3 4428	*The Bullfighter Was a Lady*	January 20, 1963
PPA3 4429	*No Room to Rhumba in a Sports Car*	January 20, 1963
PPA3 4430	*I Think I'm Gonna Like It Here*	January 20, 1963
PPA3 4431	*Bossa Nova Baby*	January 20, 1963
PPA3 4432	*You Can't Say No in Acapulco*	January 20, 1963
PPA3 4433	*Guadalajara*	January 20, 1963
Vocal—Jordanaires		Vocal—Amigos

Paramount gave RCA these tapes on October 7, 1963.

May 26–27, 1963		**RCA Nashville studio**
PPA4 2290	*Echoes of Love*	May 26, 1963
PPA4 2291	*Please Don't Drag That String Around*	May 26, 1963
PPA4 2292	*Devil in Disguise*	May 26, 1963
PPA4 2293	*Never Ending*	May 26, 1963
PPA4 2294	*What Now, What Next, Where To*	May 26, 1963
PPA4 2295	*Witchcraft*	May 26, 1963
PPA4 2296	*Finders Keepers, Losers Weepers*	May 26, 1963
PPA4 2297	*Love Me Tonight*	May 26, 1963
PPA4 0303	*Long Lonely Highway*	May 27, 1963
PPA4 0304	*Blue River*	May 27, 1963
PPA4 0305	*Western Union*	May 27, 1963
PPA4 0306	*Slowly but Surely*	May 27, 1963
Vocal—Jordanaires		

July 7 and 9, 1963		**Hollywood**
RPA3 0234	*Viva Las Vegas*	
RPA3 0235	*What'd I Say*	
	I Need Somebody to Lean On	
	C'mon, Everybody	
	If You Think I Don't Need You	
	Today, Tomorrow and Forever	
SPA1 6898	*Santa Lucia*	
WPA1 8023	*Night Life*	

WPA1 8024 *Yellow Rose of Texas/*
The Eyes of Texas
WPA1 8025 *Do the Vega*
The Lady Loves Me
Vocal—Jordanaires   Vocal—Jubilee Four
Vocal—Carol Lombard Quartet

RCA was unable to obtain permission from Ann-Margret for the use of the duet *The Lady Loves Me.* The music tracks were recorded on July 7, and Elvis recorded the voice tracks on the ninth. The movie version of *C'mon, Everybody* is slightly different from the record version. MGM gave RCA the tapes in January 1964. On March 4, 1964, number 6898 was delivered. The last three songs were not handed over until 1968.

October 11, 1963   **Hollywood**

RPA3 0218 *Kissin' Cousins*   October 11, 1963
(number 2)
RPA3 0219 *Kissin' Cousins*   October 11, 1963
RPA3 0220 *Barefoot Ballad*   October 11, 1963
RPA3 0221 *Catchin' On Fast*   October 11, 1963
RPA3 0222 *Once Is Enough*   October 11, 1963
RPA3 0223 *One Boy, Two Little*   October 11, 1963
Girls
RPA3 0224 *Smokey Mountain Boy*   October 11, 1963
RPA3 0225 *Tender Feeling*   October 11, 1963
RPA3 0226 *There's Gold in the*   October 11, 1963
Mountains
RPA3 0227 *Anyone*   October 11, 1963
Vocal—Jordanaires

MGM gave RCA the tapes on January 23, 1964.

1964

January 12, 1964   **RCA Nashville studio**
RPA4 1004 *Memphis, Tennessee*   January 12, 1964
RPA4 1005 *Ask Me*   January 12, 1964
RPA4 1006 *It Hurts Me*   January 12, 1964
Vocal—Jordanaires

January 1964   **Hollywood**
RPA3 5264 *Big Love, Big*
Heartache
RPA3 5265 *Wheels on My Heels*
RPA3 5266 *Carny Town*
RPA3 5267 *Hard Knocks*
RPA3 5268 *It's a Wonderful World*
RPA3 5269 *It's Carnival Time*
RPA3 5270 *Little Egypt*
RPA3 5271 *One-track Heart*
RPA3 5272 *Poison Ivy League*

RPA3 5273 *Roustabout*
RPA3 5274 *There's a Brand New
Day on the Horizon*
Vocal—Jordanaires
 Paramount gave RCA the tapes on August 25, 1964.

June 5 and July 8, 1964		**Hollywood**
SPA3 2001	*Girl Happy*	June 5, 1964
SPA3 2002	*Spring Fever*	July 8, 1964
SPA3 2003	*Fort Lauderdale Chamber of Commerce*	June 5, 1964
SPA3 2004	*Startin' Tonight*	June 5, 1964
SPA3 2005	*Wolf Call*	June 5, 1964
SPA3 2006	*Do Not Disturb*	July 8, 1964
SPA3 2007	*Cross My Heart and Hope to Die*	July 8, 1964
SPA3 2008	*The Meanest Girl in Town*	July 8, 1964
SPA3 2009	*Do the Clam*	June 5, 1964
SPA3 2010	*Puppet on a String*	July 8, 1964
SPA3 2011	*I've Got to Find My Baby*	July 8, 1964

Vocal—Jordanaires   Vocal—Jubilee Four
Vocal—Carol Lombard Trio

 As you can see, these songs were recorded at two different sessions: 2001, 2003, 2004, 2005, and 2009 are from the June 5 session; the other tunes are from the July 8 session. MGM gave RCA the tapes on January 26, 1965.

1965

February 24, 1965		**Hollywood**
SPA3 6751	*Go East, Young Man*	February 24, 1965
SPA3 6752	*Shake That Tambourine*	February 24, 1965
SPA3 6753	*Golden Coins*	February 24, 1965
SPA3 6754	*So Close, Yet So Far*	February 24, 1965
SPA3 6755	*Harum Holiday*	February 24, 1965
SPA3 6756	*Mirage*	February 24, 1965
SPA3 6757	*Animal Instinct*	February 24, 1965
SPA3 6758	*Kismet*	February 24, 1965
SPA3 6759	*Hey, Little Girl*	February 24, 1965
SPA3 6760	*Wisdom of the Ages*	February 24, 1965
SPA3 6761	*My Desert Serenade*	February 24, 1965

 MGM gave RCA the tapes on September 30, 1965.

March 18, 1965

SPA4 2331 *Tomorrow Night*   March 18, 1965

 Although this is listed on the official RCA recording session, it was only a mixing session. This is actually a Sun recording. RCA added lead guitar, harmonica, and choir.

173

May 13–15, 1965		United Artists Recording Studio, Los Angeles
SPA3 7374	*Come Along*	
SPA3 7375	*Petunia, the Gardener's Daughter*	
SPA3 7376	*Chesay*	
SPA3 7377	*What Every Woman Lives For*	
SPA3 7378	*Frankie and Johnny*	
SPA3 7379	*Look Out, Broadway*	
SPA3 7380	*Beginner's Luck*	
SPA3 7381	*Down by the Riverside/ When the Saints Go Marching In*	
SPA3 7382	*Shout It Out*	
SPA3 7383	*Hard Luck*	
SPA3 7384	*Please Don't Stop Loving Me*	
SPA3 7385	*Everybody Come Aboard*	

There are two versions of *Frankie and Johnny*. Donna Douglas is heard on 7375.

United Artists delivered the tapes on February 15, 1966.

July 19, 1965		Paramount Recording Studio, Hollywood
TPA3 3834	*Queenie Wahine's Papaya*	July 19, 1965
TPA3 3835	*Paradise, Hawaiian Style*	July 19, 1965
TPA3 3836	*A Dog's Life*	July 19, 1965
TPA3 3837	*Drums of the Islands*	July 19, 1965
TPA3 3838	*This Is My Heaven*	July 19, 1965
TPA3 3839	*Scratch My Back*	July 19, 1965
TPA3 3840	*Stop Where You Are*	July 19, 1965
TPA3 3841	*Stop Where You Are*	July 19, 1965
TPA3 3842	*House of Sand*	July 19, 1965
TPA3 3843	*Datin'*	July 19, 1965
TPA3 3844	*Sand Castles*	July 19, 1965

Vocal—Jordanaires

Paramount delivered the tapes on May 31, 1966.

1966

February 21, 1966		Hollywood
TPA3 5305	*Stop, Look and Listen*	February 21, 1966
TPA3 5306	*Adam and Evil*	February 21, 1966
TPA3 5307	*All That I Am*	February 21, 1966
TPA3 5308	*Never Say Yes*	February 21, 1966
TPA3 5309	*Am I Ready*	February 21, 1966
TPA3 5310	*Beach Shack*	February 21, 1966

TPA3 5311	*Spinout*	February 21, 1966
TPA3 5312	*Smorgasbord*	February 21, 1966
TPA3 5313	*I'll Be Back*	February 21, 1966

MUSICIANS:

Guitar—James Burton
Bass—Bob Moore
Drums—Murrey Harman

Piano—Floyd Cramer
Vocal—Jordanaires

MGM gave RCA the tapes on September 2, 1966.

For the first time in more than two years, Elvis returns to RCA's recording studio. This also marks the first occasion that Felton Jarvis produces Elvis.

May 25–28, 1966　　　　　　　　**RCA Nashville studio**

TPA4 0908	*Run On*	May 25, 1966
TPA4 0909	*How Great Thou Art*	May 25, 1966
TPA4 0910	*Stand by Me*	May 26, 1966
TPA4 0911	*Where No One Stands Alone*	May 26, 1966
TPA4 0912	*Down in the Alley*	May 26, 1966
TPA4 0913	*Tomorrow Is a Long Time*	May 26, 1966
TPA4 0914	*Love Letters*	May 25, 1966
TPA4 0915	*So High*	May 27, 1966
TPA4 0916	*Farther Along*	May 27, 1966
TPA4 0917	*By and By*	May 27, 1966
TPA4 0918	*In the Garden*	May 27, 1966
TPA4 0919	*Beyond the Reef*	May 27, 1966
TPA4 0920	*Somebody Bigger Than You and I*	May 27, 1966
TPA4 0921	*Without Him*	May 27, 1966
TPA4 0922	*If the Lord Wasn't Walking by My Side*	May 28, 1966
TPA4 0923	*Where Could I Go But to the Lord*	May 28, 1966
TPA4 0924	*Come What May*	May 28, 1966
TPA4 0925	*Fools Fall in Love*	

MUSICIANS:

Guitar—Harold Bradley
Guitar—Chip Young
Guitar—Scotty Moore
Bass—Bob Moore
Bass and harmonica—Charlie McCoy
Drums—Murrey Harman, D. J. Fontana

Piano—Floyd Cramer
Organ—David Briggs
Organ—Henry Slaughter
Steel guitar—Millie Kirkham
Vocal—Jordanaires
Vocal—Imperial Quartet

The Imperial Quartet: Jake Hess, Jim Murray, Gary McSpadden, Amond Morales

June 10, 1966　　　　　　　　**RCA Nashville studio**

TPA4 0982	*Indescribably Blue*	June 10, 1966
TPA4 0983	*I'll Remember You*	June 10, 1966
TPA4 0984	*If Every Day Was Like Christmas*	June 10, 1966

The same musicians who appeared on the previous session were used at this session.

175

June 26, 1966   **Hollywood**

UPA3 3934 *Double Trouble*   June 26, 1966
UPA3 3935 *Baby, if You'll Give*   June 26, 1966
            Me All of Your Love
UPA3 3936 *Could I Fall in Love*   June 26, 1966
UPA3 3937 *Long-legged Girl*   June 26, 1966
UPA3 3938 *City by Night*   June 26, 1966
UPA3 3939 *Old MacDonald*   June 26, 1966
UPA3 3940 *I Love Only One Girl*   June 26, 1966
UPA3 3941 *There Is So Much*   June 26, 1966
            World to See
UPA3 3942 *It Won't Be Long*   June 26, 1966
Vocal—Jordanaires

MGM gave RCA the tapes on March 30, 1967.

September 26, 1966   **Paramount Recording Studio,**
                                    Hollywood

UPA3 3805 *Easy Come, Easy Go*   September 26, 1966
UPA3 3806 *The Love Machine*   September 26, 1966
UPA3 3807 *Yoga Is as Yoga Does*   September 26, 1966
UPA3 3808 *You Gotta Stop*   September 26, 1966
UPA3 3809 *Sing, You Children*   September 26, 1966
UPA3 3810 *I'll Take Love*   September 26, 1966
WPA1 8027 *She's a Machine*   September 26, 1966
Vocal—Jordanaires

With the exception of 8027, which was handed over in 1968, Paramount delivered all the tapes in 1967.

1967

February 21, 1967   **RCA Nashville studio**

UPA3 8443 *Clambake*   February 21, 1967
UPA3 8444 *Who Needs Money*   February 21, 1967
UPA3 8445 *A House That Has*   February 21, 1967
            Everything
UPA3 8446 *Hey, Hey, Hey*   February 21, 1967
UPA3 8447 *The Girl I Never Loved* February 21, 1967
UPA3 8448 *How Can You Lose*   February 21, 1967
            What You Never Had
            You Don't Know Me   February 21, 1967
UPA4 2753 *Confidence*   February 21, 1967

MUSICIANS:
Guitar—Grady Martin   Piano—Floyd Cramer
Guitar—Harold Bradley   Steel guitar—Pete Drake
Bass—Bob Moore   Vocal—Jordanaires
Drums—Murrey Harman   Vocal—Millie Kirkham

United Artists paid for this session and gave the tapes to RCA on October 4, 1967. *Confidence* was overdubbed in Nashville on September 19, 1967, which explains the matrix number. *You Don't Know Me* is the film version, not the record version, which was recorded in September. Will Hutchins is the duet voice heard on 8444.

June 19, 1967			**Hollywood**
WPA1	1022	*There Ain't Nothing Like a Song*	June 19, 1967
WPA1	1023	*Your Time Hasn't Come Yet, Baby*	June 19, 1967
WPA1	1024	*Five Sleepy Heads*	June 19, 1967
WPA1	1025	*Who Are You?*	June 19, 1967
WPA1	1026	*Speedway*	June 19, 1967
WPA1	1027	[No information available]	June 19, 1967
WPA1	1028	*Suppose*	June 19, 1967
WPA1	1029	*Let Yourself Go*	June 19, 1967
WPA1	1030	*He's Your Uncle, Not Your Dad*	June 19, 1967

Vocal—Jordanaires

MGM delivered the tapes to RCA on May 14, 1968. The matrix numbers for LP releases are 1034–1037; 1038 is the matrix number given to *Your Groovy Self*, as sung by Nancy Sinatra. Nancy overdubbed her voice after the actual session.

September 10–12, 1967		**RCA Nashville studio**
UPA4	2765	*Guitar Man*	September 10, 1967
UPA4	2766	*Big Boss Man*	September 10, 1967
UPA4	2767	*Mine*	September 11, 1967
UPA4	2768	*Singing Tree*	September 11, 1967
UPA4	2769	*Just Call Me Lonesome*	September 11, 1967
UPA4	2770	*High-heel Sneakers*	September 11, 1967
UPA4	2771	*You Don't Know Me*	September 11, 1967
UPA4	2772	*We Call on Him*	September 11, 1967
UPA4	2773	*You'll Never Walk Alone*	September 11, 1967
UPA4	2774	*Singing Tree*	September 12, 1967

MUSICIANS:

Lead guitar—Scotty Moore	Piano—Floyd Cramer
Lead guitar—Jerry Reed	Harmonica—Charlie McCoy
Guitar—Grady Martin	Steel guitar—Pete Drake
Bass—Bob Moore	Vocal—Millie Kirkham
Drums—Murrey Harman	Vocal—Jordanaires

Jerry Reed appears on 2765 only.

October 4, 1967			**Hollywood**
WPA1	1001	*Goin' Home*	October 4, 1967
WPA1	1002	*Stay Away*	October 4, 1967
WPA1	8026	*All I Needed Was the Rain*	October 4, 1967
ZPA4	1054	*Stay Away, Joe*	October 4, 1967
ZPA4	1055	*Dominique*	October 4, 1967

Vocal—Jordanaires

MGM gave RCA these tapes in the early months of 1968, with the matrix numbers being assigned at a later date. Numbers 1001 and 1002 were actually given their numbers in early 1968; 8026, in connection with the 1968 TV special; and 1054 in March 1970. There have been two different versions of 1054.

177

1968

January 15–17, 1968 **RCA Nashville studio**

WPA4 1800 *Too Much Monkey* January 15, 1968
 Business
WPA4 1807 *U.S. Male* January 17, 1968

The same musicians performed this session as in the previous one, with Jerry Reed playing guitar on the January 17 session.

March 11, 1968 **MGM Sound Studio, Hollywood**

WPA1 5766 *Almost in Love* March 11, 1968
WPA1 5766 *A Little Less* March 11, 1968
 Conversation
WPA1 5768 *Wonderful World* March 11, 1968
WPA1 5769 *Edge of Reality* March 11, 1968

All these songs are from MGM's *Live a Little, Love a Little.*

WPA1 8022 *Mama*
WPA1 8023 *Night Life*
WPA1 8024 *Yellow Rose of Texas/*
 The Eyes of Texas
WPA1 8025 *Do the Vega*
WPA1 8026 *All I Needed Was the*
 Rain
WPA1 8027 *She's a Machine*
WPA1 8124 *Tonight's All Right for*
 Love

All of the above songs were recorded at an earlier date; however, they did not receive matrix numbers until 1968.

June 27 and 29, 1968 **Burbank Studios, Burbank**

WPA1 8028 *Tiger Man*
WPA1 8031 *Lawdy, Miss Clawdy*
WPA1 8032 *Baby, What You Want*
 Me to Do
WPA1 8033 *Heartbreak Hotel*
WPA1 8034 *Hound Dog*
WPA1 8035 *All Shook Up*
WPA1 8036 *Can't Help Falling in*
 Love
WPA1 8037 *Jailhouse Rock*
WPA1 8038 *Love Me Tender*
WPA1 8042 *Blue Christmas*
WPA1 8043 *One Night*
WPA1 8044 *Memories*
WPA1 8116 *Are You Lonesome*
 Tonight?
WPA1 8118 *Love Me*
WPA1 8119 *Tryin' to Get to You*
 That's All Right
 It Hurts Me

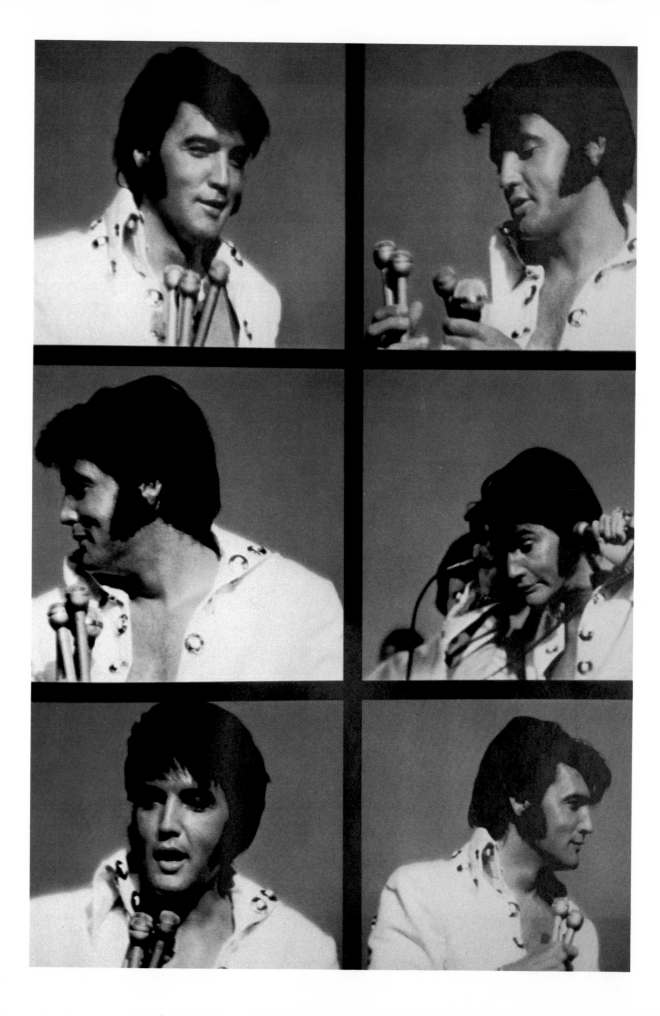

Let Yourself Go
When My Blue Moon
Turns to Gold Again
Blue Suede Shoes
Don't Be Cruel
If I Can Dream
Trouble
Blue Moon of
Kentucky
Santa Claus Is Back
in Town
Are You Lonesome
Tonight?
Baby, What You Want
Me to Do

MUSICIANS:

Guitar—Scotty Moore Guitar—Charlie Hodge
Guitar—Elvis Drums—D. J. Fontana

Elvis' career peaked in 1968 when he signed to do his NBC TV special. Elvis was recorded LIVE for the first time. He gave four shows for a small, invited audience. In his act the King was able to recapture the pure sex that initially made him. His voice was raw and savage, and RCA had its tape recorders running the whole time.

June 30, 1968 **Burbank Studios, Burbank**

WPA1 8029 *If I Can Dream* June 30, 1968
WPA1 8030 *Trouble* June 30, 1968
WPA1 8039 *Where Could I Go But* June 30, 1968
to the Lord
WPA1 8040 *Up Above My Head* June 30, 1968
WPA1 8041 *Saved* June 30, 1968
WPA1 8045 *Nothingville* June 30, 1968
WPA1 8046 *Big Boss Man* June 30, 1968
WPA1 8047 *Guitar Man* June 30, 1968
WPA1 8048 *Little Egypt* June 30, 1968

MUSICIANS:

Lead guitar—Tommy Tedesco Drums—Hal Blaine
Guitar—Mike Deasy Piano and organ—Don Randi
Bass—Larry Knectal Vocal—Blossoms
The Blossoms: Darlene Love, Jean King, and Fanita James

The NBC Orchestra, conducted by Earl Brown, provided additional music at all three sessions. The vocal on *Memories* was recorded at a later date. The matrix numbers indicate that a total of 103 tracks was given to RCA.

July 7, 1968 **Hollywood**

WPA1 8091 *Charro!* July 7, 1968
This is the title song from the film of the same name.

October 15, 1968 **Hollywood**

XPA1 3976 *Clean Up Your Own* October 15, 1968
Back Yard
XPA1 3978 *Almost* October 15, 1968
Swing Down, Sweet October 15, 1968

179

Chariot
Aura Lee   October 15, 1968
Sign of the Zodiac   October 15, 1968

Marlyn Mason is the duet voice heard on *Sign of the Zodiac*. XPA1 3976 and 3978 were overdubbed in Nashville on May 8, 1969. This is the reason for the 1969 matrix numbers. All songs are from *The Trouble with Girls*.

1969

After an absence of nearly fourteen years, Elvis returned to a Memphis recording studio, where he would produce some of the very best recordings of his career.

January 13–16 and 20–23, 1969   **American Studios, Memphis**

XPA5 1142	*Long Black Limousine*	January 13, 1969
XPA5 1143	*This Is the Story*	January 13, 1969
XPA5 1144	*Come Out, Come Out*	January 14, 1969
XPA5 1145	*Wearin' That Loved-on Look*	January 14, 1969
XPA5 1146	*You'll Think of Me*	January 14, 1969
XPA5 1147	*I'm Movin' On*	January 15, 1969
XPA5 1148	*A Little Bit of Green*	January 15, 1969
XPA5 1149	*Don't Cry, Daddy*	January 15, 1969
XPA5 1150	*Poor Man's Gold*	January 15, 1969
XPA5 1151	*Inherit the Wind*	January 16, 1969
XPA5 1152	*Mama Liked the Roses*	January 16, 1969
XPA5 1153	*My Little Friend*	January 16, 1969
XPA5 1154	*In the Ghetto*	January 21, 1969
XPA5 1155	*Gentle on My Mind*	January 15, 1969
XPA5 1156	*Rubberneckin'*	January 20, 1969
XPA5 1157	*Hey, Jude*	January 22, 1969
XPA5 1158	*From a Jack to a King*	January 21, 1969
XPA5 1159	*Without Love*	January 21, 1969
XPA5 1160	*I'll Hold You in My Heart*	January 23, 1969
XPA5 1161	*I'll Be There*	January 23, 1969
XPA5 1227	*Suspicious Minds*	

MUSICIANS:

Guitar and electric sitar —Reggie Young
Guitar and bass—Tommy Cogbill
Bass—Mike Leech
Drums—Gene Chrisman
Piano—Bobby Emmons
Organ—Glen Spreen

Vocal—Jeannie Green
Vocal—Mary and Ginger Holladay
Horn—Wayne Jackson
Horn—Bob Taylor
Horn—Ed Logan
Memphis Strings

The ending of *Suspicious Minds* was achieved by splicing three takes together, adding horns and overdubbing parts by Elvis' live group. Ronnie Milsap is singing duet on *Don't Cry, Daddy*. Elvis plays piano on *I'll Hold You in My Heart*.

February 17–22, 1969   **American Studios, Memphis**

XPA5 1265	*True Love Travels on a Gravel Road*	February 17, 1969
XPA5 1266	*Stranger in My Own Home Town*	February 17, 1969
XPA5 1267	*And the Grass Won't Pay No Mind*	February 18, 1969
XPA5 1268	*Power of My Love*	February 18, 1969
XPA5 1269	*After Loving You*	February 18, 1969
XPA5 1270	*Do You Know Who I Am*	February 19, 1969
XPA5 1271	*Kentucky Rain*	February 19, 1969
XPA5 1272	*Only the Strong Survive*	February 20, 1969
XPA5 1273	*It Keeps Right On A-hurtin'*	February 20, 1969
XPA5 1274	*Any Day Now*	February 21, 1969
XPA5 1275	*If I'm a Fool*	February 21, 1969
XPA5 1276	*The Fair's Moving On*	February 21, 1969
XPA5 1277	*Memory Revival*	February 22, 1969
XPA5 1278	*Who Am I?*	February 22, 1969

February's session included the same musicians as January's session, with the addition of vocalist Sandy Posey.

March 5–6, 1969   **MCA Studio, Hollywood**

ZPA4 1054	*Stay Away, Joe*	October 4, 1969 [mixed]
ZPA4 1055	*Let's Forget About the Stars*	[date uncertain] March 5–6, 1969
ZPA4 1056	*Have a Happy*	March 5–6, 1969
ZPA4 1057	*Let's Be Friends*	March 5–6, 1969
ZPA4 1058	*Change of Habit*	March 5–6, 1969
ZPA4 1957	*Let Us Pray*	September 22, 1969 [mixed]

1056, 1057, and 1058 are from *Change of Habit*. The film and record versions of 1957 are different.

August 22–26, 1969   **Recorded at the International Hotel, Las Vegas**

XPA5 2309	*I Got a Woman*	August 22, 1969
XPA5 2310	*All Shook Up*	August 22, 1969
XPA5 2311	*Love Me Tender*	August 22, 1969
XPA5 2312	*Suspicious Minds*	August 22, 1969
XPA5 2313	*Words*	August 22, 1969
XPA5 2314	*Johnny B. Good*	August 22, 1969
XPA5 2315	*Runaway*	August 22, 1969
XPA5 2316	*Are You Lonesome Tonight?*	August 25, 1969
XPA5 2317	*Jailhouse Rock/Don't Be Cruel*	August 25, 1969
XPA5 2318	*Yesterday/Hey, Jude*	August 25, 1969
XPA5 2319	*Memories*	August 25, 1969
XPA5 2320	*I Can't Stop Loving You*	August 25, 1969
XPA5 2374	*In the Ghetto*	August 25, 1969
XPA5 2375	*What'd I Say*	August 25, 1969
XPA5 2376	*Inherit the Wind*	August 25, 1969

XPA5 2377	*Rubberneckin'*	August 24, 1969
XPA5 2378	*This Is the Story*	August 24, 1969
XPA5 2379	*Can't Help Falling in Love*	August 24, 1969
XPA5 2380	*Heartbreak Hotel*	August 24, 1969
XPA5 2381	*My Babe*	August 24, 1969
XPA5 2382	*Funny How Time Slips Away*	August 26, 1969
XPA5 2383	*Blue Suede Shoes*	August 26, 1969
XPA5 2384	*Hound Dog*	August 26, 1969
XPA5 2385	*Baby, What You Want Me to Do*	August 26, 1969
XPA5 2386	*Mystery Train/Tiger Man*	August 26, 1969

MUSICIANS:

Lead guitar—James Burton
Guitar—John Wilkinson
Guitar and vocal—Charlie Hodge
Bass—Jerry Scheff
Drums—Ronnie Tutt

Piano—Larry Muhoberac
Vocal—Millie Kirkham
Vocal—Sweet Inspirations
Vocal—Imperial Quartet
Joe Guercio Orchestra

The Sweet Inspirations: Emily Houston, Myrna Smith, Sylvia Shenwell, Estelle Brown

This was Elvis' first live performance in over nine years. RCA recorded four shows.

1970

February 16–19, 1970   **International Hotel, Las Vegas**

ZPA5 1286	*All Shook Up*	February 16, 1970
ZPA5 1287	*In the Ghetto*	February 16, 1970
ZPA5 1288	*Suspicious Minds*	February 16, 1970
ZPA5 1289	*Proud Mary*	February 17, 1970
ZPA5 1290	*See See Rider*	February 17, 1970
ZPA5 1291	*Let It Be Me*	February 17, 1970
ZPA5 1292	*Don't Cry, Daddy*	February 17, 1970
ZPA5 1293	*Sweet Caroline*	February 18, 1970
ZPA5 1294	*Release Me*	February 18, 1970
ZPA5 1295	*Kentucky Rain*	February 18, 1970
ZPA5 1296	*Long Tall Sally*	February 18, 1970
ZPA5 1297	*Walk a Mile in My Shoes*	February 18, 1970
ZPA5 1298	*Polk Salad Annie*	February 18, 1970
ZPA5 1299	*I Can't Stop Loving You*	February 18, 1970
ZPA5 1300	*The Wonder of You*	February 19, 1970

MUSICIANS:

Lead guitar—James Burton
Guitar—John Wilkinson
Guitar and vocal—Charlie Hodge

Piano—Glenn D. Hardin
Vocal—Millie Kirkham
Vocal—Sweet Inspirations

RECORDING SESSIONS

Bass—Jerry Scheff	Vocal—Imperial Quartet	
Drums—Ronnie Tutt	Joe Guercio Orchestra	

June 4–8, 1970   **RCA Nashville studio**

ZPA4 1593	*Twenty Days and Twenty Nights*	June 4, 1970
ZPA4 1594	*I've Lost You*	June 4, 1970
ZPA4 1595	*I Was Born About 10,000 Years Ago*	June 4, 1970
ZPA4 1596	*The Sound of Your Cry*	June 4, 1970
ZPA4 1597	*The Fool*	June 4, 1970
ZPA4 1598	*Little Cabin on the Hill*	June 4, 1970
ZPA4 1599	*Cindy, Cindy*	June 4, 1970
ZPA4 1600	*Bridge over Troubled Water*	June 5, 1970
ZPA4 1601	*Got My Mojo Working/ Keep Your Hands*	June 5, 1970
ZPA4 1602	*How the Web Was Woven*	June 5, 1970
ZPA4 1603	*It's Your Baby, You Rock It*	June 5, 1970
ZPA4 1604	*Stranger in the Crowd*	June 5, 1970
ZPA4 1605	*I'll Never Know*	June 5, 1970
ZPA4 1606	*Mary in the Morning*	June 5, 1970
ZPA4 1607	*It Ain't No Big Thing*	June 6, 1970
ZPA4 1608	*You Don't Have to Say You Love Me*	June 6, 1970
ZPA4 1609	*Just Pretend*	June 6, 1970
ZPA4 1610	*This Is Our Dance*	June 6, 1970
ZPA4 1613	*Life*	June 6, 1970
ZPA4 1614	*Heart of Rome*	June 6, 1970
ZPA4 1615	*When I'm over You*	June 7, 1970
ZPA4 1616	*I Really Don't Want to Know*	June 7, 1970
ZPA4 1617	*Faded Love*	June 7, 1970
ZPA4 1618	*Tomorrow Never Comes*	June 7, 1970
ZPA4 1619	*The Next Step Is Love*	June 7, 1970
ZPA4 1620	*Make the World Go Away*	June 7, 1970
ZPA4 1621	*Funny How Time Slips Away*	June 7, 1970
ZPA4 1622	*I Washed My Hands in Muddy Water*	June 7, 1970
ZPA4 1623	*Love Letters*	June 7, 1970
ZPA4 1624	*There Goes My Everything*	June 8, 1970
ZPA4 1625	*If I Were You*	June 8, 1970
ZPA4 1626	*Only Believe*	June 8, 1970
ZPA4 1627	*Sylvia*	June 8, 1970
ZPA4 1628	*Patch It Up*	June 8, 1970

MUSICIANS:

Lead guitar—James Burton	Vocal—Millie Kirkham
Guitar—Chip Young	Vocal—Jeannie Green

Bass—Norbert Putnam
Drums—Jerry Carrigan
Piano—David Briggs
Harmonica—Charlie McCoy

Vocal—Mary and Ginger Holladay
Vocal—Jordanaires
Vocal—Imperial Quartet
Vocal—Nashville Edition

Got My Mojo Working/Keep Your Hands was a studio jam and not meant to be recorded. However, someone left the tape running. All strings, horns, and voices were overdubbed at a later date.

July–August 1970

MGM Recording Studio, Los Angeles

Words
The Next Step Is Love
Polk Salad Annie
That's All Right
Little Sister
What'd I Say
Stranger in the Crowd
How the Web Was Woven
I Just Can't Help Believin'
You Don't Have to Say You Love Me

MUSICIANS:

Lead guitar—James Burton
Guitar—John Wilkinson
Guitar—Charlie Hodge

Bass—Jerry Scheff
Drums—Ronnie Tutt
Piano—Glenn D. Hardin

These were rehearsals for Elvis' August 1970 Vegas engagement. MGM filmed and recorded them for inclusion in *That's the Way It Is*. Tapes were not given to RCA.

August 1970

International Hotel, Las Vegas

Bridge over Troubled Water
You've Lost That Lovin' Feelin'
Mary in the Morning
Polk Salad Annie

These, too, were rehearsals for *That's the Way It Is*.

August 10, 1970

International Hotel, Las Vegas

That's All Right   August 10, 1970
I've Lost You   August 10, 1970
Patch It Up   August 10, 1970
Love Me Tender   August 10, 1970
You've Lost That Lovin' Feelin'   August 10, 1970
Sweet Caroline
I Just Can't Help Believing
Tiger Man
Bridge over Troubled

Water
Heartbreak Hotel
One Night
Blue Suede Shoes
All Shook Up
Polk Salad Annie
Can't Help Falling in
Love

Here are more recordings by MGM for *That's the Way It Is.*

		International Hotel, Las Vegas
August 13–15, 1970		
ZPA5 1862	*I Just Can't Help Believing*	August 13, 1970
ZPA5 1863	*Patch It Up*	August 13, 1970
ZPA5 1864	*You've Lost That Lovin' Feelin'*	August 14, 1970
ZPA5 1865	*I've Lost You*	August 14, 1970
ZPA5 1866	*Bridge over Troubled Water*	August 15, 1970

MUSICIANS:

Lead guitar—James Burton
Guitar—John Wilkinson
Guitar and vocal—Charlie Hodge
Bass—Jerry Scheff
Drums—Ronnie Tutt

Piano—Glenn D. Hardin
Vocal—Millie Kirkham
Vocal—Sweet Inspirations
Vocal—Imperial Quartet
Joe Guercio Orchestra

These are the five songs taped and released by RCA.

		Veterans Coliseum, Phoenix, Arizona
September 9, 1970		
	Mystery Train/Tiger Man	September 9, 1970

MUSICIANS:

Lead guitar—James Burton
Guitar—John Wilkinson
Guitar and vocal—Charlie Hodge
Bass—Jerry Scheff

Piano—Glenn D. Hardin
Vocal—Kathy Westmoreland
Vocal—Sweet Inspirations
Joe Guercio Orchestra

The above medley can be heard over the opening credits for *That's the Way It Is.*

		RCA Nashville studio
September 22, 1970		
ZPA4 1797	*Snowbird*	September 22, 1970
ZPA4 1798	*Where Did They Go, Lord*	September 22, 1970
ZPA4 1799	*Whole Lotta Shakin' Goin' On*	September 22, 1970
ZPA4 1800	*Rags to Riches*	September 22, 1970

MUSICIANS:

Lead guitar—Edward Hinton
Guitar—Chip Young
Bass—Norbert Putnam
Drums—Jerry Carrigan

Organ—Charlie McCoy
Vocal—Jeannie Green
Vocal—Jordanaires
Piano—David Briggs

All strings, horns, and voices were dubbed at a later date. Elvis had the horns removed from 1799.

1971

March 15, 1971		**RCA Nashville studio**
APA4	*The First Time Ever I Saw Your Face*	March 15, 1971
APA4	*Amazing Grace*	March 15, 1971
APA4	*Early Mornin' Rain*	March 15, 1971
APA4	*For Lovin' Me*	March 15, 1971

MUSICIANS:

Lead guitar—James Burton	Vocal—Millie Kirkham
Guitar—Chip Young	Vocal—Jeannie Green
Bass—Norbert Putnam	Vocal—Mary and Ginger Holladay
Drums—Jerry Carrigan	Vocal—Imperial Quartet
Piano—David Briggs	Vocal—Nashville Edition
Harmonica—Charlie McCoy	

Elvis was scheduled to record at least enough for an LP, but the sessions had to be canceled when he came down with an eye infection.

May 15–21, 1971			**RCA Nashville studio**
APA4	1259	*Miracle of the Rosary*	May 15, 1971
APA4	1260	*It Won't Seem Like Christmas*	May 15, 1971
APA4	1261	*If I Get Home on Christmas Day*	May 15, 1971
APA4	1262	*Padre*	May 15, 1971
APA4	1263	*Holly Leaves and Christmas Trees*	May 15, 1971
APA4	1264	*Merry Christmas, Baby*	May 15, 1971
APA4	1265	*Silver Bells*	May 15, 1971
APA4	1266	*I'll Be Home on Christmas Day*	May 16, 1971
APA4	1267	*On a Snowy Christmas Night*	May 16, 1971
APA4	1268	*Winter Wonderland*	May 16, 1971
APA4	1269	*Don't Think Twice, It's All Right*	May 16, 1971
APA4	1270	*O Come, All Ye Faithful*	May 16, 1971
APA4	1271	*The First Noel*	May 16, 1971
APA4	1272	*The Wonderful World of Christmas*	May 16, 1971
APA4	1273	*Help Me Make It Through the Night*	May 16, 1971
APA4	1274	*Until It's Time for You to Go*	May 17, 1971
APA4	1275	*Lead Me, Guide Me*	May 17, 1971
APA4	1276	*Fools Rush In*	May 18, 1971
APA4	1277	*He Touched Me*	May 18, 1971
APA4	1278	*I've Got Confidence*	May 18, 1971
APA4	1279	*An Evening Prayer*	May 18, 1971

APA4 1280	*Seeing Is Believing*	May 19, 1971
APA4 1281	*A Thing Called Love*	May 19, 1971
APA4 1282	*It's Still Here*	May 19, 1971
APA4 1283	*I'll Take You Home Again, Kathleen*	May 19, 1971
APA4 1284	*I Will Be True*	May 19, 1971
APA4 1285	*I'm Leavin'*	May 20, 1971
APA4 1286	*We Can Make the Morning*	May 20, 1971
APA4 1287	*It's Only Love*	May 20, 1971
APA4 1288	*Love Me, Love the Life I Lead*	May 21, 1971

MUSICIANS:

Lead guitar—James Burton
Guitar—Chip Young
Bass—Norbert Putnam
Drums—Jerry Carrigan
Piano—David Briggs

Harmonica—Charlie McCoy
Vocal—Millie Kirkham
Vocal—Ginger Holladay
Vocal—Temple Riser
Vocal—Imperial Quartet

The voices were dubbed at a later date than the session dates. The strings were added on June 21 and 22 in Hollywood. *Don't Think Twice, It's All Right* was an eight-minute jam and was released in an edited form some two years later. After the session ended, Elvis sat down at the piano and recorded *It's Still Here; I'll Take You Home Again, Kathleen;* and *I Will Be True* alone.

June 8–9, 1971   **RCA Nashville studio**

APA4 1289	*Until It's Time for You to Go*	June 8, 1971
APA4 1290	*Put Your Hand in the Hand*	June 8, 1971
APA4 1291	*Reach Out to Jesus*	June 8, 1971
APA4 1292	*He Is My Everything*	June 8, 1971
APA4 1293	*There Is No God But God*	June 9, 1971
APA4 1294	*I John*	June 9, 1971
APA4 1295	*The Bosom of Abraham*	June 9, 1971
APA4 1296	*I'll Be Home for Christmas*	June 9, 1971

MUSICIANS:

Lead guitar—James Burton
Guitar—Chip Young
Bass—Norbert Putnam
Drums—Jerry Carrigan
Drums—Kenneth Buttrey
Piano—David Briggs

Organ—Glen Spreen
Harmonica—Charlie McCoy
Vocal—Millie Kirkham
Vocal—June Page
Vocal—Sonja Montgomery
Vocal—Imperial Quartet

Elvis attempted to remake 1289 and 1296, but his attempt was less than successful. The versions from the May sessions were released.

1972

February 14–17, 1972	**Hilton Hotel, Las Vegas**
BPA5 1142 *Never Been to Spain*	February 14, 1972
BPA5 1143 *You Gave Me a Mountain*	February 15, 1972
BPA5 1144 *A Big Hunk o' Love*	February 15, 1972
BPA5 1145 *It's Impossible*	February 16, 1972
BPA5 1146 *The Impossible Dream*	February 16, 1972
BPA5 1147 *An American Trilogy*	February 17, 1972

MUSICIANS:

Lead guitar—James Burton	Vocal—Kathy Westmoreland
Guitar—John Wilkinson	Vocal—Sweet Inspirations
Guitar and vocal—Charlie Hodge	Vocal—J. D. Sumner and
Bass—Jerry Scheff	the Stamps
Drums—Ronnie Tutt	Joe Guercio Orchestra
Piano—Glenn D. Hardin	

The Sweet Inspirations: Myrna Smith, Sylvia Shenwell, Estelle Brown
J. D. Sumner and the Stamps: J. D. Sumner, Donnie Sumner, Bill Baize,
Ed Enoch, Richard Staborn

These songs were to appear on the *Standing Room Only* LP, LSP 4762.
RCA chose not to release it.

March 27–29, 1972	**MGM Recording Studio, Los Angeles**
BPA3 1149 *Separate Ways*	March 27, 1972
BPA3 1150 *For the Good Times*	March 27, 1972
BPA3 1151 *Where Do I Go from Here*	March 27, 1972
BPA3 1257 *Burning Love*	March 28, 1972
BPA3 1258 *Fool*	March 28, 1972
BPA3 1259 *Always on My Mind*	March 29, 1972
BPA3 1260 *It's a Matter of Time*	March 29, 1972

MUSICIANS:

Lead Guitar—James Burton	Piano—Glenn D. Hardin
Guitar—John Wilkinson	Vocal—J. D. Sumner and
Bass—Emory Gordy	the Stamps
Drums—Ronnie Tutt	

Some of these songs can be found on the *On Tour* film. This is the first
session in which Elvis used his live band in the studio.

MGM recorded backstage and in hotel rooms during this concert tour.

April 9, 1972	**Coliseum, Hampton Roads, Virginia**
April 10, 1972	**Coliseum, Richmond, Virginia**

April 18, 1972

**Convention Center,
San Antonio, Texas**

*Johnny B. Good
See See Rider
Polk Salad Annie
Proud Mary
Never Been to Spain
Burning Love
Love Me Tender
Until It's Time for You
to Go
Suspicious Minds
Bridge over Troubled
Water
Funny How Time Slips
Away
American Trilogy
I Got a Woman
A Big Hunk o' Love
You Gave Me a
Mountain
Lawdy, Miss Clawdy
Can't Help Falling in
Love*

MUSICIANS:

Lead guitar—James Burton
Guitar—John Wilkinson
Guitar and vocal—Charlie Hodge
Bass—Jerry Scheff
Drums—Ronnie Tutt
Piano—Glenn D. Hardin

Vocal—Kathy Westmoreland
Vocal—Sweet Inspirations
Vocal—J. D. Sumner and
the Stamps
Joe Guercio Orchestra

All of these were live recordings from the April tour.

*For the Good Times
Lead Me, Guide Me
Bosom of Abraham
I John*

MUSICIANS:

Piano and vocal—Charlie Hodge
Vocal—Sweet Inspirations

Vocal—J. D. Sumner and
the Stamps

The above songs were recorded by RCA during a late-night jam session.

June 10, 1972

**Madison Square Garden,
New York**

BPA5 6797	*Also Sprach Zarathustra*	June 10, 1972
BPA5 6774	*That's All Right*	June 10, 1972
BPA5 6775	*Proud Mary*	June 10, 1972
BPA5 6776	*Never Been to Spain*	June 10, 1972
BPA5 6777	*You Don't Have to Say You Love Me*	June 10, 1972
BPA5 6778	*You've Lost That Lovin' Feelin'*	June 10, 1972
BPA5 6779	*Polk Salad Annie*	June 10, 1972
BPA5 6780	*Love Me*	June 10, 1972
BPA5 6781	*All Shook Up*	June 10, 1972

BPA5 6782	*Heartbreak Hotel*	June 10, 1972
BPA5 6783	*Teddy Bear/Don't Be Cruel*	June 10, 1972
BPA5 6794	Introductions by Elvis	June 10, 1972
BPA5 6784	*The Impossible Dream*	June 10, 1972
BPA5 6785	*Hound Dog*	June 10, 1972
BPA5 6786	*Suspicious Minds*	June 10, 1972
BPA5 6787	*For the Good Times*	June 10, 1972
BPA5 6788	*American Trilogy*	June 10, 1972
BPA5 6789	*Funny How Time Slips Away*	June 10, 1972
BPA5 6790	*I Can't Stop Loving You*	June 10, 1972
BPA5 6791	*I Can't Stop Loving You*	June 10, 1972
BPA5 6792	*Can't Help Falling in Love*	June 10, 1972
BPA5 6793	Closing	June 10, 1972

MUSICIANS:

Lead guitar—James Burton
Guitar—John Wilkinson
Guitar and vocal—Charlie Hodge
Bass—Jerry Scheff
Drums—Ronnie Tutt
Piano—Glenn D. Hardin

Vocal—Kathy Westmoreland
Vocal—Sweet Inspirations
Vocal—J. D. Sumner and the Stamps
Joe Guercio Orchestra

The evening show was recorded in its entirety.

1973

January 14, 1973   **H.I.C. Arena, Hawaii**

CPA5 4723	*Also Sprach Zarathustra*	January 14, 1973
CPA5 4724	*See See Rider*	January 14, 1973
CPA5 4725	*Burning Love*	January 14, 1973
CPA5 4726	*Something*	January 14, 1973
CPA5 4727	*You Gave Me a Mountain*	January 14, 1973
CPA5 4728	*Steamroller Blues*	January 14, 1973
CPA5 4729	*My Way*	January 14, 1973
CPA5 4730	*Love Me*	January 14, 1973
CPA5 4731	*Johnny B. Good*	January 14, 1973
CPA5 4732	*It's Over*	January 14, 1973
CPA5 4733	*Blue Suede Shoes*	January 14, 1973
CPA5 4734	*I'm So Lonesome I Could Cry*	January 14, 1973
CPA5 4735	*I Can't Stop Loving You*	January 14, 1973
CPA5 4736	*Hound Dog*	January 14, 1973
CPA5 4737	*What Now, My Love*	January 14, 1973
CPA5 4738	*Fever*	January 14, 1973

CPA5 4739	*Welcome to My World*	January 14, 1973
CPA5 4740	*Suspicious Minds*	January 14, 1973
CPA5 4741	Introductions by Elvis	January 14, 1973
CPA5 4742	*I'll Remember You*	January 14, 1973
CPA5 4743	*Long Tall Sally/Whole Lotta Shakin' Goin' On*	January 14, 1973
CPA5 4744	*American Trilogy*	January 14, 1973
CPA5 4745	*A Big Hunk o' Love*	January 14, 1973
CPA5 4746	*Can't Help Falling in Love*	January 14, 1973
CPA5 4747	Closing vamp	January 14, 1973
CPA5 4756	*Blue Hawaii*	January 14, 1973
CPA5 4757	*Ku-u-i-po*	January 14, 1973
CPA5 4758	*No More*	January 14, 1973
CPA5 4759	*Hawaiian Wedding Song*	January 14, 1973
CPA5 4760	*Early Mornin' Rain*	January 14, 1973

MUSICIANS:

Lead guitar—James Burton
Guitar—John Wilkinson
Guitar and vocal—Charlie Hodge
Bass—Jerry Scheff
Piano—Glenn D. Hardin

Vocal—Kathy Westmoreland
Vocal—Sweet Inspirations
Vocal—J. D. Sumner and the Stamps

J. D. Sumner and the Stamps: J. D. Sumner, Donnie Sumner, Bill Baize, Ed Enoch, Ed Wideman.

This was Elvis' first live recording to be made Quadrophonic. The last five songs were recorded at RCA's New York studio for use in the "Aloha" TV special.

July 21–25, 1973 — **Stax Recording Studio, Memphis**

CPA5 4761	*If You Don't Come Back*	July 21, 1973
CPA5 4762	*Three Corn Patches*	July 21, 1973
CPA5 4763	*Take Good Care of Her*	July 21, 1973
CPA5 4764	*Find Out What's Happening*	July 22, 1973
CPA5 4765	*I've Got a Thing About You, Baby*	July 22, 1973
CPA5 4766	*Just a Little Bit*	July 22, 1973
CPA5 4767	*Raised on Rock*	July 23, 1973
CPA5 4768	*For Ol' Times Sake*	July 23, 1973
CPA5 4769	*Girl of Mine*	July 24, 1973
CPA5 4770	*Good, Bad, but Beautiful*	July 24, 1973
CPA5 4771	*Color My Rainbow*	July 25, 1973
CPA5 4772	*Sweet Angeline*	July 25, 1973
CPA5 4773	*The Wonders You Perform*	July 25, 1973

MUSICIANS:

Lead guitar—James Burton
Guitar—Reggie Young
Guitar—Johnny Christopher

Organ—Bobby Emmons
Vocal—Kathy Westmoreland
Vocal—Jeannie Green

191

Bass—Tommy Cogbill
Drums—Jerry Carrigan
Drums—Ronnie Tutt
Piano—Bobby Wood

Vocal—Mary and Ginger
Holladay
Vocal—J. D. Sumner and
the Stamps

All strings and voices were overdubbed on September 28, 1973, in Nashville. The vocal backing on 4772 is the group Voice.

September 24, 1973   **Elvis' home, Palm Springs**

| CPA5 4774 | *I Miss You* | September 24, 1974 |
| CPA5 4775 | *Are You Sincere* | September 24, 1974 |

Vocal—Voice
Voice: Donnie Sumner, Tim Batey, Sherril Nielson

December 10–16, 1973   **Stax Studio, Memphis**

CPA5 1617	*I Got a Feelin' in My Body*	December 10, 1973
CPA5 1618	*It's Midnight*[1]	December 10, 1973
CPA5 1619	*You Asked Me To*	December 11, 1973
CPA5 1620	*If You Talk in Your Sleep*	December 11, 1973
CPA5 1621	*Mr. Songman*	December 12, 1973
CPA5 1622	*Thinking About You*	December 12, 1973
CPA5 1623	*Love Song of the Year*	December 12, 1973
CPA5 1624	*Help Me*	December 12, 1973
CPA5 1625	*Loving Arms*	December 13, 1973
CPA5 1626	*Good-time Charlie's Got the Blues*	December 13, 1973
CPA5 1627	*Talk About the Good Times*	December 14, 1973
CPA5 1628	*Promised Land*	December 15, 1973
CPA5 1629	*Your Love's Been a Long Time Coming*	December 15, 1973
CPA5 1630	*My Boy*	December 15, 1973
CPA5 1631	*There's a Honky Tonk Angel*	December 15, 1973
CPA5 1632	*If That Isn't Love*	December 15, 1973
CPA5 1633	*Spanish Eyes*	December 16, 1973
CPA5 1634	*She Wears My Ring*	December 16, 1973

MUSICIANS:
Lead guitar—James Burton
Guitar—Johnny Christopher
Bass—Norbert Putnam
Drums—Ronnie Tutt
Piano and organ—David Briggs
Piano—Pete Hullin
Vocal—Kathy Westmoreland

Vocal—Jeannie Green
Vocal—Mary Holladay
Vocal—Susan Pilkington
Vocal—J. D. Sumner and the
Stamps
Vocal—Voice

The strings were overdubbed in Hollywood on January 11, 1974. The horns were added on January 15, 1974, in Nashville.

[1] *It's Midnight* was not satisfactorily recorded until January 10, 1974.

1974

March 20, 1974		**Mid-South Coliseum, Memphis**
DPA5 0903	*See See Rider*	March 20, 1974
DPA5 0904	*I Got a Woman*	March 20, 1974
DPA5 0905	*Love Me*	March 20, 1974
DPA5 0906	*Tryin' to Get to You*	March 20, 1974
DPA5 0907	*All Shook Up*	March 20, 1974
DPA5 0908	*Steamroller Blues*	March 20, 1974
DPA5 0909	*Teddy Bear/ Don't Be Cruel*	March 20, 1974
DPA5 0910	*Love Me Tender*	March 20, 1974
DPA5 0911	*Long Tall Sally/ Whole Lotta Shakin' Goin' On/ Your Mama Won't Dance/ Flip, Flop, Fly/ Jailhouse Rock/ Hound Dog*	March 20, 1974
DPA5 0912	*Fever*	March 20, 1974
DPA5 0913	*Polk Salad Annie*	March 20, 1974
DPA5 0914	*Why Me, Lord*	March 20, 1974
DPA5 0915	*How Great Thou Art*	March 20, 1974
DPA5 0916	*Suspicious Minds*	March 20, 1974
DPA5 0917	Introductions by Elvis	March 20, 1974
DPA5 0918	*Blueberry Hill/ I Can't Stop Loving You*	March 20, 1974
DPA5 0919	*Help Me*	March 20, 1974
DPA5 0920	*An American Trilogy*	March 20, 1974
DPA5 0921	*Let Me Be There*	March 20, 1974
DPA5 0926	*My Baby Left Me*	March 20, 1974
DPA5 0927	*Lawdy, Miss Clawdy*	March 20, 1974
DPA5 0928	*Funny How Time Slips Away*	March 20, 1974
DPA5 0929	*Can't Help Falling in Love*	March 20, 1974
DPA5 0930	Closing vamp	March 20, 1974

MUSICIANS:
Lead guitar—James Burton
Guitar—John Wilkinson
Guitar and vocal—Charlie Hodge
Bass—Duke Bardwell
Piano—Glenn D. Hardin
Vocal—Kathy Westmoreland

Vocal—Sweet Inspirations
Vocal—J. D. Sumner and the Stamps
Vocal—Voice
Joe Guercio Orchestra

   This was probably Elvis' best live recording, although the album did not sell and consequently RCA deleted it.

1975

May 10–12, 1975		**Hollywood**
EPA3 1594	*Fairytale*	May 10, 1975
EPA3 1595	*Green, Green Grass of Home*	May 10, 1975
EPA3 1596	*I Can Help*	May 10, 1975
EPA3 1597	*And I Love You So*	May 10 and 11, 1975
EPA3 1598	*Susan When She Tried*	May 10 and 11, 1975
EPA3 1599	*T-R-O-U-B-L-E*	May 10 and 11, 1975
EPA3 1600	*Woman Without Love*	May 11 and 12, 1975
EPA3 1601	*Shake a Hand*	May 11 and 12, 1975
EPA3 1602	*Bringing It Back*	May 11 and 12, 1975
EPA3 1603	*Pieces of My Life*	May 12, 1975

MUSICIANS:

Lead guitar—James Burton
Piano—Glenn D. Hardin
Guitar—John Wilkinson
Guitar—Charlie Hodge
Drums—Ronnie Tutt

Clarinet—David Briggs
Bass—Duke Bardwell
Vocal—Voice
Vocal—Mary and Ginger Holladay

1976

Release Date: January 1976
April 11, 1956; September 5, 1957;
April 3, 1960; April 4, 1960; May 25,
1966

Recording Locations:
Texas, Nashville, and Hawaii

EPA3	2742	*Harbor Lights*[2]	
EPA5	2744	Interview with Elvis[3]	
G2WB	0270	*I Want You, I Need You, I Love You*	April 11, 1956
WPA1	8117	*Blue Suede Shoes*	NBC TV show, 1968
H2PB	5525	*Blue Christmas*	September 5, 1957
H2WB	6779	*Jailhouse Rock*	May 2, 1957
L2WB	0100	*It's Now or Never*	April 3, 1960
SPA3	6743	*Cane and a High Starched Collar*	February 9, 1961
EPA3	2743	Presentation of Awards to Elvis	March 25, 1961
CPA5	4756	*Blue Hawaii*	
L2WB	0105	*Such a Night*	April 4, 1960
WPA1	8120	*Baby, What You Want Me to Do*	NBC TV show, 1968
TPA4	0909	*How Great Thou Art*	May 25, 1966
WPA1	8029	*If I Can Dream*	NBC TV Show, 1968

[2] *Harbor Lights,* 1954: Sun master—no record of personnel.
[3] Interview with Elvis in Texas, April 10, 1956.

RECORDING SESSIONS

MUSICIANS:
Guitar—Elvis, Scotty Moore, Chet Atkins, Hank Garland, Charlie Hodge; Harold Bradley, Chip Young, Jerry Stembridge (on TPA4 0909)
Steel guitar—Pete Drake (on TPA4 0909)
Bass—Bill Black, Bob Moore, Charlie McCoy
Piano—Marvin Hughes, Dudley Brooks, Floyd Cramer, Henry Slaughter, Mike Stoller
Drums—D. J. Fontana, Murrey Harman

Saxophone—Homer (Boots) Randolph, Rufus Long
Vocals—J. D. Sumner and the Stamps; Imperial Quartet; Jordanaires; Ben Speer; Brock Speer; Gordon Stoker; Millie Kirkham; Neil Matthews, Jr.; Hoyt Hawkins; Hugh Jarrett; Raymond Walker; Jake Hess; Charles S. Nielsen; Gary McSpadden; Amond Morales; June Page; Dolores Edgin

Release Date: March 1976

Recording Location: Sun studio, Memphis

F2WB 8040	*That's All Right*	July 1954
F2WB 8041	*Blue Moon of Kentucky*	July 1954
F2WB 8042	*I Don't Care If the Sun Don't Shine*	September 1954
F2WB 8043	*Good Rockin' Tonight*	September 1954
F2WB 8044	*Milkcow Blues Boogie*	December 1954
F2WB 8045	*You're a Heartbreaker*	December 1954
F2WB 8046	*Baby, Let's Play House*	February 1955
F2WB 8047	*I'm Left, You're Right, She's Gone*	July 1955
F2WB 8001	*Mystery Train*	February 1955
F2WB 8000	*I Forgot to Remember to Forget*	July 1955
F2WB 8116	*I'll Never Let You Go*	January 1955
G2WB 1086	*I Love You Because* (first version)	July 1954
F2WB 8039	*Tryin' to Get to You*	July 1955
F2WB 8117	*Blue Moon*	July 1954
F2WB 8118	*Just Because*	September 1954
G2WB 1087	*I Love You Because* (second version)	July 1954

February 2–8, 1976

Memphis

FWA5 0665	*Bitter They Are, Harder They Fall*	February 2–3, 1976
FWA5 0667	*The Last Farewell*	February 2–3, 1976
FWA5 0668	*Solitaire*	February 3–4, 1976
FWA5 0670	*I'll Never Fall in Love Again*	February 4–5, 1976
FWA5 0671	*For the Heart*	February 5–6, 1976
FWA5 0672	*Hurt*	February 5–6, 1976
FWA5 0673	*Danny Boy*	February 5–6, 1976
FWA5 0674	*Never Again*	February 6–7, 1976
FWA5 0675	*Love Coming Down*	February 6–7, 1976
FWA5 0676	*Blue Eyes Crying in the Rain*	February 7–8, 1976

195

FWA5 0678 *She Thinks I Still Care* February 2–3, 1976
FWA5 0679 *Moody Blue* February 3–4, 1976

MUSICIANS:

Lead guitar—James Burton
Piano—Glenn D. Hardin
Guitar—John Wilkinson
Guitar—Charlie Hodge

Drums—Ronnie Tutt
Electric piano—David Briggs
Bass—Jerry Scheff

On *Blue Eyes Crying in the Rain:* Piano—David Briggs; Electric piano—Bobby Emmons; Bass—Norbert Putnam; Electric guitar—Billy Sanford Vocals—J. D. Sumner and the Stamps, Ed Hill, Larry Strickland, Kathy Westmoreland, Myrna Smith

Release Date: 1976
January 15, 1969; February 18, 1970;
June 7, 1970; May 17, 1971; May 20,
1972; January 14, 1973

Recording Locations: Memphis, Las Vegas, Nashville, New York, and Hawaii

XPA5 1155 *Gentle on My Mind* January 15, 1969
ZPA5 1294 *Release Me (and* February 18, 1970
Let Me Love Again)
ZPA4 1616 *I Really Don't Want* June 7, 1970
to Know
ZPA4 1620 *Make the World Go* June 7, 1970
Away
APA3 1273 *Help Me Make It* May 17, 1971
Through the Night
BPA5 6788 *For the Good Times* May 20, 1972
CPA5 4734 *I'm So Lonesome I* January 14, 1973
Could Cry
CPA5 4739 *Welcome to My* January 14, 1973
World
I Can't Stop Loving You June 10, 1972

MUSICIANS:

Guitar—James Burton, John Wilkinson, Charlie Hodge; Reggie Young (on XPA5 1155); Jerry Stembridge (on APA3 1273)
Piano—Glenn D. Hardin, David Briggs; Ronnie Milsap (on XPA5 1155)
Drums—Ronnie Tutt; Kenneth Buttrey (on APA3 1273)

Bass—Jerry Scheff; Norbert Putnam (on APA3 1273); Tommy Cogbill (on XPA5 1155)
Organ—Bobby Emmons
Vocals—J. D. Sumner and the Stamps, Imperial Quartet, Jordanaires, Jeannie Green, Mary and Ginger Holladay, Millie Kirkham, Sandra P. Robinson

1977

Release Date: June 1977
March 20, 1974; October 29–31,
1976; April 25, 1977
DPA5 0926 *Let Me Be There*

Recording Locations: Memphis;
Murfreesboro, Tennessee;
Saginaw, Michigan
March 20, 1974

RECORDING SESSIONS

FWA5 1048	*It's Easy for You*	October 29, 1977
FWA5 1049	*Way Down*	October 29, 1976
FWA5 1051	*There's a Fire Below*	October 30, 1976
FWA5 1052	*He'll Have to Go*	October 31, 1976
GWA5 2574	*If You Love Me*	April 25, 1977
GWA5 2575	*Little Darlin'*	April 25, 1977
GWA5 2576	*Unchained Melody*	April 25, 1977

MUSICIANS:

Lead guitar—James Burton
Guitar—John Wilkinson
Guitar—Charlie Hodge
Guitar—Jerry Stembridge
Bass—Jerry Scheff
Bass—Duke Bardwell (on DPA5 0926)
Piano—Sonny Brown
Piano—Glenn D. Hardin (on DPA5 0926)

Electric piano—David Briggs
Drums—Ronnie Tutt
Vocals—J. D. Sumner, Ed Enoch, Ed Hill, Larry Strickland, Kathy Westmoreland, Myrna Smith, Sherril Nielson, Gary Buckles, Estelle Brown, Sylvia Shenwell

BOOK 4

DISCOGRAPHY
AND FILMS

American Records

It is with great pleasure that I write this chapter. In the following pages I will attempt to remind you of facts you may have forgotten, or perhaps never knew. The Elvis Unique Record Club boasts the most accurate and complete Elvis discography in the world. The facts contained here were found through love and twenty-two years of painstaking research. It is true that Elvis is the King, and it is also true that the listings on these pages are what made him King. There is no other entertainer in the history of show business who has compiled the record-shattering statistics that Elvis has. Consider the following:

1. Elvis has had the most records on *Billboard*'s Hot 100 chart.

2. Elvis has 40 top-ten songs to his credit. This is more than any other artist.

3. Elvis holds the record for retaining the most weeks (forty-seven) at the top number 1 position (1957).

4. Elvis has had 14 number 1 records.

5. Elvis has had 47 two-sided record hits.

6. Elvis' records have appeared on *Billboard*'s charts for twenty-three consecutive years, another all-time record.

7. Elvis has had 737 different records listed on *Billboard*'s charts.

8. Elvis has had 29 top-ten singles.

9. *All Shook Up* was on the charts for thirty weeks in 1957.

10. Elvis has had 3 number 1 records in less than three weeks.

Take a moment to digest the above before I mention that Elvis has also had many 45 EPs on the charts. Elvis has had fifty-eight LPs on the Top 100 chart. The trophy room at Graceland looks like Fort Knox, the walls literally lined with gold. No one person could be more deserving of these awards than Elvis, for never in the recorded history of mankind has anyone ever done so much for pop culture.

It is this author's opinion that you could have removed all of the glitter and glamour, even the shrewd business mind of Colonel Tom Parker, and you would still have had an American pop original. Put the boy on the stage and he'd begin to rock. Leave him there for twenty-three years and you'd find the man still all alone, number one, the undisputed King of Rock and Roll.

SUN 45 RPM AND 78 RPM SINGLES

Elvis had five records on Sam Phillips' Sun label. All five were released simultaneously as 45s and 78s.

1. **Sun 209**   August 1954
   That's All Right [Mama]/ Blue Moon of Kentucky

2. **Sun 210**   October 1954
   Good Rockin' Tonight/ I Don't Care if the Sun Don't Shine

3. **Sun 215**   January 1955
   Milkcow Blues Boogie/ You're a Heartbreaker

4. **Sun 217**   May 1955
   I'm Left, You're Right, She's Gone/ Baby, Let's Play House
   On July 6, 1955, *Baby, Let's Play House* reached the number 10 position on *Billboard*'s Country chart. It remained on the chart for fifteen weeks.

5. **Sun 223**   August 1955
   Mystery Train/ I Forgot to Remember to Forget
   On September 7, 1955, both sides of this record reached number 1 on the Country chart. They remained on the chart for forty weeks.

RCA 45 RPM AND 78 RPM SINGLES

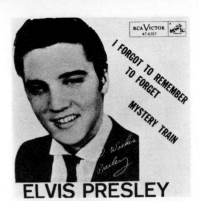

From November 1955 to October 1958 RCA released twenty-four singles by Elvis. All twenty-four were available as 45 rpm's and 78 rpm's.

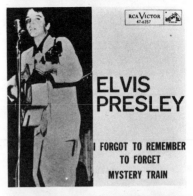

1. **RCA 6357**   November 1955

   Mystery Train/I Forgot to Remember to Forget

   BLACK LABEL   DOG ON TOP

2. **RCA 6380**   November 1955

   That's All Right, Mama/Blue Moon of Kentucky

   BLACK LABEL   DOG ON TOP

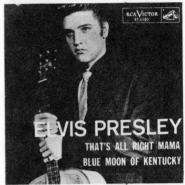

3. **RCA 6381**   November 1955

   Good Rockin' Tonight/I Don't Care if the Sun Don't Shine

   BLACK LABEL   DOG ON TOP

   I Don't Care if the Sun Don't Shine made *Billboard*'s Hot 100 chart on October 3, 1956, at the number 74 slot and remained on the chart for six weeks.

4. **RCA 6382**   November 1955

   Milkcow Blues Boogie/You're a Heartbreaker

   BLACK LABEL   DOG ON TOP

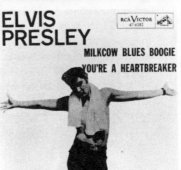

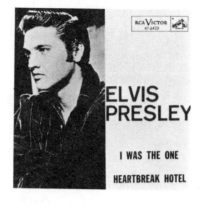

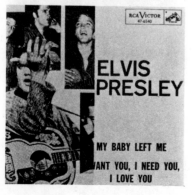

5. RCA 6383   November 1955

    I'm Left, You're Right, She's Gone/Baby, Let's Play House

BLACK LABEL   DOG ON TOP

6. RCA 6420   January 1956

    Heartbreak Hotel/I Was the One

BLACK LABEL   DOG ON TOP

Heartbreak Hotel made *Billboard*'s Hot 100 chart on February 22, 1956. It became Elvis' first national number 1. It remained on the chart for twenty-seven weeks and held the number 1 position for seven weeks. It remained on the Country charts also for twenty-seven weeks, reaching number 1 on the same day. It made the Rhythm and Blues chart on April 4, 1956, at the number 5 slot. It remained on this chart for thirteen weeks.

    I Was the One numbered 23 on the Hot 100 chart on February 29, 1956, and remained on the chart for sixteen weeks.

7. RCA 6540   May 1956

    I Want You, I Need You, I Love You/My Baby Left Me

BLACK LABEL   DOG ON TOP

I Want You, I Need You, I Love You entered *Billboard*'s Hot 100 chart on May 16, 1956, at number 3. It remained on the chart for twenty-four weeks. The Country chart had *I Want You, I Need You, I Love You* at number 1 on May 23. It remained on the Country chart for twenty weeks. On June 6 this song was numbered at 10 on the Rhythm and Blues chart, where it would remain for eleven weeks.

    My Baby Left Me entered the Hot 100 at number 31 on May 16. It entered the Country chart on May 23 at number 1 and remained on the chart for twenty weeks, with *I Want You, I Need You, I Love You.*

204

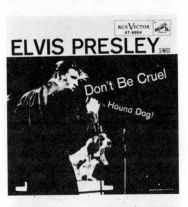

8. **RCA 6604**   July 1956

   Hound Dog/Don't Be Cruel

BLACK LABEL   DOG ON TOP

Hound Dog was on the Hot 100 chart on July 25, 1956, at number 2. It remained on this chart for twenty-eight weeks. It entered the Country chart on the same day at the number 1 position and remained for twenty-nine weeks. The Rhythm and Blues chart listed *Hound Dog* on August 8 at the number 1 slot; it remained on this chart for eight weeks.

   Don't Be Cruel was number 1 on *Billboard*'s Hot 100 on August 8, 1956. It remained on the chart for twenty-seven weeks and was number 1 for seven weeks. The Country chart acquired *Don't Be Cruel* on July 25 and positioned it at number 1. It remained on this chart for twenty-nine weeks. On August 8 it could be found on the Rhythm and Blues chart, where it would stay for eight weeks, one week holding the number 1 position.

9. **RCA 6636**   September 1956

   Blue Suede Shoes/Tutti Frutti

BLACK LABEL   DOG ON TOP

On March 28, 1957, *Blue Suede Shoes* entered the Hot 100 at number 24; it remained on the chart for twelve weeks.

10. **RCA 6637**   September 1956

    I'm Counting on You/I Got a Woman

BLACK LABEL   DOG ON TOP

11. **RCA 6638**   September 1956

    I'll Never Let You Go/I'm Gonna Sit Right Down and Cry over You

BLACK LABEL   DOG ON TOP

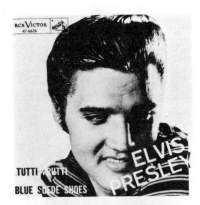

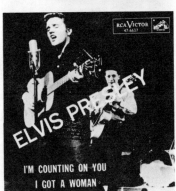

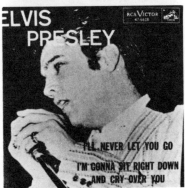

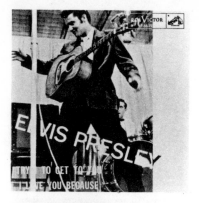

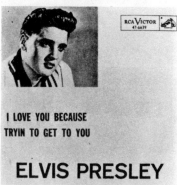

12. **RCA 6639**   September 1956

Tryin' to Get to You/I Love You Because

BLACK LABEL   DOG ON TOP

13. **RCA 6640**   September 1956

Blue Moon/Just Because

BLACK LABEL   DOG ON TOP

Blue Moon entered Billboard's Hot 100 chart on September 19, 1956, at number 55. It remained on the chart for seventeen weeks.

14. **RCA 6641**   September 1956

Money Honey/One-sided Love Affair

BLACK LABEL   DOG ON TOP

Money Honey was number 76 on the Hot 100 on May 5, 1957. It remained on the chart for five weeks.

15. **RCA 6642**   September 1956

Shake, Rattle and Roll/Lawdy, Miss Clawdy

BLACK LABEL   DOG ON TOP

16. **RCA 6643**   September 1956

Love Me Tender/Any Way You Want Me

BLACK LABEL   DOG ON TOP

Love Me Tender entered *Billboard's* Hot 100 chart on October 10, 1956, at the number 1 position. It remained number 1 for four weeks, and on the chart for twenty-three weeks.[1] On the same day this song was slotted at number 3 on the Country chart, where it remained for eighteen weeks, and was positioned at number 4 on the Rhythm and Blues chart, where it stayed for thirteen weeks.

[1] This record was available with three different covers.

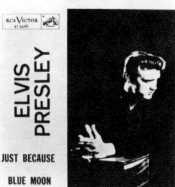

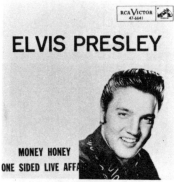

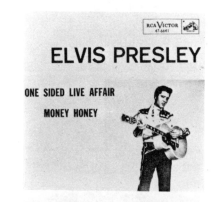

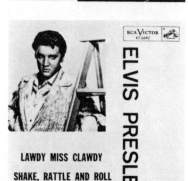

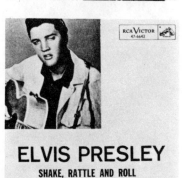

17. RCA 6800   January 1957

Too Much/Playing for Keeps

BLACK LABEL   DOG ON TOP

On January 16, 1957, *Too Much* was number 2 on the Hot 100 and stayed on this chart for seventeen weeks. It remained for fourteen weeks on the Country chart, where it was number 5 on January 23. The Rhythm and Blues chart displayed *Too Much* at number 7 and kept it on the chart for eight weeks.

Playing for Keeps was number 34 on the Hot 100 on January 23. It remained on the chart for nine weeks.

18. RCA 6870   March 1957

All Shook Up/That's When Your Heartaches Begin

BLACK LABEL   DOG ON TOP

All Shook Up was number 1 on the Country chart and the Rhythm and Blues chart on April 3, 1957. On March 27 it was number 1 on the Hot 100. The Hot 100 held this song on its chart for thirty weeks, eight of which were number 1 positions. The Country chart kept this record on its chart for sixteen weeks; the Rhythm and Blues, for fourteen weeks, four of them at number 1.

That's When Your Heartaches Begin entered the Hot 100 chart on April 3 at the number 58 position. It remained on this chart for seven weeks.

19. RCA 7000   June 1957

Teddy Bear/Loving You

BLACK LABEL   DOG ON TOP

On June 19, 1957, the Hot 100 had *Teddy Bear* in the number 1 position. It remained number 1 for seven weeks and stayed on the chart for twenty-five weeks. It was number 1 on the Country chart on June 22 and remained on this chart for sixteen weeks. The Rhythm and Blues chart had *Teddy Bear* at number 1 on June 29; it remained on the R&B chart for twelve weeks.

Loving You was on *Billboard*'s Hot 100 chart on June 19 at number 28. It stayed on the chart for twenty-two weeks. The Rhythm and Blues chart had *Loving You* in the number 1 position on June 29. It remained on this chart for twelve weeks.

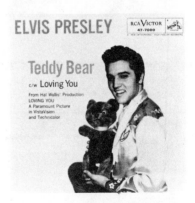

20. RCA 7035   September 1957

Jailhouse Rock/Treat Me Nice

BLACK LABEL   DOG ON TOP

October 5, 1957, found *Jailhouse Rock* on the Hot 100 at the number 1 position. This song was number 1 for six weeks and was on the chart for twenty-seven weeks. On the same day the Country chart had the song in the same position. It remained on the Country chart for twenty-four weeks. It also entered the R&B chart at the same position on the fifth. It remained on the Rhythm and Blues chart for fifteen weeks.

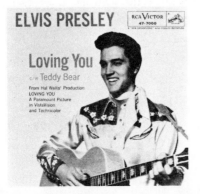
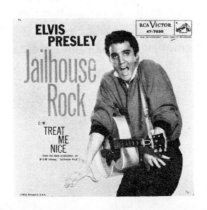

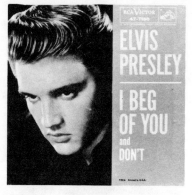

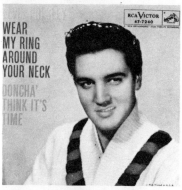

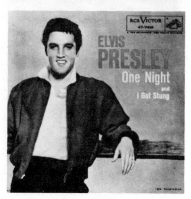

The Hot 100 chart cast *Treat Me Nice* in the number 27 spot on October 12. It stayed on the chart for ten weeks. On October 5 *Treat Me Nice* was number 1 on the R&B chart, where it would rank for fifteen weeks.

21. RCA 7150   December 1957
Don't/I Beg of You

BLACK LABEL   DOG ON TOP

Don't entered the Hot 100 chart on January 18, 1958, at the number 1 slot. It remained on the chart for twenty weeks. On January 25 this song also showed on the R&B and Country charts. It hit the number 2 position on the Country chart and held for eighteen weeks. *Don't* was number 4 on the Rhythm and Blues chart. It remained on the R&B chart for ten weeks.

I Beg of You was on the Hot 100 chart on the same day as its flip side, in the number 8 position, and remained on the chart for the same twenty weeks as *Don't*. On January 25, it was number 2 on the Country chart, where it remained for eighteen weeks, and number 4 on the R&B chart, remaining on the chart for ten weeks.

22. RCA 7240   April 1958
Wear My Ring Around Your Neck/Doncha' Think It's Time

BLACK LABEL   DOG ON TOP

Wear My Ring Around Your Neck entered both the Hot 100 and the Country charts on April 12, 1958, at the number 3 position and remained on both charts for fifteen weeks. It also entered the Rhythm and Blues chart on the twelfth, but in the number 7 position, and remained on the chart for eleven weeks.

Doncha' Think It's Time made the Hot 100 chart on the same day. It numbered 21 and remained on the chart for six weeks.

23. RCA 7280   June 1958
Hard-headed Woman/Don't Ask Me Why

BLACK LABEL   DOG ON TOP

On June 21, 1958, *Hard-headed Woman* entered *Billboard*'s Hot 100, Country, and Rhythm and Blues charts at the number 2 position. It remained for thirteen weeks on the Hot 100, sixteen on the Country, and ten weeks on the R&B chart.

Don't Ask Me Why was the number 28 song on the Hot 100 chart on June 28; it remained on this chart for nine weeks. It was number 2 on the R&B chart on the June 21 and remained for ten weeks.

24. RCA 7410[2]   October 1958
I Got Stung/One Night

BLACK LABEL   DOG ON TOP

Billboard listed *I Got Stung* on its Hot 100 chart in the number 8 position on November 9, 1958. It remained on this chart for sixteen weeks.

One Night numbered 4 on the Hot 100 chart on November 16. It stayed on the Hot 100 for seventeen weeks. On December 28 the Country chart listed this song at number 24, and it remained on this chart for three weeks. Number 10 was the position *One Night* held on the R&B chart, where it remained for fifteen weeks after entering on November 23.

[2] RCA 7410 was the last Elvis record to be issued as a 78.

25. **RCA 7506**   March 1959

    A Fool Such as I/I Need Your Love Tonight[3]

BLACK LABEL   DOG ON TOP

    A Fool Such as I entered *Billboard*'s Hot 100 on March 29, 1959, in the number 2 slot. It remained on the chart for fifteen weeks. On April 19, 1959, this song held the number 16 position on the Rhythm and Blues chart, where it showed for the next seven weeks.

    Billboard listed *I Need Your Love Tonight* on its Hot 100 chart on April 5 in the number 4 position. It remained on the chart for thirteen weeks.

26. **RCA 7600**   June 1959

    A Big Hunk o' Love/My Wish Came True

BLACK LABEL   DOG ON TOP

    A Big Hunk o' Love was number 1 on July 12, 1959, on the Hot 100, which kept it on the chart for fourteen weeks. The Rhythm and Blues chart made this song number 10 on August 2. It remained on the R&B chart for seven weeks.

    Billboard's Hot 100 listed *My Wish Came True* as number 12 on July 7; it stayed on the chart for eleven weeks. The R&B chart listed this tune at number 15 and kept it for three weeks.

27. **RCA 7740**   March 1960

    Stuck on You/Fame and Fortune

BLACK LABEL   DOG ON TOP

    Stuck on You was number 1 on the Hot 100 chart for four weeks, beginning April 10, 1960. It was on this chart for 14 weeks. It numbered 6 on the R&B chart upon entering the list on April 1, 1960. It remained on the chart for nine weeks.

    Fame and Fortune numbered 17 on *Billboard*'s Hot 100 chart on April 17, 1960; it remained on the Hot 100 for ten weeks.

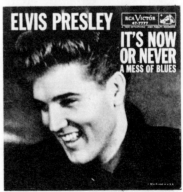

28. **RCA 7777**   July 1960

    It's Now or Never/A Mess of Blues

BLACK LABEL   DOG ON TOP

    It's Now or Never was number 1 for five weeks out of twenty weeks on the Hot 100 chart, having entered on July 24, 1960. This song arrived on the Country chart on August 14 in the number 7 position. It remained on this chart for seven weeks.

    A Mess of Blues was listed on the Hot 100 on July 31, 1960, and held the number 32 position. It remained on the Hot 100 for eleven weeks.

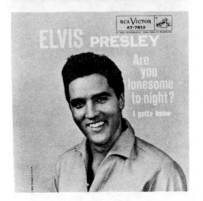

29. **RCA 7810**   November 1960

    Are You Lonesome Tonight?/I Gotta Know

BLACK LABEL   DOG ON TOP

    On November 20, 1960, the number 1 song on *Billboard*'s Hot 100 was *Are You Lonesome Tonight?* It was number 1 for six weeks and remained on the chart for a total of sixteen weeks. The Country chart listed this song for six weeks; it numbered 22 upon its arrival on December 18. The R&B chart listed it at number 3 on December 4. It remained on the Rhythm and Blues chart for ten weeks.

    I Gotta Know entered the Hot 100 on the same day that its flip side entered, and settled in the number 20 position. It remained on the chart for eleven weeks.

[3] *A Fool Such as I/I Need Your Love Tonight* was available with two different covers.

209

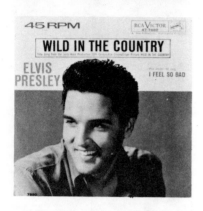

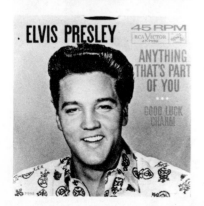

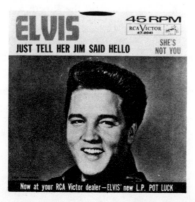

30. **RCA 7850**   February 1961

Surrender/Lonely Man

BLACK LABEL   DOG ON TOP

Surrender was number 1 on the Hot 100 chart on February 26, 1961. It remained on the chart for twelve weeks.

Lonely Man entered the chart on March 5, 1961, in the number 32 position. It remained on the chart for five weeks.

31. **RCA 7880**   May 1961

I Feel So Bad/Wild in the Country

BLACK LABEL   DOG ON TOP

Billboard's Hot 100 posted *I Feel So Bad* in the number 5 position on May 21, 1961. It stayed on the chart for nine weeks. The R&B chart listed this song at number 15 on June 11; it remained on the chart for three weeks.

Wild in the Country was number 26 on the Hot 100 chart on June 11. It remained on the chart for five weeks.

32. **RCA 7908**   August 1961

Little Sister/His Latest Flame

BLACK LABEL   DOG ON TOP

Little Sister entered *Billboard*'s Hot 100 chart on August 27, 1961. It held the number 5 position and remained on the chart for thirteen weeks.

His Latest Flame was number 4 on the same chart on September 3; it remained on the chart for eleven weeks.

33. **RCA 7968**   November 1961

Can't Help Falling in Love/Rock-a-hula Baby

BLACK LABEL   DOG ON TOP

Can't Help Falling in Love was number 2 on the Hot 100 on December 10, 1961. This classic remained on the Hot 100 chart for fourteen weeks.

On that same day *Rock-a-hula Baby* was number 23 on the Hot 100. It remained on the chart for nine weeks.

34. **RCA 7992**   February 1962

Good Luck Charm/Anything That's Part of You

BLACK LABEL   DOG ON TOP

On March 17, 1962, *Good Luck Charm* was at the top of *Billboard*'s Hot 100 chart. This song remained on the Hot 100 for thirteen weeks.

Billboard posted *Anything That's Part of You* at number 31 on the same day. It remained on the chart for eight weeks.

35. **RCA 8041**   July 1962

She's Not You/Just Tell Her Jim Said Hello

BLACK LABEL   DOG ON TOP

The Hot 100 had *She's Not You* in the number 5 position on their chart on August 4, 1962. It remained on the chart for ten weeks. The Rhythm and

Blues chart entered this song at the number 13 position on September 8. It remained on this chart for five weeks.

On August 11, 1962, *Just Tell Her Jim Said Hello* was number 30; it remained on the chart for seven weeks.

36. **RCA 8100**   October 1962

Return to Sender/Where Do You Come From

BLACK LABEL   DOG ON TOP

On October 20, 1962, *Billboard*'s Hot 100 chart had *Return to Sender* in the number 2 position. It remained on the chart for sixteen weeks. The Rhythm and Blues chart showed this song on the November 10 at number 5. The R&B chart kept this song for twelve weeks.

Number 99 was the position *Where Do You Come From* held on the Hot 100 on October 27. It remained on the chart for one week.

37. **RCA 8134**   January 1963

One Broken Heart for Sale/They Remind Me Too Much of You

BLACK LABEL   DOG ON TOP

One Broken Heart for Sale entered *Billboard*'s Hot 100 on February 16, 1963, in the number 11 position. It remained on the chart for nine weeks. The Rhythm and Blues chart cast this song in the number 21 position on March 23, 1963. It remained on the R&B chart for four weeks.

On February 23 *They Remind Me Too Much of You* was on the Hot 100 chart in the number 53 slot. It remained on the chart for four weeks.

38. **RCA 8188**   July 1963

Devil in Disguise/Please Don't Drag That String Around

BLACK LABEL   DOG ON TOP

June 29, 1963, was the day that *Devil in Disguise* entered the Hot 100. It was in the number 3 position and remained on the chart for eleven weeks. The R&B chart cast this tune in the number 9 position on July 27, 1963, and it remained on the chart for eight weeks.

39. **RCA 8243**   October 1963

Bossa Nova Baby/Witchcraft

BLACK LABEL   DOG ON TOP

Number 8 was the position that *Bossa Nova Baby* held upon entering *Billboard*'s Hot 100 chart on October 19, 1963. It remained on the Hot 100 for ten weeks. *Bossa Nova Baby* was the last record to appear on the Rhythm and Blues chart for Elvis. It was number 20 on this chart on November 16, 1963, and stayed on the chart for two weeks.

Witchcraft entered *Billboard*'s Hot 100 on October 19 in the number 37 position and remained on the chart for seven weeks.

40. **RCA 8307**   February 1964

Kissin' Cousins/It Hurts Me

BLACK LABEL   DOG ON TOP

Billboard's Hot 100 chart placed *Kissin' Cousins* in its number 12 position on February 22, 1964, and it remained on the chart for nine weeks.

It Hurts Me entered the Hot 100 on February 29 in the number 29 position. It remained on the chart for seven weeks.

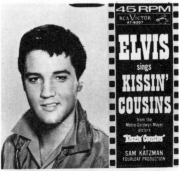

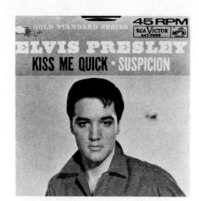

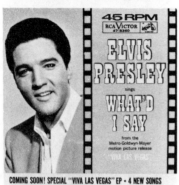

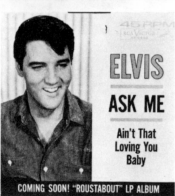

41. **RCA 0639**   April 1964
    Kiss Me Quick/ Suspicion
BLACK LABEL   DOG ON TOP
    Kiss Me Quick entered the Hot 100 chart on May 2, 1964, in the number 34 slot and remained on the chart for six weeks.

42. **RCA 8360**   May 1964
    Viva Las Vegas/ What'd I Say
BLACK LABEL   DOG ON TOP
    On May 9, 1964, *Viva Las Vegas* entered *Billboard*'s Hot 100 list at number 29 and remained on the chart for seven weeks.
    At number 21 was *What'd I Say,* which entered the Hot 100 on May 23 and remained for six weeks.

43. **RCA 8400**   July 1964
    Such a Night/ Never Ending
BLACK LABEL   DOG ON TOP
    Billboard's Hot 100 chart listed *Such a Night* at number 16 on July 25, 1964. It remained on the chart for eight weeks.

44. **RCA 8440**   September 1964
    Ain't That Loving You, Baby/ Ask Me
BLACK LABEL   DOG ON TOP
    For ten weeks *Ain't That Loving You, Baby* remained on the Hot 100, where it entered on October 10, 1964, in the number 16 position.
    On the same day *Ask Me* was in the number 12 position, and it stayed on the chart for twelve weeks.

45. **RCA 0720**   November 1964
    Blue Christmas/ Wooden Heart
BLACK LABEL   DOG ON TOP

46. **RCA 8500**   March 1965
    Do the Clam/ You'll Be Gone
BLACK LABEL   DOG ON TOP
    Do the Clam was on *Billboard*'s Hot 100 chart for eight weeks, after entering the chart in the number 21 position on February 27, 1965.

47. **RCA 0643**   April 1965
    Crying in the Chapel/ I Believe in the Man in the Sky[4]
BLACK LABEL   DOG ON SIDE
    On April 24, 1965, *Billboard* placed *Crying in the Chapel* in the number 3 position on its Hot 100 chart. It remained on this chart for fourteen weeks.

[4] At this point, RCA discontinued the dog on the top of the label. Nipper would now be appearing on the side.

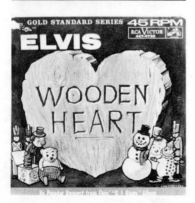

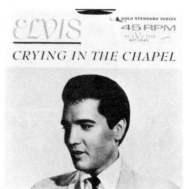

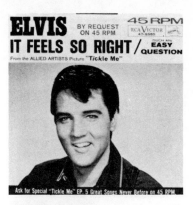

48. **RCA 8585**   May 1965

    (Such an) Easy Question/It Feels So Right

BLACK LABEL   DOG ON SIDE

  (Such an) Easy Question entered the Hot 100 chart on June 19, 1965, in the number 11 place and remained on this list for eight weeks.

  On the same day *It Feels So Right* was number 55, and it remained on the Hot 100 for eleven weeks.

49. **RCA 8657**   August 1965

    I'm Yours/(It's a) Long Lonely Highway

BLACK LABEL   DOG ON SIDE

  I'm Yours was number 11 on the Hot 100 on August 28, 1965, and continued to show on the chart for eleven weeks.

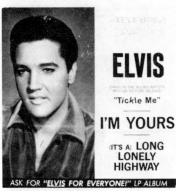

50. **RCA 0650**   October 1965

    Puppet on a String/Wooden Heart

BLACK LABEL   DOG ON SIDE

  Puppet on a String entered *Billboard*'s Hot 100 in the number 14 position on November 13, 1965. It remained on this chart for ten weeks.

51. **RCA 0647**   November 1965

    Blue Christmas/Santa Claus Is Back in Town

BLACK LABEL   DOG ON SIDE

52. **RCA 8740**   January 1966

    Tell Me Why/Blue River

BLACK LABEL   DOG ON SIDE

  On January 1, 1966, both *Tell Me Why* and *Blue River* entered *Billboard*'s Hot 100 chart, *Tell Me Why* being in the number 33 position and remaining on the list for seven weeks, and *Blue River* number 95 and remaining on the chart for only one week.

53. **RCA 0651**   February 1966

    Joshua Fit the Battle/Known Only to Him

BLACK LABEL   DOG ON SIDE

54. **RCA 0652**   February 1966

    Milky White Way/Swing Down, Sweet Chariot

BLACK LABEL   DOG ON SIDE

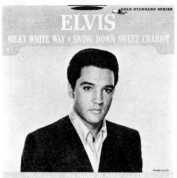

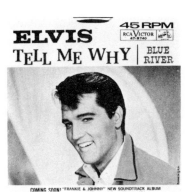

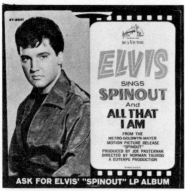

55. RCA 8780   March 1966

Frankie and Johnny/Please Don't Stop Loving Me

BLACK LABEL   DOG ON SIDE

Frankie and Johnny appeared on *Billboard*'s Hot 100 list on March 19, 1966. It was number 25, and it remained on this chart for eight weeks.

Please Don't Stop Loving Me remained on the chart for the same amount of weeks, after entering on the same day at number 45.

56. RCA 8870   June 1966

Love Letters/Come What May

BLACK LABEL   DOG ON SIDE

On July 2, 1966, *Billboard*'s Hot 100 showed *Love Letters* in the number 19 position. It remained on the chart for seven weeks.

57. RCA 8941   October 1966

Spinout/All That I Am

BLACK LABEL   DOG ON SIDE

Spinout entered the Hot 100 on October 8, 1966, in the number 40 position and remained on the chart for seven weeks.

On the same day *All That I Am* was right behind it at number 41 and remained for two weeks.

58. RCA 8950   November 1966

If Every Day Was Like Christmas/How Would You Like to Be

BLACK LABEL   DOG ON SIDE

59. RCA 9056   January 1967

Indescribably Blue/Fools Fall in Love

BLACK LABEL   DOG ON SIDE

On January 28, 1967, *Indescribably Blue* was number 33 on the Hot 100 roster. It remained on this chart for eight weeks.

60. RCA 9115   May 1967

Long-legged Girl (with the Short Dress On)/That's Someone You Never Forget

BLACK LABEL   DOG ON SIDE

On May 20, 1967, *Long-legged Girl* was number 63 on *Billboard*'s Hot 100. It appeared on the chart for five weeks.

The flip side, *That's Someone You Never Forget,* was number 92 on the Hot 100 on May 27 and remained on the chart for one week.

214

61. RCA 9287 August 1967

There's Always Me/Judy

BLACK LABEL   DOG ON SIDE

For six weeks *There's Always Me* showed on the Hot 100 after its entry on August 26, 1967. It numbered 7.

Judy entered this chart on September 9, 1967, at number 78 and remained on the list for five weeks.

62. RCA 9341 September 1967

Big Boss Man/You Don't Know Me

BLACK LABEL   DOG ON SIDE

Big Boss Man was 38 on the Hot 100 on October 14, 1967. It remained on the roster for six weeks.

You Don't Know Me also held a position for six weeks, upon entering the Hot 100 at number 44 on the same day.

63. RCA 9425 January 1968

Guitar Man/High-heel Sneakers

BLACK LABEL   DOG ON SIDE

January 27, 1968, found *Guitar Man* in the number 43 position on the Hot 100. It would remain on this chart for six weeks.

64. RCA 9465 March 1968

U.S. Male/Stay Away

BLACK LABEL   DOG ON S!DE

U.S. Male entered the Country chart on April 6, 1968, at number 55 and remained on this chart for six weeks. The Hot 100 posted this song on March 23 in the number 28 position. It remained on this chart for nine weeks.

On March 16, 1968, *Stay Away* entered *Billboard*'s Hot 100 chart at number 67 and remained on the chart for five weeks.

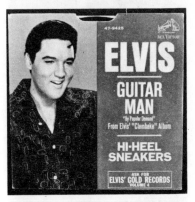

65. RCA 9600 April 1968

You'll Never Walk Alone/ We Call on Him

BLACK LABEL   DOG ON S!DE

You'll Never Walk Alone was on the Hot 100 at number 90 on April 20, 1968. It remained on the chart for two weeks.

66. RCA 9547 May 1968

Let Yourself Go/Your Time Hasn't Come Yet, Baby

BLACK LABEL   DOG ON S'DE

On June 15, 1968, the number 71 song on the Hot 100 was *Let Yourself Go*. It remained on the chart for five weeks.

On June 22, 1968, *Your Time Hasn't Come Yet, Baby* was number 72, and it remained on the chart for seven weeks. The Country chart included this tune on June 29, 1968. It was number 50 and could be found on the chart for eight weeks.

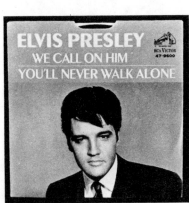

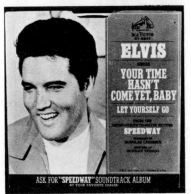

215

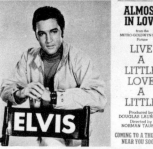

67. RCA 9610   September 1968

    A Little Less Conversation/ Almost in Love

BLACK LABEL   DOG ON SIDE

    Almost in Love was number 95 on the Hot 100 on September 28, 1968. It remained on the chart for two weeks.

    Billboard cast *A Little Less Conversation* in the number 63 slot of its Hot 100 chart on October 12, 1968, and it stayed on the list for four weeks.

68. RCA 9670   October 1968

    If I Can Dream/ Edge of Reality[5]

ORANGE LABEL

    If I Can Dream was number 12 on *Billboard*'s Hot 100 chart on November 30, 1968, and it remained on the Hot 100 for thirteen weeks.

69. RCA 9731   March 1969

    Memories/ Charro!

ORANGE LABEL

    On February 22, 1969, *Memories* was number 37 on the Hot 100 chart and it remained on this chart for seven weeks. The Country chart posted this song at number 56 on April 19, 1969, and it remained on the chart for two weeks.

70. RCA 0130   April 1969

    How Great Thou Art/ His Hand in Mine

ORANGE LABEL

71. RCA 9741   April 1969

    In the Ghetto/ Any Day Now

ORANGE LABEL

    Billboard's Hot 100 chart posted *In the Ghetto* in the number 3 position on May 3, 1969. It remained on the chart for thirteen weeks. On June 14, 1969, this song was number 60 on the Country chart, and it was on the chart for seven weeks.

72. RCA 9747   June 1969

    Clean Up Your Own Back Yard/ The Fair Is Moving On

ORANGE LABEL

    Clean Up Your Own Back Yard was number 35 on the Hot 100 on July 5, 1969. It was on the chart for eight weeks.

    On August 16 this tune was number 74 on the Country chart, and it remained on the chart for three weeks.

[5] Beginning with 9670, you will notice that Nipper, the RCA dog, has stopped appearing on the label, and the label's color has changed to orange.

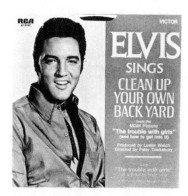

73. **RCA 9764** August 1969

Suspicious Minds/You'll Think of Me

ORANGE LABEL

The number 1 song on *Billboard*'s Hot 100 chart on September 13, 1969, was (you guessed it) *Suspicious Minds*. It made a showing on this chart for fifteen weeks.

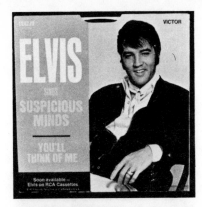

74. **RCA 9768** November 1969

Don't Cry, Daddy/Rubberneckin'

ORANGE LABEL

On November 29, 1969, *Don't Cry, Daddy* was number 6 on the Hot 100, and it remained on the chart for thirteen weeks. The Country chart had this song in the number 13 position on December 20, 1969. It stayed on this chart for eleven weeks.

Rubberneckin' made a number 6 place showing on November 29, 1969, and remained on the chart for thirteen weeks.

75. **RCA 9791** January 1970

Kentucky Rain/My Little Friend

ORANGE LABEL

Kentucky Rain positioned number 16 on February 14, 1970, and remained on *Billboard*'s Hot 100 chart for nine weeks. The Country chart had this song in the number 31 slot on February 28, 1970. It remained on this chart for ten weeks.

76. **RCA 9835** May 1970

The Wonder of You/Mama Liked the Roses

ORANGE LABEL

The Wonder of You settled in the number 9 position on *Billboard*'s Hot 100 chart, tied with *Mama Liked the Roses* on May 16, 1970. They both remained for twelve weeks. On June 6 *The Wonder of You* entered the Country chart in the number 37 position and stayed on this chart for ten weeks.

77. **RCA 9873** July 1970

I've Lost You/The Next Step Is Love

ORANGE LABEL

Both sides of this 45 entered *Billboard*'s Hot 100 chart on August 1, 1970; they were tied at number 32; and both remained on the chart for nine weeks.

On August 24, both entered the Country chart, *The Next Step Is Love* being number 51 and *I've Lost You* positioning number 57. Together they remained on the chart for six weeks.

217

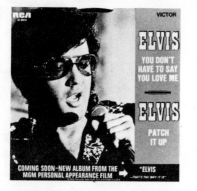

78. RCA 9916 October 1970

You Don't Have to Say You Love Me/Patch It Up

ORANGE LABEL

On October 24, 1970, *You Don't Have to Say You Love Me* and *Patch It Up* entered the Hot 100 chart together, tied in the number 11 position. They both remained on the chart for ten weeks. On December 5, 1970, *You Don't Have to Say You Love Me* entered the Country chart at number 56 and remained for five weeks.

79. RCA 9960 December 1970

I Really Don't Want to Know/There Goes My Everything

ORANGE LABEL

On December 26, 1970, *I Really Don't Want to Know* and *There Goes My Everything* entered *Billboard*'s Hot 100 chart tied at number 21, both remaining for nine weeks.

On January 1, 1971, both entered the Country chart, tied at number 9, and both remained on this chart for thirteen weeks.

80. RCA 9980 March 1971

Rags to Riches/Where Did They Go, Lord

ORANGE LABEL

On March 13, 1971, *Rags to Riches* and *Where Did They Go, Lord* were on the Hot 100 chart tied at number 33, and both remained on this chart for seven weeks.

Where Did They Go, Lord also appeared on the Country chart for eight weeks. It was number 55 and entered on March 27.

81. RCA 9985 May 1971

Life/Only Believe

ORANGE LABEL

Both sides of the 45 appeared on *Billboard*'s Hot 100 chart on May 15, 1971. They made number 53 and remained on the chart for seven weeks.

Life also made the Country chart on June 5. It was number 34 and was on this chart for eight weeks.

82. RCA 9998 August 1971

I'm Leavin'/Heart of Rome

ORANGE LABEL

I'm Leavin' settled in at number 36 on July 10, 1971, and remained on the Hot 100 for nine weeks.

83. RCA 1017 October 1971

It's Only Love/The Sound of Your Cry

ORANGE LABEL

It's Only Love entered *Billboard*'s Hot 100 chart at number 51 on October 9, 1971. It was on the chart for six weeks.

218

84. **RCA 0572** November 1971

   Merry Christmas, Baby/O Come, All Ye Faithful
ORANGE LABEL

85. **RCA 0619** January 1972

   Until It's Time for You to Go/We Can Make the Morning
ORANGE LABEL

   Until It's Time for You to Go appeared on the Hot 100 on January 29, 1972. It was number 40, and it remained on this chart for nine weeks.

   The Country chart posted this song at 68 on March 4, 1972, and it remained on the chart for two weeks.

86. **RCA 0651** March 1972

   He Touched Me/The Bosom of Abraham
ORANGE LABEL

87. **RCA 0672** April 1972

   An American Trilogy/The First Time Ever I Saw Your Face
ORANGE LABEL

   An American Trilogy was number 66 on the Hot 100 on May 6, 1972, and remained on this chart for six weeks.

88. **RCA 0769** August 1972

   Burning Love/It's a Matter of Time
GRAY AND ORANGE LABELS[6]

   On August 19, 1972, *Burning Love* was number 2 on *Billboard*'s Hot 100. It stayed on this chart for fifteen weeks.

   It's a Matter of Time entered the Country chart at number 10 on September 9, 1972. It remained on the Country chart for thirteen weeks.

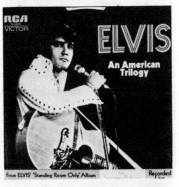

89. **RCA 0815** November 1972

   Always on My Mind/Separate Ways
ORANGE LABEL

   Separate Ways was number 20 on the Hot 100 on December 2, 1972. It remained on the Hot 100 for twelve weeks, as well as twelve weeks on the Country chart, where it entered at number 10 on December 16.

   Always on My Mind entered the Country chart on December 9 at number 10. This song remained on the Country chart for thirteen weeks.

[6] This record was available on both a gray and an orange label.

90. **RCA 0910** March 1973

Fool/Steamroller Blues

ORANGE LABEL

Fool and *Steamroller Blues* entered the Hot 100 on April 14, 1973. Together they held the number 17 position, and both remained on this chart for twelve weeks.

Both sides were posted at number 31 on April 28, 1973, on *Billboard*'s Country chart. They remained on the chart for ten weeks.

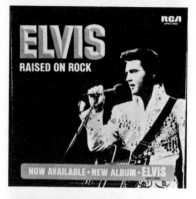

91. **RCA 0088** September 1973

Raised on Rock/For Ol' Times Sake

ORANGE LABEL

Billboard cast both sides at number 41 on October 27, 1973, and both songs remained on the Hot 100 for nine weeks.

For Ol' Times Sake also made the Country chart. It was number 42 on October 6, 1973, and remained on this chart for ten weeks.

92. **RCA 0196** January 1974

Take Good Care of Her/I've Got a Thing About You, Baby

ORANGE LABEL

I've Got a Thing About You, Baby entered *Billboard*'s Hot 100 at number 39 on February 9, 1974. It remained on this chart for twelve weeks. The Country chart cast this song a week later (February 16) in its number 4 position. It remained on this chart for thirteen weeks.

Take Good Care of Her entered both the Hot 100 and the Country charts on March 16. It was number 39 on the Hot 100, remaining for seven weeks; and number 4 on the Country chart, remaining for thirteen weeks.

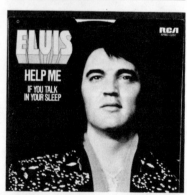

93. **RCA 0280** May 1974

Help Me/If You Talk in Your Sleep

ORANGE LABEL

Help Me was number 6 on the Country chart on June 8, 1974. It remained on the Country chart for fifteen weeks.

On June 8, 1974, *If You Talk in Your Sleep* entered the Hot 100 at number 17 and the Country chart at number 6. It remained on the Hot 100 for thirteen weeks, and on the Country chart for fifteen weeks.

94. **RCA 10074** October 1974

It's Midnight/Promised Land

GRAY, BROWN, AND ORANGE LABELS[7]

It's Midnight appeared on the Hot 100 on October 26, 1974, in the number 9 position and remained on the Hot 100 for fourteen weeks.

Promised Land entered both the Hot 100 and Country charts on October 26, 1974. It was number 14 on the Hot 100 while remaining for thirteen weeks, and number 9 on the Country chart, remaining for fourteen weeks.

[7] This 45 was issued on gray, brown, and orange labels.

95. RCA 10191   January 1975

My Boy/Thinking About You
BROWN AND ORANGE LABELS[8]

On January 25, 1975, *My Boy* entered the Hot 100, where it stayed for eleven weeks. It was number 20. The Country chart had this song in its number 14 slot on February 8, 1975. It remained on this chart for ten weeks.

96. RCA 10278   April 1975

T-R-O-U-B-L-E/Mr. Songman
BROWN AND ORANGE LABELS[9]

On May 10, 1975, *Billboard* posted *T-R-O-U-B-L-E* on its Hot 100 chart at number 35, where it began its nine-week stay.

The Country chart held this song for thirteen weeks, beginning on May 17, when it was number 11.

97. RCA 10401   October 1975

Bringing It Back/Pieces of My Life
BROWN LABEL[10]

Bringing It Back was on *Billboard*'s Hot 100 chart on October 25, 1975. It was number 65 and remained on this chart for five weeks.

Pieces of My Life entered the Country chart on October 18 at number 33 and remained on this chart for ten weeks.

98. RCA 10601   March 1976

Hurt/For the Heart
BROWN LABEL

Hurt and *For the Heart* entered *Billboard*'s Country and Hot 100 chart on May 16, 1976. The Hot 100 cast these songs tied at number 20; they remained for thirteen weeks. The Country chart positioned them tied at number 6, and they remained for sixteen weeks.

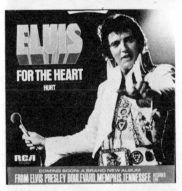

99. RCA 10857   December 1976

Moody Blue/She Thinks I Still Care
BLACK LABEL[11]   DOG AT TOP RIGHT-HAND CORNER

Moody Blue reached number 2 on the Easy Listening chart. It stayed on this chart for seven weeks. Both *Moody Blue* and *She Thinks I Still Care* peaked at number 31 on the Hot 100 chart, and both remained on the chart for eleven weeks. Both songs were on the Country chart for twelve weeks, and both sides reached number 1.

[8] This record was available on a brown or orange label.
[9] This record also was available on a brown or orange label.
[10] This record brought an end to orange labels; it was available on a brown label only.
[11] As part of RCA's Seventy-fifth Jubilee Anniversary, it returns to a black label. "Nipper" once again can be found on the label, this time in the top right-hand corner.

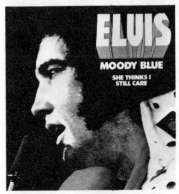

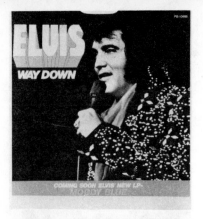

100. RCA 10998   June 1977

Way Down / Pledging My Love

BLACK LABEL   DOG AT TOP RIGHT-HAND CORNER

Elvis' death affected the chart positions of both sides of this single. The record had peaked, but because of the great tragedy it began to climb on the charts again.

The positions of both sides on the charts as of 9/17/77 follow: *Way Down* was number 16 after twelve weeks on the Easy Listening chart. After thirteen weeks, both *Way Down* and *Pledging My Love* were number 1 on the Hot Country chart. The Hot 100 chart showed *Way Down* at the number 21 position with a bullet (a bullet indicates records that are on the rise). *Way Down* has stayed on the chart for thirteen weeks.

RCA 45 RPM EXTENDED-PLAY ALBUMS

The initials EP stand for "extended play." RCA issued Elvis EPs from 1956 to 1967, when they deleted the mini LP. The records came in a cardboard picture cover. It was standard procedure for an extended play to feature four songs. This was the case with all of Elvis' EPs with the exception of EPB-1254, EPA-4114, EPA-4371, EPA-4383, and EPA-4387. Because the majority of Elvis' EPs were released in the fifties, the covers featured some of the best early stage shots. These unique mini-albums are missed by many of us, and unless RCA should decide to reissue them, they will continue to be among the most cherished and sought-after Elvis records.

1. RCA EPB-1254   March 1956

Elvis Presley

BLACK LABEL/DOG ON TOP

This EP is very rare and was available with eight songs. Another version (RCA SP-23—see "Rare Records" section) featured twelve songs. This is Elvis' only double EP released to the public. The following are the songs on the double EP:

Side 1: *Blue Suede Shoes; I'm Counting on You*

Side 2: *I Got a Woman; One-sided Love Affair*

Side 3: *Tutti Frutti; Tryin' to Get to You*

Side 4: *I'm Gonna Sit Right Down and Cry; I'll Never Let You Go*

2. RCA EPA-747   March 1956

Elvis Presley

BLACK LABEL/DOG ON TOP

BLACK LABEL/DOG ON SIDE

ORANGE LABEL

This EP was available with three different covers.

Side 1: *Blue Suede Shoes; Tutti Frutti*

Side 2: *I Got a Woman; Just Because*

This record was on *Billboard*'s Hot 100 chart on March 28, 1956, in the number 24 position and remained on the chart for twelve weeks.

222

3. **RCA EPA-821**   May 1956

Heartbreak Hotel

BLACK LABEL/DOG ON TOP

BLACK LABEL/DOG ON SIDE

ORANGE LABEL

This EP was available with two different covers.

Side 1: *Heartbreak Hotel; I Was the One*

Side 2: *Money Honey; I Forgot to Remember to Forget*

This EP entered *Billboard*'s Hot 100 chart on May 2, 1956, at number 75 and remained on the chart for five weeks.

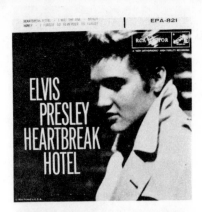

4. **RCA EPA-830**   September 1956

Shake, Rattle and Roll

BLACK LABEL/DOG ON TOP

BLACK LABEL/DOG ON SIDE

ORANGE LABEL

Side 1: *Shake, Rattle and Roll; I Love You Because*

Side 2: *Blue Moon; Lawdy, Miss Clawdy*

This EP was on the Hot 100 on September 19, 1956, at number 55 and remained on the chart for seventeen weeks.

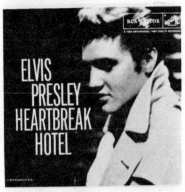

5. **RCA EPA-965**   October 1956

Any Way You Want Me

BLACK LABEL/DOG ON TOP

BLACK LABEL/DOG ON SIDE

ORANGE LABEL

Three of the four songs on the EP were Sun recordings. This EP had two different covers.

Side 1: *Any Way You Want Me; I'm Left, You're Right, She's Gone*

Side 2: *I Don't Care if the Sun Don't Shine; Mystery Train*

Billboard's Hot 100 cast his EP in the number 74 position on October 3, 1956. It remained on the chart for six weeks.

6. **RCA EPA-940**   September 1956

The Real Elvis

BLACK LABEL/DOG ON TOP

This classic was available for five years.

Side 1: *Don't Be Cruel; I Want You, I Need You, I Love You*

Side 2: *Hound Dog; My Baby Left Me*

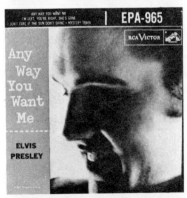

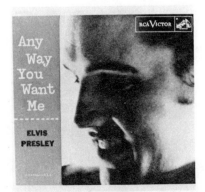

7. **RCA EPA-5120 (Gold Standard)**   April 1961

The Real Elvis

BLACK LABEL/DOG ON TOP

BLACK LABEL/DOG ON SIDE

ORANGE LABEL

This is the first of Elvis' Gold Standard EPs. It features the same songs as EPA-940. Of special interest is the fact that this EP was originally released on a maroon label with the dog on the top, as were the other six Gold Standard EPs.

8. **RCA EPA-992**   November 1956

Elvis, Volume I

BLACK LABEL/DOG ON TOP

BLACK LABEL/DOG ON SIDE

ORANGE LABEL

This EP had two different picture covers.

Side 1: *Rip It Up; Love Me*

Side 2: *When My Blue Moon Turns to Gold Again; Paralyzed*

This EP entered *Billboard*'s Hot 100 chart on November 7, 1956, at number 6 and remained on the chart for nineteen weeks.

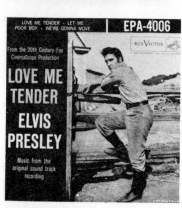

9. **RCA EPA-4006**   December 1956

Love Me Tender

BLACK LABEL/DOG ON TOP

BLACK LABEL/DOG ON SIDE

ORANGE LABEL

All four songs from the film were included. This EP had two different covers.

Side 1: *Love Me Tender; Let Me*

Side 2: *Poor Boy; We're Gonna Move*

On December 19, 1956, this EP was number 35 on the Hot 100, and it remained on the chart for eleven weeks.

10. **RCA EPA-993**   December 1956

Elvis, Volume II

BLACK LABEL/DOG ON TOP

BLACK LABEL/DOG ON SIDE

ORANGE LABEL

Side 1: *So Glad You're Mine; Old Shep*

Side 2: *Ready Teddy; Anyplace Is Paradise*

This EP remained on the Hot 100 for two weeks; it entered on December 19, 1956, in the number 47 position.

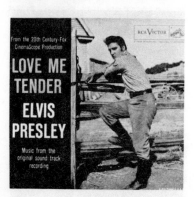

RCA 45 RPM EXTENDED-PLAY ALBUMS

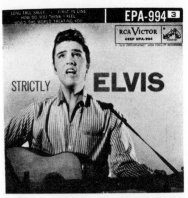

11. RCA EPA-994   January 1957

Strictly Elvis

BLACK LABEL/DOG ON TOP

BLACK LABEL/DOG ON SIDE

ORANGE LABEL

This EP was available with two different covers.

Side 1: *Long Tall Sally; First in Line*

Side 2: *How Do You Think I Feel; How's the World Treating You*

12. RCA EPA-1-1515   June 1957

Loving You, Volume I

BLACK LABEL/DOG ON TOP

BLACK LABEL/DOG ON SIDE

ORANGE LABEL

This EP had two different covers.

Side 1: *Loving You; Party*

Side 2: *(Let Me Be Your) Teddy Bear; True Love*

13. RCA EPA-2-1515   June 1957

Loving You, Volume II

BLACK LABEL/DOG ON TOP

BLACK LABEL/DOG ON SIDE

ORANGE LABEL

Two different covers.

Side 1: *Lonesome Cowboy; Hot Dog*

Side 2: *Mean Woman Blues; Got a Lot o' Livin' to Do!*

14. RCA EPA-4041   September 1957

Just for You

BLACK LABEL/DOG ON TOP

BLACK LABEL/DOG ON SIDE

ORANGE LABEL

Also available with two different covers.

Side 1: *I Need You So; Have I Told You Lately That I Love You*

Side 2: *Blueberry Hill; Is It So Strange*

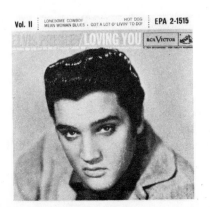

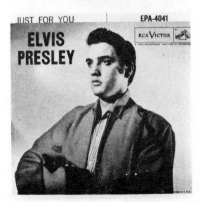

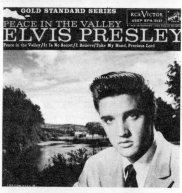

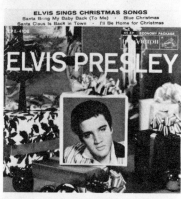

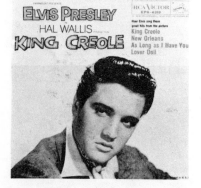

15. **RCA EPA-4054** April 1957

Peace in the Valley

BLACK LABEL/DOG ON TOP

This was Elvis' first religious recording.

Side 1: (*There'll Be*) *Peace in the Valley* (*for Me*); *It Is No Secret* (*What God Can Do*)

Side 2: *I Believe; Take My Hand, Precious Lord*

This EP entered the Hot 100 chart on April 3, 1957, at number 39 and remained on the chart for ten weeks.

16. **RCA EPA-5121 (Gold Standard)** April 1961

Peace in the Valley

BLACK LABEL/DOG ON TOP

BLACK LABEL/DOG ON SIDE

ORANGE LABEL

This was the second Gold Standard EP. It featured the same songs as EPA-4054 and was issued on a maroon label with the dog at the top.

17. **RCA EPA-4108** November 1957

Elvis Sings Christmas Songs

BLACK LABEL/DOG ON TOP

BLACK LABEL/DOG ON SIDE

ORANGE LABEL

This EP had the same front cover as LOC-1035 (33⅓ LP).

Side 1: *Santa, Bring My Baby Back* (*To Me*); *Blue Christmas*

Side 2: *Santa Claus Is Back in Town; I'll Be Home for Christmas*

18. **RCA EPA-4114** November 1957

Jailhouse Rock

BLACK LABEL/DOG ON TOP

BLACK LABEL/DOG ON SIDE

ORANGE LABEL

This EP featured five songs and was Elvis' best-selling EP.

Side 1: *Jailhouse Rock; Young and Beautiful*

Side 2: *I Want to Be Free; Don't Leave Me Now; Baby, I Don't Care*

19. **RCA EPA-4319** October 1958

King Creole, Volume 1

BLACK LABEL/DOG ON TOP

Side 1: *King Creole; New Orleans*

Side 2: *As Long As I Have You; Lover Doll*

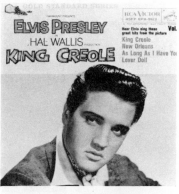

20. RCA EPA-5122 (Gold Standard) April 1961

King Creole, Volume I

BLACK LABEL/DOG ON TOP

BLACK LABEL/DOG ON SIDE

ORANGE LABEL

The third Elvis EP to be issued as a Gold Standard. This was originally released with a maroon label with the dog at the top.

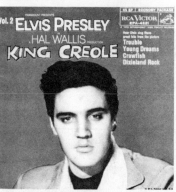

21. RCA EPA-4321 October 1958

King Creole, Volume II

BLACK LABEL/DOG ON TOP

BLACK LABEL/DOG ON SIDE

ORANGE LABEL

Side 1: *Trouble; Young Dreams*

Side 2: *Crawfish; Dixieland Rock*

22. RCA EPA-4325 March 1959

Elvis Sails

BLACK LABEL/DOG ON TOP

This is the first interview record released to the public by RCA. The back cover has a 1959 calendar with important dates in Elvis' career circled.

Side 1: Press interviews with Elvis

Side 2: More press interviews with Elvis

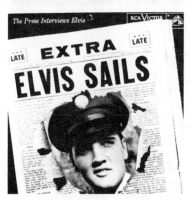

23. RCA EPA-5157 (Gold Standard) April 1961

Elvis Sails

BLACK LABEL/DOG ON TOP

BLACK LABEL/DOG ON SIDE

ORANGE LABEL

This Gold Standard had a different back cover. It was originally issued with a maroon label, dog at the top. It has the same contents as EPA-4325.

24. RCA EPA-4340 November 1958

Christmas with Elvis

BLACK LABEL/DOG ON TOP

BLACK LABEL/DOG ON SIDE

ORANGE LABEL

Side 1: *White Christmas; Here Comes Santa Claus*

Side 2: *O Little Town of Bethlehem; Silent Night*

25. RCA EPA-5088 (Gold Standard)   April 1961

   A Touch of Gold, Volume I

BLACK LABEL/DOG ON TOP

BLACK LABEL/DOG ON SIDE

ORANGE LABEL

"A Touch of Gold" is just what this EP was, as it featured four of Elvis' biggest hits. It was originally released as a Gold Standard with a maroon label, dog on the top.

Side 1: *Hard-headed Woman; Good Rockin' Tonight*

Side 2: *Don't; I Beg of You*

26. RCA EPA-5101 (Gold Standard)   April 1961

   A Touch of Gold, Volume II

BLACK LABEL/DOG ON TOP

BLACK LABEL/DOG ON SIDE

ORANGE LABEL

This EP was originally issued with a maroon label and the dog on the top.

Side 1: *Wear My Ring Around Your Neck; Treat Me Nice*

Side 2: *One Night; That's All Right*

27. RCA EPA-5141 (Gold Standard)   April 1961

   A Touch of Gold, Volume III

BLACK LABEL/DOG ON TOP

BLACK LABEL/DOG ON SIDE

ORANGE LABEL

A maroon label, with the dog at the top, could be found on this EP.

Side 1: *All Shook Up; Don't Ask Me Why*

Side 2: *Too Much; Blue Moon of Kentucky*

28. RCA-4368   May 1962

   Follow That Dream

BLACK LABEL/DOG ON TOP

BLACK LABEL/DOG ON SIDE

ORANGE LABEL

Side 1: *Follow That Dream; Angel*

Side 2: *What a Wonderful Life; I'm Not the Marrying Kind*

This EP made *Billboard*'s Hot 100 chart on May 12, 1962. It was number 15 and remained on the chart for ten weeks.

29. RCA EPA-4371   September 1962

   Kid Galahad

BLACK LABEL/DOG ON TOP

BLACK LABEL/DOG ON SIDE

ORANGE LABEL

There are six outstanding songs from the film on this EP.

Side 1: *King of the Whole Wide World; This Is Living; Riding the Rainbow*

Side 2: *Home Is Where the Heart Is; I Got Lucky; A Whistling Tune*

On September 22, 1962, this EP made the Hot 100, where it entered at number 30. It remained on the chart for seven weeks.

228

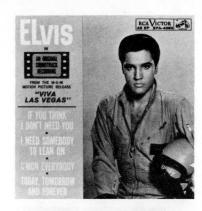

30. **RCA EPA-4382**   July 1964
Viva Las Vegas
BLACK LABEL/DOG ON TOP
BLACK LABEL/DOG ON SIDE
ORANGE LABEL
Side 1: *If You Think I Don't Need You; I Need Somebody to Lean On*
Side 2: *C'mon, Everybody; Today, Tomorrow and Forever*
Billboard cast this EP in the number 92 position on their Hot 100 chart on July 4, 1964. It remained on this chart for one week.

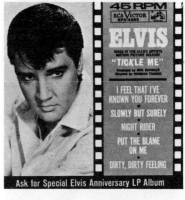

31. **RCA EPA-4383**   July 1965
Tickle Me
BLACK LABEL/DOG ON SIDE
ORANGE LABEL
This EP featured five songs from the film. *Tickle Me* has three different covers.
Side 1: *I Feel That I've Known You Forever; Slowly but Surely*
Side 2: *Night Rider; Put the Blame on Me; Dirty, Dirty Feeling*
This EP appeared on *Billboard*'s Hot 100 on July 10, 1965, at number 70. It remained on the chart for seven weeks.

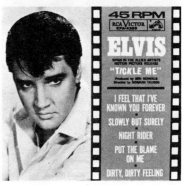

32. **RCA EPA-4387**   May 1967
Easy Come, Easy Go
BLACK LABEL/DOG ON SIDE
ORANGE LABEL
This was the final Elvis EP that RCA released to the public. There were six songs from the film on this record.
Side 1: *Easy Come, Easy Go; The Love Machine; Yoga Is as Yoga Does*
Side 2: *You Gotta Stop; Sing, You Children; I'll Take Love*

RCA 33 1/3 RPM EXTENDED-PLAY ALBUMS

1. **RCA LPC-128**   April 1961
Elvis by Request
BLACK LABEL/DOG ON TOP
"LPC" indicated "Long Playing Compact." This is the only EP that RCA made in 33⅓ and released to the public.
Side 1: *Flaming Star; Summer Kisses, Winter Tears*
Side 2: *Are You Lonesome Tonight; It's Now or Never*
This LPC was on *Billboard*'s Hot 100 chart on April 23, 1961, at number 14. It remained on the chart for seven weeks.

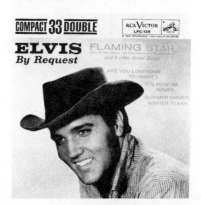

RCA 33 1/3 RPM LONG-PLAYING ALBUMS

RCA has released sixty-five Elvis LPs to date, not including television LPs, budget LPs (Camden), and the Boxcar LP. In the twenty-one years Elvis has been recording for RCA, only thirteen of his LPs have been deleted (put out of print). In some cases the deleted LP has resurfaced as a budget LP. The first thirty-two LPs were available in both monaural and stereo.

All listing and prefixes are for the original RCA releases.

1. **LPM-1254**   April 1956

Elvis Presley

BLACK LABEL   DOG ON TOP

The front cover had the RCA logo in green and black with "Nipper," the RCA dog, in pink and white (front, top right-hand corner). The back cover had four pictures of Elvis. There was a square with instructions regarding the "New Orthophonic High Fidelity." Nipper was also pictured in the square (bottom right-hand corner).

Side 1: *Blue Suede Shoes; I'm Counting on You; I Got a Woman; One-sided Love Affair; I Love You Because; Just Because*

Side 2: *Tutti Frutti; Tryin' to Get to You; I'm Gonna Sit Right Down and Cry; I'll Never Let You Go; Blue Moon; Money Honey*

This LP made *Billboard*'s Hot LP chart on March 31, 1956; it was number 1 for ten weeks. It remained on the chart for a total of forty-nine weeks.

2. **LPM-1382**   October 1956

Elvis

BLACK LABEL   DOG ON TOP

The front cover gave photo credit to David B. Hecht (bottom left-hand corner). The back cover had excellent liner notes and was available in six different variations.

Side 1: *Rip It Up; Love Me; When My Blue Moon Turns to Gold Again; Long Tall Sally; First in Line; Paralyzed*

Side 2: *So Glad You're Mine; Old Shep; Ready Teddy; Anyplace Is Paradise; How's the World Treating You; How Do You Think I Feel*

Elvis entered *Billboard*'s Hot LP chart on November 10, 1956, at number 1. It remained on the chart for thirty-two weeks.

3. **LPM-1515**   July 1957

Loving You

BLACK LABEL   DOG ON TOP

The original front cover had no black margin at the top. The song listings were different and no photo credit was given on the back cover.

Side 1: *Mean Woman Blues; (Let Me Be Your) Teddy Bear; Loving You; Got a Lot o' Livin' to Do; Lonesome Cowboy; Hot Dog; Party*

Side 2: *Blueberry Hill; True Love; Don't Leave Me Now; Have I Told You Lately That I Love You?; I Need You So*

Loving You appeared on the Hot LP list on July 13, 1957, at number 1 and remained on the chart for twenty-nine weeks.

4. LOC-1035 (DELETED)   November 1957

Elvis' Christmas Album

BLACK LABEL   DOG ON TOP

This beautiful package featured a booklike cover. It contained a 10-page book of beautiful color photos. The back cover had an outstanding color portrait and featured a gold sticker that read "To_____, From _____" and listed song titles.

Side 1: *Santa Claus Is Back in Town; White Christmas; Here Comes Santa Claus; I'll Be Home for Christmas; Blue Christmas; Santa, Bring My Baby Back (to Me).*

Side 2: *O Little Town of Bethlehem; Silent Night; (There'll Be) Peace in the Valley (for Me); I Believe; Take My Hand, Precious Lord; It Is No Secret (What God Can Do)*

This LP was on *Billboard*'s Hot LP chart at number 1 on November 23, 1957. It remained on the chart for seven weeks. It was number 1 for four weeks.

5. LPM-1707   March 1958

Elvis' Golden Records

BLACK LABEL   DOG ON TOP

The title was written in light blue on the front cover. The back cover had interesting liner notes.

Side 1: *Hound Dog; Loving You; All Shook Up; Heartbreak Hotel; Jailhouse Rock; Love Me; Too Much*

Side 2: *Don't Be Cruel; That's When Your Heartaches Begin; Teddy Bear; Love Me Tender; Treat Me Nice; Any Way You Want Me; I Want You, I Need You, I Love You*

LPM-1707 entered *Billboard*'s Hot LP list on April 12, 1958, at number 3. It remained on this chart for fifty weeks.

6. LPM-1884   August 1958

King Creole

BLACK LABEL   DOG ON TOP

The front cover had the RCA logo and Nipper in light blue (top right-hand corner).

Side 1: *King Creole; As Long As I Have You; Hard-headed Woman; T-R-O-U-B-L-E; Dixieland Rock*

Side 2: *Don't Ask Me Why; Lover Doll; Crawfish; Young Dreams; Steadfast, Loyal and True; New Orleans*

King Creole entered the Hot LP chart on September 6, 1958, at number 2, remaining on the chart for fifteen weeks.

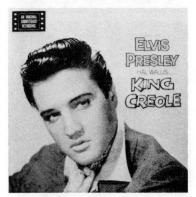

7. LPM-1951 (DELETED)   November 1958

Elvis' Christmas Album

BLACK LABEL   DOG ON TOP

RCA reissued *Elvis' Christmas Album* with a new cover and prefix. The front cover had the RCA logo and Nipper in blue (top right-hand corner). The back featured four color photos showing Elvis with his new Army look.

This LP had the same tracks as LOC-1035.

8. **LPM-1990** February 1959

For LP Fans Only

BLACK LABEL DOG ON TOP

This LP didn't show Elvis' name anywhere on the front or back cover. This was another first for the record industry. The title of the LP was in the box with the RCA logo and Nipper (top right-hand corner). The back cover showed Elvis in his Army dress uniform.

Side 1: *That's All Right; Lawdy, Miss Clawdy; Mystery Train; Playing for Keeps; Poor Boy*

Side 2: *My Baby Left Me; I Was the One; Shake, Rattle and Roll; I'm Left, You're Right, She's Gone; You're a Heartbreaker*

On March 14, 1959, this LP entered *Billboard*'s Hot LP chart at number 19, and it remained on the chart for eight weeks.

9. **LPM-2011** September 1959

A Date with Elvis

BLACK LABEL DOG ON TOP

This package opened into a double cover, the inside displaying a telegram from Elvis to his many fans. It also showed photos of Elvis waving good-by as his boat left for Germany. The front cover showed the song titles in a red block. A calendar was featured on the back cover.

Side 1: *Blue Moon of Kentucky; Young and Beautiful; Baby, I Don't Care; Milkcow Blues Boogie; Baby, Let's Play House*

Side 2: *Good Rockin' Tonight; Is It So Strange; We're Gonna Move; I Want to Be Free; I Forgot to Remember to Forget*

This LP was number 32 on *Billboard*'s Hot LP chart on September 20, 1959. It remained on the chart for eight weeks.

10. **LPM-2075** December 1959

50,000,000 Elvis Fans Can't Be Wrong

BLACK LABEL DOG ON TOP

Elvis wore his famous suit of gold on the cover of his second greatest-hits LP.

Side 1: *I Need Your Love Tonight; Don't; Wear My Ring Around Your Neck; My Wish Came True; I Got Stung*

Side 2: *One Night; A Big Hunk o' Love; I Beg of You; A Fool Such as I; Doncha' Think It's Time*

On February 19, 1960, this LP entered the Hot LP chart in the number 31 position. It remained on the chart for six weeks.

NOTE: RCA began releasing Elvis' LPs in true living stereo. No longer would there be a noticeable difference between the stereo and mono covers.

---

11. **LSP/LPM-2231** April 1960

Elvis Is Back!

BLACK LABEL DOG ON TOP

Side 1: *Make Me Know It; Fever; The Girl of My Best Friend; I Will Be Home Again; Dirty, Dirty Feeling; Thrill of Your Love*

Side 2: *Soldier Boy; Such a Night; It Feels So Right; The Girl Next Door (Went Awalking); Like a Baby; Reconsider, Baby*

Elvis Is Back! made the Hot LP chart at number 2 on May 13, 1960. It remained on the chart for fifty-six weeks.

12. **LSP/LPM-2256**   October 1960

   G.I. Blues

BLACK LABEL   DOG ON TOP

Side 1: *Tonight Is So Right for Love; What's She Really Like; Frankfort
        Special; Wooden Heart; G.I. Blues*

Side 2: *Pocketful of Rainbows; Shoppin' Around; Big Boots; Didja Ever;
        Blue Suede Shoes; Doin' the Best I Can*

On October 30, 1960, this LP was number 1. It remained on the chart for
a total of 111 weeks. It was number 1 for 10 weeks.

13. **LSP/LPM-2328**   (DELETED)   December 1960

   His Hand in Mine

BLACK LABEL   DOG ON TOP

This album was Elvis' first religious album.

Side 1: *His Hand in Mine; I'm Gonna Walk Dem Golden Stairs; In My
        Father's House; Milky White Way; Known Only to Him; I Be-
        lieve in the Man in the Sky*

Side 2: *Joshua Fit the Battle; Jesus Knows Just What I Need; Swing Down,
        Sweet Chariot; Mansion over the Hilltop; If We Never Meet Again;
        Working on the Building*

This LP made *Billboard*'s Hot LP chart on January 15, 1961. It was number 13, and remained on the chart for twenty weeks.

14. **LSP/LPM-2370**   June 1961

   Something for Everybody

BLACK LABEL   DOG ON TOP

The back cover had a picture from the film *Wild in the Country*. It also
featured advertisements for the 33⅓ single *Wild in the Country* and the
33⅓ EP *Elvis by Request*.

Side 1: *There's Always Me; Give Me the Right; It's a Sin; Sentimental
        Me; Starting Today; Gently*

Side 2: *I'm Comin' Home; In Your Arms; Put the Blame on Me; Judy; I
        Want You with Me; I Slipped, I Stumbled, I Fell*

On July 16, 1961, this LP was number 1 on the Hot LP chart. It remained
on the chart for twenty-five weeks.

15. **LSP/LPM-2426**   October 1961

   Blue Hawaii

BLACK LABEL   DOG ON TOP

Side 1: *Blue Hawaii; Almost True; Aloha Oe; No More; Can't Help Fall-
        ing in Love; Rock-a-hula Baby; Moonlight Swim*

Side 2: *Ku-u-i-po; Ito Eats; Slicin' Sand; Hawaiian Sunset; Beach Boy
        Blues; Island of Love; Hawaiian Wedding Song*

Blue Hawaii was number 1 on *Billboard*'s Hot LP chart on October 29,
1961. It remained on the chart for seventy-nine weeks.

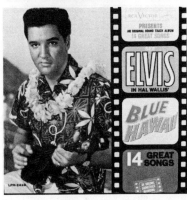

233

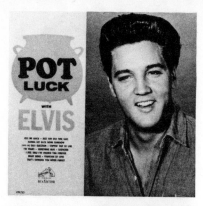

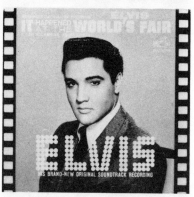

16. **LSP/LPM-2523**   June 1962

  Pot Luck

BLACK LABEL   DOG ON TOP

Side 1: *Kiss Me Quick; Just for Old Time Sake; Gonna Get Back Home Somehow; (Such an) Easy Question; Steppin' Out of Line; I'm Yours*

Side 2: *Something Blue; Suspicion; I Feel That I've Known You Forever; Night Rider; Fountain of Love; That's Someone You Never Forget*

Billboard cast this LP at number 4 on July 14, 1962. It remained on the chart for thirty-one weeks.

17. **LSP/LPM-2621**   November 1962

  Girls! Girls! Girls

BLACK LABEL   DOG ON TOP

Side 1: *Girls! Girls! Girls!; I Don't Wanna Be Tied; Where Do You Come From; I Don't Want To; We'll Be Together; A Boy Like Me, a Girl Like You; Earth Boy*

Side 2: *Return to Sender; Because of Love; Thanks to the Rolling Sea; Song of the Shrimp; The Walls Have Ears; We're Comin' In Loaded*

December 8, 1962, was when this LP entered *Billboard*'s Hot LP chart at number 3. It remained on the chart for thirty-two weeks.

18. **LSP/LPM-2697**   (DELETED)   April 1963

  It Happened at the World's Fair

BLACK LABEL   DOG ON TOP

Side 1: *Beyond the Bend; Relax; Take Me to the Fair; They Remind Me Too Much of You; One Broken Heart for Sale*

Side 2: *I'm Falling in Love Tonight; Cotton Candy Land; A World of Our Own; How Would You Like to Be; Happy Ending*

On April 20, 1963, the number 4 position on the Hot LP chart was held by this LP. It remained on the chart for twenty-six weeks.

19. **LSP/LPM-2765**   September 1963

  Elvis' Golden Records, Volume III

BLACK LABEL   DOG ON TOP

Side 1: *It's Now or Never; Stuck on You; Fame and Fortune; I Gotta Know; Surrender; I Feel So Bad*

Side 2: *Are You Lonesome Tonight?; His Latest Flame; Little Sister; Good Luck Charm; Anything That's Part of You; She's Not You*

Billboard posted this LP on September 14, 1963. It was number 3 on the Hot LP chart and remained on the chart for forty weeks.

20. **LSP/LPM-2756**   December 1963

  Fun in Acapulco

BLACK LABEL   DOG ON TOP

Side 1: *Fun in Acapulco; Vino, Dinero y Amor; Mexico; El Toro; Marguerita; The Bullfighter Was a Lady; No Room to Rhumba in a Sports Car*

Side 2: *I Think I'm Gonna Like It Here; Bossa Nova Baby; You Can't Say No in Acapulco; Guadalajara; Love Me Tonight; Slowly but Surely*

Billboard cast this LP on its Hot LP chart on December 21, 1963. It was number 3 and remained on the chart for twenty-four weeks.

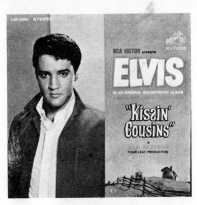

21. **LSP/LPM-2894**   March 1964

Kissin' Cousins

BLACK LABEL   DOG ON TOP

The original cover did not include the photograph of Elvis' movie family, the Tatums (front cover, bottom right-hand corner).

Side 1: *Kissin' Cousins; Smokey Mountain Boy; There's Gold in the Mountains; One Boy, Two Little Girls; Catchin' On Fast; Tender Feeling*

Side 2: *Anyone; Barefoot Ballad; Once Is Enough; Kissin' Cousins/Echoes of Love; Long Lonely Highway*

Number 6 was the position this LP held on April 11, 1964. It remained on the Hot LP chart for thirty weeks.

22. **LSP/LPM-2999**   October 1964

Roustabout

BLACK LABEL   DOG ON TOP

Side 1: *Roustabout; Little Egypt; Poison Ivy League; Hard Knocks; It's a Wonderful World; Big Love, Big Heartache*

Side 2: *One-track Heart; It's Carnival Time; Carny Town; There's a Brand New Day on the Horizon; Wheels on My Heels*

On November 14, 1964, *Roustabout* was number 1 on *Billboard*'s Hot LP chart. It remained on the chart for twenty-seven weeks.

23. **LSP/LPM-3338**   April 1965

Girl Happy

BLACK LABEL   DOG ON TOP

Side 1: *Girl Happy; Spring Fever; Fort Lauderdale Chamber of Commerce; Startin' Tonight; Wolf Call; Do Not Disturb*

Side 2: *Cross My Heart and Hope to Die; The Meanest Girl in Town; Do the Clam; Puppet on a String; I've Got to Find My Baby; You'll Be Gone*

Girl Happy entered the Hot LP list at number 8 on April 17, 1965. It remained on the chart for thirty-one weeks.

24. **LSP/LPM-3450**   July 1965

Elvis for Everyone

BLACK LABEL   DOG ON TOP

Side 1: *Your Cheatin' Heart; Summer Kisses, Winter Tears; Finders Keepers, Losers Weepers; In My Way; Tomorrow Night; Memphis, Tennessee*

Side 2: *For the Millionth and the Last Time; Forget Me Never; Sound Advice; Santa Lucia; I Met Her Today; When It Rains, It Really Pours*

On August 14, 1965, this LP was number 10 on the Hot LP chart. It remained on the chart for twenty-seven weeks.

235

25. **LSP/LPM-3468** (DELETED)   October 1965

Harum Scarum

BLACK LABEL   DOG ON TOP

This LP came with a bonus picture.

Side 1: *Harum Holiday; My Desert Serenade; Go East, Young Man; Mirage; Kismet; Shake That Tambourine*

Side 2: *Hey, Little Girl; Golden Coins; So Close, Yet So Far; Animal Instinct; Wisdom of the Ages*

Harum Scarum was number 8 on the Hot LP chart on November 13, 1965. It remained on the chart for twenty-three weeks.

26. **LSP/LPM-3553** (DELETED)   April 1966

Frankie and Johnny

BLACK LABEL   DOG ON TOP

RCA included a reproduction of a beautiful oil painting by June Kelly with this package.

Side 1: *Frankie and Johnny; Come Along; Petunia, the Gardener's Daughter; Chesay; What Every Woman Lives For; Look Out, Broadway*

Side 2: *Beginner's Luck; Down by the Riverside/When the Saints Go Marching In; Shout It Out; Hard Luck; Please Don't Stop Loving Me; Everybody Come Aboard*

This LP was number 20 on the Hot LP chart on April 23, 1966. It remained on the chart for nineteen weeks.

27. **LSP/LPM-3643**   June 1966

Paradise, Hawaiian Style

BLACK LABEL   DOG ON TOP

Side 1: *Paradise, Hawaiian Style; Queenie Wahine's Papaya; Scratch My Back; Drums of the Islands; Datin'*

Side 2: *A Dog's Life; House of Sand; Stop Where You Are; This Is My Heaven; Sand Castles*

On July 16, 1966, this LP was number 15 on the Hot LP chart. It remained on the chart for nineteen weeks.

28. **LSP/LPM-3702** (DELETED)   October 1966

Spinout

BLACK LABEL   DOG ON TOP

There was a bonus color photo included with the LP.

Side 1: *Stop, Look and Listen; Adam and Evil; All That I Am; Never Say Yes; Am I Ready; Beach Shack*

Side 2: *Spinout; Smorgasbord; I'll Be Back; Tomorrow Is a Long Time; Down in the Alley; I'll Remember You*

October 29, 1966, was the entry date for *Spinout* on *Billboard*'s Hot LP chart. It positioned at number 18 and remained on the chart for thirty-two weeks.

29. **LSP/LPM-3758**   March 1967

How Great Thou Art

BLACK LABEL   DOG ON TOP

Side 1: *How Great Thou Art; In the Garden; Somebody Bigger Than You and I; Farther Along; Stand by Me; Without Him*

Side 2: *So High; Where Could I Go But to the Lord; By and By; If the*

Lord Wasn't Walking by My Side; Run On; Where No One Stands Alone; Crying in the Chapel

This LP entered *Billboard*'s Hot LP chart on March 25, 1967, in the number 13 position. It stayed on this chart for twenty weeks.

30. **LSP/LPM-3787** (DELETED)   June 1967

Double Trouble

BLACK LABEL   DOG ON TOP

There was a special full-color photo included with this LP.

Side 1: *Double Trouble; Baby, if You'll Give Me All of Your Love; Could I Fall in Love; Long-legged Girl; City by Night; Old MacDonald*

Side 2: *I Love Only One Girl; There Is So Much World to See; It Won't Be Long; Never Ending; Blue River; What Now, What Next, Where To*

Billboard cast this LP in the number 47 position on its Hot LP chart. It entered on June 24, 1967, and remained on the chart for twenty weeks.

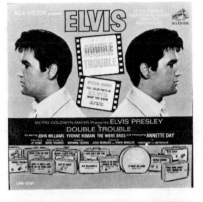

31. **LSP/LPM-3893** (DELETED)   November 1967

Clambake

BLACK LABEL   DOG ON TOP

A wedding photo of Elvis and Priscilla was included with this package.

Side 1: *Guitar Man; Clambake; Who Needs Money; A House That Has Everything; Confidence; Hey, Hey, Hey*

Side 2: *You Don't Know Me; The Girl I Never Loved; How Can You Lose What You Never Had; Big Boss Man; Singing Tree; Just Call Me Lonesome*

On December 2, 1967, this LP entered the Hot LP chart at number 33. It remained on the chart for twenty-two weeks.

32. **LSP/LPM-3921**   February 1968

Elvis' Gold Records, Volume 4

BLACK LABEL   DOG ON TOP

Side 1: *Love Letters; Witchcraft; It Hurts Me; What'd I Say; Please Don't Drag That String Around; Indescribably Blue*

Side 2: *(You're the) Devil in Disguise; Lonely Man; A Mess of Blues; Ask Me; Ain't That Loving You, Baby; Just Tell Her Jim Said Hello*

On March 2, 1968, this LP was number 33 on *Billboard*'s Hot LP chart. It remained on this chart for twenty-two weeks.

NOTE: RCA, along with all the other major record companies, discontinued all mono LPs. All future Elvis LPs would be available in stereo only, except on rare occasions when an LP would feature either live cuts or vintage Presley.

237

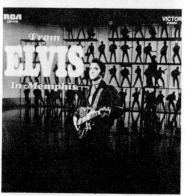

33. LSP-3989 June 1968

Speedway

BLACK LABEL DOG ON TOP

Once again RCA included a color photo of Elvis with this release.

Side 1: *Speedway; There Ain't Nothing Like a Song; Your Time Hasn't Come Yet, Baby; Who Are You?; He's Your Uncle, Not Your Dad; Let Yourself Go*

Side 2: *Your Groovy Self; Five Sleepy Heads; Western Union; Mine; Goin' Home; Suppose*

This LP would be found on *Billboard*'s Hot LP chart for thirteen weeks after its entry on July 6, 1968, when it was number 82.

34. LPM-4088 December 1968

Elvis—TV Special[1]

ORANGE LABEL

Side 1: *Trouble/Guitar Man; Lawdy, Miss Clawdy/Baby, What You Want Me to Do; Heartbreak Hotel; Hound Dog; All Shook Up/Can't Help Falling in Love; Jailhouse Rock/*(Dialogue)*; Love Me Tender*

Side 2: (Dialogue)*; Where Could I Go But to the Lord; Up Above My Head/Saved; Blue Christmas/One Night; Memories;* Medley: *Nothingville/Big Boss Man/Guitar Man/Little Egypt; T-R-O-U-B-L-E; Guitar Man; If I Can Dream*

This LP positioned number 8 on the Hot LP chart on December 21, 1968. It was on the chart for thirty-two weeks.

35. LSP-4155 June 1969

From Elvis in Memphis

ORANGE LABEL

The package included a color photo.

Side 1: *Wearin' That Loved-on Look; Only the Strong Survive; I'll Hold You in My Heart; Long Black Limousine; It Keeps Right on A-hurtin'; I'm Movin' On*

Side 2: *Power of My Love; Gentle on My Mind; After Loving You; True Love Travels on a Gravel Road; Any Day Now; In the Ghetto*

Billboard showed this LP on its Hot LP chart on June 14, 1969. It was number 13 and remained on the chart for thirty-four weeks.

36. LSP-6020 November 1969

From Memphis to Vegas/From Vegas to Memphis

ORANGE LABEL

RCA released Elvis' first double LP, and half of the LP was live. There were two bonus pictures included with this package.

Side 1: *Blue Suede Shoes; Johnny B. Good; All Shook Up; Are You Lonesome Tonight?; Hound Dog; I Can't Stop Loving You; My Babe*

Side 2: *Mystery Train/Tiger Man; Words; In the Ghetto; Suspicious Minds; Can't Help Falling in Love*

Side 3: *Inherit the Wind; This Is the Story; Stranger in My Own Home Town; A Little Bit of Green; And the Grass Won't Pay No Mind*

Side 4: *Do You Know Who I Am; From a Jack to a King; The Fair's Moving On; You'll Think of Me; Without Love (There Is Nothing)*

On November 29, 1969, this double LP was number 12 on the Hot LP chart. It remained on the chart for twenty-four weeks.

[1] RCA retires Nipper and changes the color of the label to orange.

37. **LSP-4428**   February 1970

   Elvis in Person

ORANGE LABEL

This LP featured the same tracks as the live segments from LSP 6020 (sides 1 and 2).

38. **LSP-4362**   June 1970

   On Stage, February, 1970

ORANGE LABEL

Side 1: *See See Rider; Release Me; Sweet Caroline; Runaway; The Wonder of You*

Side 2: *Polk Salad Annie; Yesterday; Proud Mary; Walk a Mile in My Shoes; Let It Be Me*

On Stage was number 13 on the Hot LP chart upon entering on June 20, 1970. It was on this chart for twenty weeks.

39. **LPM-6401**   August 1970

   Elvis: Worldwide 50 Gold Award Hits, Volume 1

ORANGE LABEL

This four-record set came with a photo book.

Side 1: *Heartbreak Hotel; I Was the One; I Want You, I Need You, I Love You; Don't Be Cruel; Hound Dog; Love Me Tender*

Side 2: *Any Way You Want Me; Too Much; Playing for Keeps; (I'm) All Shook Up; That's When Your Heartaches Begin; Loving You*

Side 3: *Teddy Bear; Jailhouse Rock; Treat Me Nice; I Beg of You; Don't; Wear My Ring Around Your Neck; Hard-headed Woman*

Side 4: *I Got Stung; A Fool Such as I; A Big Hunk o' Love; Stuck on You; A Mess of Blues; It's Now or Never*

Side 5: *I Gotta Know; Are You Lonesome Tonight?; Surrender; I Feel So Bad; Little Sister; Can't Help Falling in Love*

Side 6: *Rock-a-hula Baby; Anything That's Part of You; Good Luck Charm; She's Not You; Return to Sender; Where Do You Come From; One Broken Heart for Sale*

Side 7: *(You're the) Devil in Disguise; Bossa Nova Baby; Kissin' Cousins; Viva Las Vegas; Ain't That Loving You, Baby; Wooden Heart*

Side 8: *Crying in the Chapel; If I Can Dream; In the Ghetto; Suspicious Minds; Don't Cry, Daddy; Kentucky Rain;* Excerpts from *Elvis Sails*

The box set positioned number 45 on *Billboard*'s Hot LP chart on August 22, 1970. It remained on the chart for twenty-two weeks.

40. **LSP-4429**   November 1970

   Back in Memphis

ORANGE LABEL

This LP featured the studio tracks from LSP 6020 (sides 3 and 4). It entered *Billboard*'s Hot LP chart on November 21, 1970, at the number 183 position and remained on the chart for three weeks.

239

41. **LSP-4445**   December 1970

    That's the Way It Is

ORANGE LABEL

Side 1: *I Just Can't Help Believin'; Twenty Days and Twenty Nights; How the Web Was Woven; Patch It Up; Mary in the Morning; You Don't Have to Say You Love Me*

Side 2: *You've Lost That Lovin' Feelin'; I've Lost You; Just Pretend; Stranger in the Crowd; The Next Step Is Love; Bridge over Troubled Water*

On December 12, 1970, this LP was number 21 on the Hot LP chart. It remained on the chart for twenty-three weeks.

42. **LSP-4460**   January 1971

    Elvis Country

ORANGE LABEL

A bonus photo was included with this LP.

Side 1: *Snowbird; Tomorrow Never Comes; Little Cabin on the Hill; Whole Lotta Shakin' Goin' On; Funny How Time Slips Away; I Really Don't Want to Know*

Side 2: *There Goes My Everything; It's Your Baby, You Rock It; The Fool; Faded Love; I Washed My Hands in Muddy Water; Make the World Go Away*

On January 23, 1971, this LP was number 12 on the Hot LP chart. It remained on the chart for twenty-one weeks.

43. **LSP-4530**   June 1971

    Love Letters from Elvis

ORANGE LABEL

The original had the RCA logo at center top, and *Love Letters from* all on one line. Colonel Parker was not happy with this, so very few copies were released with this cover. The reissue cover had *Love Letters from* on two lines, and the RCA logo appeared in the lower right-hand corner, with *R.E.* (for "reissue") in the lower left-hand corner.

Side 1: *Love Letters; When I'm over You; If I Were You; Got My Mojo Working; Heart of Rome*

Side 2: *Only Believe; This Is Our Dance; Cindy, Cindy; I'll Never Know; It Ain't No Big Thing; Life*

This LP entered the Hot LP list on June 26, 1971, at the number 33 position and remained on the chart for fifteen weeks.

44. **LPM 6402**   August 1971

    Elvis: The Other Sides; Worldwide Gold Award Hits, Volume 2

ORANGE LABEL

This four-record box set includes a piece of Elvis' clothing and a poster.

Side 1: *Puppet on a String; Witchcraft; T-R-O-U-B-L-E; Poor Boy; I Want to Be Free; Doncha' Think It's Time; Young Dreams*

Side 2: *The Next Step Is Love; You Don't Have to Say You Love Me; Paralyzed; My Wish Came True; When My Blue Moon Turns to Gold Again; Lonesome Cowboy*

Side 3: *My Baby Left Me; It Hurts Me; I Need Your Love Tonight; Tell Me Why; Please Don't Drag That String Around; Young and Beautiful*

Side 4: *Hot Dog; New Orleans; We're Gonna Move; Crawfish; King Creole; I Believe in the Man in the Sky; Dixieland Rock*

Side 5: *The Wonder of You; They Remind Me Too Much of You; Mean Woman Blues; Lonely Man; Any Day Now; Don't Ask Me Why*

Side 6: *His Latest Flame; I Really Don't Want to Know; Baby, I Don't Care; I've Lost You; Let Me; Love Me*

Side 7: *Got a Lot o' Livin' to Do; Fame and Fortune; Rip It Up; There Goes My Everything; Lover Doll; One Night*

Side 8: *Just Tell Her Jim Said Hello; Ask Me; Patch It Up; As Long As I Have You; You'll Think of Me; Wild in the Country*

This LP held the number 120 position on the Hot LP chart on August 28, 1971. It remained on the chart for seven weeks.

45. **LSP-4579** (DELETED)   October 1971

The Wonderful World of Christmas

ORANGE LABEL

A Christmas card from Elvis was included.

Side 1: *O Come, All Ye Faithful; The First Noel; On a Snowy Christmas Night; Winter Wonderland; The Wonderful World of Christmas; It Won't Seem Like Christmas (Without You)*

Side 2: *I'll Be Home on Christmas Day; If I Get Home on Christmas Day; Holly Leaves and Christmas Trees; Merry Christmas, Baby; Silver Bells*

46. **LSP-4671**   January 1972

Elvis Now

ORANGE LABEL

Side 1: *Help Me Make It Through the Night; Miracle of the Rosary; Hey, Jude; Put Your Hand in the Hand; Until It's Time for You to Go*

Side 2: *We Can Make the Morning; Early Mornin' Rain; Sylvia; Fools Rush In; I Was Born About 10,000 Years Ago*

On February 12, 1972, this LP was number 43 on the Hot LP list. It remained on the chart for nineteen weeks.

47. **LSP-4690**   April 1972

He Touched Me

ORANGE LABEL

Side 1: *He Touched Me; I've Got Confidence; Amazing Grace; Seeing Is Believing; He Is My Everything; Bosom of Abraham*

Side 2: *An Evening Prayer; Lead Me, Guide Me; There Is No God But God; A Thing Called Love; I John; Reach Out to Jesus*

Number 79 was the position where this LP settled on the Hot LP chart on April 22, 1972. It stayed on the chart for ten weeks.

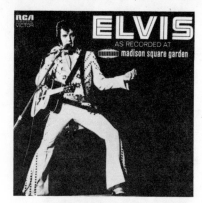

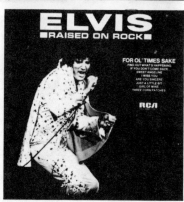

48. **LSP-4776**   June 1972

Elvis As Recorded at Madison Square Garden

ORANGE LABEL

Side 1: *Also Sprach Zarathustra; That's All Right; Proud Mary; Never Been to Spain; You Don't Have to Say You Love Me; You've Lost That Lovin' Feelin'; Polk Salad Annie; Love Me; All Shook Up; Heartbreak Hotel;* Medley: *Teddy Bear/Don't Be Cruel/Love Me Tender*

Side 2: *The Impossible Dream;* Introductions by Elvis; *Hound Dog; Suspicious Minds; For the Good Times; American Trilogy; Funny How Time Slips Away; I Can't Stop Loving You; Can't Help Falling in Love*

This LP entered the Hot LP chart in the number 11 position on July 8, 1972. It was on the chart for thirty-four weeks.

49. **VPX-6089**   February 1973

Elvis: Aloha from Hawaii

ORANGE LABEL

This LP was released as a two-record set. This was the first RCA Quadra Disc.

Side 1: *Also Sprach Zarathustra; See See Rider; Burning Love; Something; Lord, This Time You Gave Me a Mountain; Steamroller Blues*

Side 2: *My Way; Love Me; Johnny B. Good; It's Over; Blue Suede Shoes; I'm So Lonesome I Could Cry; I Can't Stop Loving You; Hound Dog*

Side 3: *What Now, My Love; Fever; Welcome to My World; Suspicious Minds;* Introductions by Elvis

Side 4: *I'll Remember You;* Medley: *Long Tall Sally/Whole Lotta Shakin' Goin' On; American Trilogy; A Big Hunk o' Love; Can't Help Falling in Love*

On February 24, 1973, *Elvis: Aloha from Hawaii* entered *Billboard*'s Hot LP chart in the number 1 position. It remained on the chart for approximately one year.

50. **APL-0283**   (DELETED)   June 1973

Elvis

ORANGE LABEL

Side 1: *Fool; Where Do I Go from Here; Love Me, Love the Life I Lead; It's Still Here; It's Impossible*

Side 2: *For Lovin' Me; Padre; I'll Take You Home Again, Kathleen; I Will Be True; Don't Think Twice, It's All Right*

Elvis appeared on the Hot LP chart on July 21, 1973, in the number 52 position. It was on the chart for thirteen weeks.

51. **APL-0388**   (DELETED)   October 1973

Raised on Rock

ORANGE LABEL

Side 1: *Raised on Rock; Are You Sincere; Find Out What's Happening; I Miss You; Girl of Mine*

Side 2: *For Ol' Times Sake; If You Don't Come Back; Just a Little Bit; Sweet Angeline; Three Corn Patches*

Billboard cast this LP in slot number 50 on November 24, 1973. It remained on the chart for thirteen weeks.

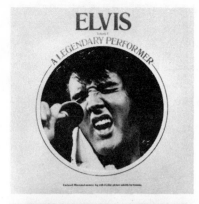

52. **CPL-0341**   January 1974

A Legendary Performer, Volume 1

BLACK LABEL

Side 1: *That's All Right; I Love You Because; Heartbreak Hotel; Don't Be Cruel; Love Me; Tryin' to Get to You*

Side 2: *Love Me Tender; Peace in the Valley; A Fool Such as I; Tonight's All Right for Love; Are You Lonesome Tonight?; Can't Help Falling in Love*

This LP entered the Hot LP chart on February 2, 1974, at number 43. It was on the chart for fourteen weeks.

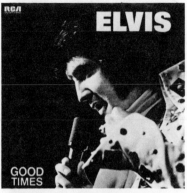

53. **CPL-0475**   (DELETED)   March 1974

Good Times

ORANGE LABEL

Side 1: *Take Good Care of Her; Loving Arms; I Got a Feelin' in My Body; If That Isn't Love; She Wears My Ring*

Side 2: *I've Got a Thing About You, Baby; My Boy; Spanish Eyes; Talk About the Good Times; Good-time Charlie's Got the Blues*

On April 6, 1974, this LP was number 90 on the Hot LP chart. It was on the chart for eight weeks.

54. **CPL-0606**   (DELETED)   June 1974

Elvis: Recorded Live on Stage in Memphis

ORANGE LABEL

This LP was also available in Quad.

Side 1: *See See Rider; I Got a Woman; Love Me; Tryin' to Get to You; Medley: Long Tall Sally/Whole Lotta Shakin' Goin' On/Your Mama Won't Dance/Flip, Flop and Fly/Jailhouse Rock/Hound Dog; Why Me, Lord; How Great Thou Art*

Side 2: *Medley: Blueberry Hill/I Can't Stop Loving You; Help Me; An American Trilogy; Let Me Be There; My Baby Left Me; Lawdy, Miss Clawdy; Can't Help Falling in Love; Closing vamp*

This LP appeared on *Billboard*'s Hot LP chart on July 27, 1974. It was number 33, and it remained on the chart for thirteen weeks.

55. **CPM-0818**   October 1974

Having Fun with Elvis on Stage

ORANGE LABEL

This was a talking album only. Both sides consist of excerpts of dialogue from Elvis' live concerts. It was on the Hot LP chart at number 130 on November 2, 1974, and remained on the chart for nine weeks.

56. **APL-0873**   January 1975

Promised Land

ORANGE LABEL

This LP was available in Quad.

Side 1: *Promised Land; There's a Honky Tonk Angel; Help Me; Mr. Songman; Love Song of the Year*

Side 2: *It's Midnight; Your Love's Been a Long Time Coming; If You Talk in Your Sleep; Thinking About You; You Asked Me To*

Promised Land entered *Billboard*'s Hot LP chart on February 1, 1975, in the number 47 position. It was on the chart for twelve weeks.

243

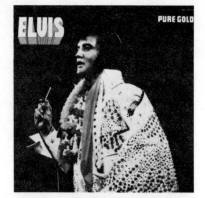

57. ANL-0971   March 1975

Pure Gold

ORANGE LABEL

Side 1: *Kentucky Rain; Fever; It's Impossible; Jailhouse Rock; Don't Be Cruel*

Side 2: *I Got a Woman; All Shook Up; Loving You; In the Ghetto; Love Me Tender*

58. APL-1039   June 1975

Today

ORANGE LABEL

This album is also available in Quad.

Side 1: *T-R-O-U-B-L-E; And I Love You So; Susan When She Tried; Woman Without Love; Shake a Hand*

Side 2: *Pieces of My Life; Fairytale; I Can Help; Bringing It Back; Green, Green Grass of Home*

This LP entered the Hot LP chart on June 7, 1975, in the number 57 position. It remained on the chart for thirteen weeks.

59. CPL-1349   January 1976

A Legendary Performer, Volume 2

BLACK LABEL[2]

Side 1: *Harbor Lights;* Interview with Elvis; *I Want You, I Need You, I Love You; Blue Suede Shoes; Blue Christmas; Jailhouse Rock; It's Now or Never*

Side 2: *A Cane and a High Starched Collar;* Presentation of Awards to Elvis; *Blue Hawaii; Such a Night; Baby, What You Want Me to Do; How Great Thou Art; If I Can Dream*

On February 15, 1976, this LP entered the Hot LP chart in the number 50 position. It was on the chart for eleven weeks.

60. ANL-1319   March 1976

His Hand in Mine

ORANGE LABEL

This LP is an RCA reissue on the Pure Gold series. It has the same selections as LSP/LPM 2328.

61. APM-1675   March 1976

The Sun Sessions

BROWN LABEL

RCA begins to use a brown label.

Side 1: *That's All Right; Blue Moon of Kentucky; I Don't Care if the Sun Don't Shine; Good Rockin' Tonight; Milkcow Blues Boogie; You're a Heartbreaker; I'm Left, You're Right, She's Gone; Baby, Let's Play House*

Side 2: *Mystery Train; I Forgot to Remember to Forget; I'll Never Let You Go; I Love You Because; Tryin' to Get to You; Blue Moon; Just Because; I Love You Because*

The Sun Sessions entered *Billboard*'s Hot LP chart on March 19, 1976, in the number 48 position. It was on the chart for fourteen weeks.

[2] RCA now discontinued the orange labels, except for the Pure Gold series.

244

62. **APL-1506**   May 1976

From Elvis Presley Boulevard, Memphis, Tennessee

BROWN LABEL

Side 1: *Hurt; Never Again; Blue Eyes Crying in the Rain; Danny Boy; The Last Farewell*

Side 2: *For the Heart; Bitter They Are, Harder They Fall; Solitaire; Love Coming Down; I'll Never Fall in Love Again*

This album was on the Country chart on May 28, 1976, at number 1. It remained on the chart for ten weeks.

63. **ANL-1936**   November 1976

The Wonderful World of Christmas

ORANGE LABEL

This LP is an RCA reissue on the Pure Gold series. It has the same selections as LSP-4579. The back cover is different from that of the original release.

64. **APL-2274**   March 1977

Welcome to My World

BLACK LABEL[3]   DOG AT TOP RIGHT-HAND CORNER

All songs with the exception of *I Can't Stop Loving You*, which was recorded live at Madison Square Garden during the June 10, 1972, Saturday afternoon performance, were previously released.

Side 1: *Welcome to My World* (live); *Help Me Make It Through the Night; Release Me (and Let Me Love Again)* (live); *I Really Don't Want to Know; For the Good Times* (live)

Side 2: *Make the World Go Away* (live); *Gentle on My Mind; I'm So Lonesome I Could Cry* (live); *Your Cheatin' Heart; I Can't Stop Loving You* (live—unreleased)

Welcome to My World reached number 44 on the Hot LP chart. It remained on the chart for ten weeks. It reached number 4 on the Country chart and remained on the chart for eleven weeks.

65. **AFL-2428**   June 1977

Moody Blue

BLACK LABEL   DOG AT TOP RIGHT-HAND CORNER

RCA pressed the first 250,000 copies of this LP on translucent blue plastic. Those of you who purchased this LP when it was first released own a real collector's item.

Side 1: *Unchained Melody; If You Love Me (Let Me Know); Little Darlin'; He'll Have to Go; Let Me Be There*

Side 2: *Way Down; Pledging My Love; Moody Blue; She Thinks I Still Care; It's Easy for You*

After ten weeks on the Hot Country chart, *Moody Blue* could be found at the number 1 position. *Moody Blue* was at the number 3 position on the Hot 100 chart.

It is interesting to note that in the three weeks following Elvis' death, fifteen of his LPs reappeared on the nation's charts.

[3] All RCA records once again have a black label and feature "Nipper." This time the famous trademark dog appears in the top right-hand corner. This was done as part of RCA's Seventy-fifth Jubilee Anniversary.

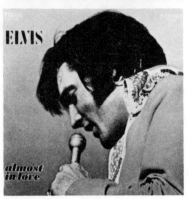

33 1/3 RPM CAMDEN LP'S RELEASED BY RCA

In 1975 RCA sold all of the rights to Elvis' Camden LPs to Pickwick Records. All of Elvis' Camden LPs are now deleted.

1. **CAS-2304**   (DELETED)   April 1969
   Elvis Sings Flaming Star
   BLUE LABEL
   Side 1: *Flaming Star; Wonderful World; Night Life; All I Needed Was the Rain; Too Much Monkey Business*
   Side 2: *Yellow Rose of Texas/The Eyes of Texas; She's a Machine; Do the Vega; Tiger Man*
   This LP was number 96 on *Billboard*'s Hot LP chart on April 19, 1969. It remained on the chart for sixteen weeks.

2. **CAS-2408**   (DELETED)   April 1970
   Let's Be Friends
   BLUE LABEL
   Side 1: *Stay Away, Joe; If I'm a Fool; Let's Be Friends; Let's Forget About the Stars; Mama*
   Side 2: *I'll Be There; Almost; Change of Habit; Have a Happy*
   This LP appeared on the Hot LP chart on May 9,.1970, in the number 105 position. It was on the chart for eleven weeks.

3. **CAL-2428**   (DELETED)   November 1970
   Elvis' Christmas Album
   BLUE LABEL
   Side 1: *Blue Christmas; Silent Night; White Christmas; Santa Claus Is Back in Town; I'll Be Home for Christmas*
   Side 2: *If Every Day Was Like Christmas; Here Comes Santa Claus; O Little Town of Bethlehem; Santa, Bring My Baby Back (to Me); Mama Liked the Roses*

4. **CAS-2440**   November 1970
   Almost in Love
   BLUE LABEL
   The original release lists the song *Stay Away, Joe* as recorded in stereo. The reissue lists the song as *Stay Away*, recorded in mono.
   Side 1: *Almost in Love; Long-legged Girl; Edge of Reality; My Little Friend; A Little Less Conversation*
   Side 2: *Rubberneckin'; Clean Up Your Own Back Yard; U.S. Male; Charro; Stay Away, Joe*
   Almost in Love was on the Hot LP chart on November 21, 1970, in the number 65 position. It remained on the chart for eighteen weeks.

5. **CALX-2472** (DELETED)   March 1971

   You'll Never Walk Alone

BLUE LABEL

Side 1: *You'll Never Walk Alone; Who Am I?; Let Us Pray; Peace in the Valley; We Call on Him*

Side 2: *I Believe; It Is No Secret; Sing, You Children; Take My Hand, Precious Lord*

This LP was number 69 on the Hot LP chart on March 20, 1971. It was on the chart for twelve weeks.

6. **CAL-2518** (DELETED)   July 1971

   C'mon Everybody

BLUE LABEL

Side 1: *C'mon, Everybody; Angel; Easy Come, Easy Go; A Whistling Tune; Follow That Dream*

Side 2: *King of the Whole Wide World; I'll Take Love; Today, Tomorrow and Forever; I'm Not the Marrying Kind; This Is Living*

Billboard cast this LP in the number 70 position on the Hot LP chart on July 24, 1971. It remained on the chart for eleven weeks.

7. **CAL-2533** (DELETED)   November 1971

   I Got Lucky

BLUE LABEL

Side 1: *I Got Lucky; What a Wonderful Life; I Need Somebody to Lean On; Yoga Is as Yoga Does; Riding the Rainbow*

Side 2: *Fools Fall in Love; The Love Machine; Home Is Where the Heart Is; You Gotta Stop; If You Think I Don't Need You*

On November 27, 1971, this LP was number 104 on the Hot LP chart. It was on the chart for eight weeks.

8. **CAS-2567** (DELETED)   June 1972

   Elvis Sings Hits from His Movies, Volume 1

BLUE LABEL

Side 1: *Down by the Riverside/When the Saints Go Marching In; They Remind Me Too Much of You; Confidence; Frankie and Johnny; Guitar Man*

Side 2: *Long-legged Girl; You Don't Know Me; How Would You Like to Be; Big Boss Man; Old MacDonald*

This LP was in the number 87 position on the Hot LP chart on July 8, 1972, and remained on the chart for fifteen weeks.

9. **CAS-2595** (DELETED)   November 1972

   Burning Love and Hits from His Movies, Volume 2

BLUE LABEL

A photo was included with this LP.

Side 1: *Burning Love; Tender Feeling; Am I Ready; Tonight Is So Right for Love; Guadalajara*

Side 2. *It's a Matter of Time; No More; Santa Lucia; We'll Be Together; I Love Only One Girl*

On November 11, 1972, this album entered the Hot LP chart in the number 22 position. It remained on the list for twenty-five weeks.

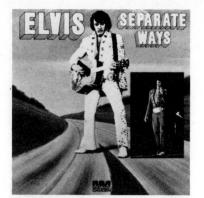

10. **CAS-2611** (DELETED)   January 1973
   Separate Ways
BLUE LABEL
A photo was included with this LP.
Side 1: *Separate Ways; Sentimental Me; In My Way; I Met Her Today;
        What Now, What Next, Where To*
Side 2: *Always on My Mind; I Slipped, I Stumbled, I Fell; Is It So Strange;
        Forget Me Never; Old Shep*
On January 27, 1973, this LP was number 46 on the Hot LP chart. It re-
mained on the chart for eighteen weeks.

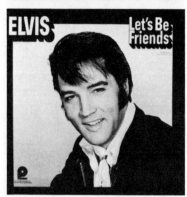

33 1/3 RPM LP'S RELEASED BY PICKWICK

   After purchasing Elvis' Camden catalogue, Pickwick reissued all the LPs
with the same numbers. It changed the covers on four of the LPs and also
issued two new releases. The first was a two-record set consisting of material
contained on the other Camden LPs. The second was a reissue of a deleted
soundtrack LP. The Pickwick label is black.
   The following LPs have different covers from those of original Camden releases.

1. **CAS-2408**   January 1976
   Let's Be Friends
BLACK LABEL
Same tracks as Camden LP.

2. **CAS-2440**   January 1976
   Almost in Love
BLACK LABEL
Same tracks as Camden LP.

3. **CAS-2611**   January 1976
   Separate Ways
BLACK LABEL
Same tracks as Camden LP.

4. **DL2-5001**   January 1976
   Double Dynamite
BLACK LABEL
Side 1 (first record): *Rubberneckin'; U.S. Male; Frankie and Johnny; If
                       You Think I Don't Need You; Easy Come, Easy Go*
Side 2 (first record): *Separate Ways; Peace in the Valley; Big Boss Man;
                       It's a Matter of Time*
Side 1 (second record): *Burning Love; I'll Be There; Fools Fall in Love;
                        Follow That Dream; You'll Never Walk Alone*
Side 2 (second record): *Flaming Star; Yellow Rose of Texas; Old Shep;
                        Mama*

5. **CAS-2428**   November 1976

Elvis' Christmas Album

BLACK LABEL

Same tracks as Camden LP.

6. **ACI-7007**   November 1976

Frankie and Johnny

BLACK LABEL

This album has a new cover and is missing three songs from the original soundtrack album LSP-3553.

Side 1: *What Every Woman Lives For; Please Don't Stop Loving Me; Hard Luck; Come Along*

Side 2: *Down by the Riverside/When the Saints Go Marching In; Shout It Out; Beginner's Luck; Frankie and Johnny; Petunia, the Gardener's Daughter*

Rare Records

The following is a complete American listing of the rarest Elvis Presley records in existence.

78 AND 45 RPM SINGLES AND EP'S

1. **Sun 272**　　　　　　　　45 rpm

   Foolish Heart/Greenback Dollar, Watch and Chain
   Elvis plays piano on this Ray Harris single.

2. **Sun 1129**　　　　　　　　45 rpm

   That's All Right/Blue Moon of Kentucky
   This controversial record has had Elvis collectors baffled for years. Is that Elvis singing? In my opinion, it is he. The background music has been re-recorded using studio musicians. Sun employees informed me that the vocal track is an outtake from the original Sun sessions. The record was originally released without giving any artist credit. RCA took Sun to court, and the record was reissued giving credit to an artist by the name of Jimmy Ellis.

3. **RCA 8705**　　　　　　　　45 rpm　　　　　BLUE LABEL

   TV Guide Presents Elvis Presley
   This is perhaps the most valuable of all Elvis records. This 45 had a light blue label. The logo read: "RCA Victor Custom-Made Record." It featured an open-end interview that had Elvis explaining his "Pelvis" nickname, among other things!

250

4. **RCA 0808**   45 rpm   DOG ON RIGHT-HAND
                                                                   SIDE

Blue Christmas

This record had a white label and featured *Blue Christmas* on both sides. It was pulled from the LOC-1035 33⅓ LP in 1957. It is in the top five when it comes to evaluating Elvis rarities.

5. **RCA CR-15**   45 rpm   WHITE LABEL/DOG ON
                                                                   TOP

Old Shep

The disc jockey single is a shorter version of *Old Shep*.

6. **RCA CR-25**   45 rpm   WHITE LABEL/DOG ON
                                                                   TOP

Ready Teddy

This disc jockey record would be the only time *Ready Teddy* was issued as an RCA single.

In the early years of the 45 rpm, RCA issued special "Record Prevue" discs for radio stations. The following is a complete listing of every Elvis "Record Prevue":

A. **RCA 6357**   Record Prevue   WHITE LABEL/DOG ON
                                                                   RIGHT-HAND SIDE

Mystery Train/I Forgot to Remember to Forget

B. **RCA 6382**   Record Prevue   WHITE LABEL/DOG ON
                                                                   RIGHT-HAND SIDE

You're a Heartbreaker/Milkcow Blues Boogie

C. **RCA 6383**   Record Prevue   WHITE LABEL/DOG ON
                                                                   RIGHT-HAND SIDE

I'm Left, You're Right, She's Gone/Baby, Let's Play House

D. **RCA 6466**   Record Prevue   WHITE LABEL/DOG ON
                                                                   RIGHT-HAND SIDE

Tutti Frutti/One-sided Love Affair

E. RCA 6492   Record Prevue   WHITE LABEL/DOG ON RIGHT-HAND SIDE

Blue Suede Shoes/I'm Counting on You

F. RCA 6540   Record Prevue   WHITE LABEL/DOG ON RIGHT-HAND SIDE

I Want You, I Need You, I Love You/My Baby Left Me

G. RCA 6639   Record Prevue   WHITE LABEL/DOG ON RIGHT-HAND SIDE

I Love You Because/Tryin' to Get to You

H. RCA 6643   Record Prevue   WHITE LABEL/DOG ON RIGHT-HAND SIDE

Any Way You Want Me/Love Me Tender

I. RCA 6689   Record Prevue   WHITE LABEL/DOG ON RIGHT-HAND SIDE

I Got a Woman/Money Honey

J. RCA 6870   Record Prevue   WHITE LABEL/DOG ON RIGHT-HAND SIDE

That's When Your Heartaches Begin/All Shook Up

K. RCA 7035   Record Prevue   WHITE LABEL/DOG ON RIGHT-HAND SIDE

Treat Me Nice/Jailhouse Rock

L. RCA 7066   Record Prevue   WHITE LABEL/DOG ON RIGHT-HAND SIDE

Have I Told You Lately That I Love You?/Mean Woman Blues

M. RCA 7150   Record Prevue   WHITE LABEL/DOG ON RIGHT-HAND SIDE

Don't/I Beg of You

N. **RCA 7240**   Record Prevue   WHITE LABEL/DOG ON
                                               RIGHT-HAND SIDE

Wear My Ring Around Your Neck/Doncha' Think It's Time

7. **RCA DJ-7**   45 EP   WHITE LABEL/DOG ON
                                               RIGHT-HAND SIDE

Love Me Tender/Any Way You Want Me
This special disc jockey EP had two Elvis songs on one side, and two by
Jean Chapel on the other.

8. **RCA DJ-56**   45 EP   WHITE LABEL/DOG ON
                                               RIGHT-HAND SIDE

Too Much/Playing for Keeps
This special disc jockey EP had two songs by Elvis on one side, and two
by Dinah Shore on the other side.

RCA released five "Living Stereo" 45s. They had black labels with the
dog on the top. They also released one "Living Stereo" 33⅓ single (see E).

9. **RCA 61-7740**   45 rpm Living
                         Stereo Single

Fame and Fortune/Stuck on You

A. **RCA 61-7777**   45 rpm Living
                         Stereo Single

Now or Never/A Mess of Blues

B. **RCA 61-7810**   45 rpm Living
                         Stereo Single

Are You Lonesome Tonight/I Gotta Know

C. **RCA 61-7850**   45 rpm Living
                         Stereo Single

Surrender/Lonely Man

D. **RCA 61-7880**   45 rpm Living
                         Stereo Single

I Feel So Bad/Wild in the Country

E. **RCA 68-7850**   33⅓ Living
                         Stereo Single

Surrender/Lonely Man

10. **RCA 37-7850**   33⅓ rpm Single   BLACK LABEL/DOG ON TOP

Surrender/ Lonely Man
Every Elvis collector seems to be looking for Elvis 33⅓ singles. This was the first released by RCA.

11. **RCA 37-7880**   33⅓ rpm Single   BLACK LABEL/DOG ON TOP

Wild in the Country/I Feel So Bad
This was the second 33⅓ single.

12. **RCA 74-0651**   33⅓ Single   ORANGE LABEL
The Bosom of Abraham/ He Touched Me
RCA released this record with a 45 rpm hole, but it played at 33⅓. Only 10,000 copies had been released before RCA found out about the error and recalled the copies that had been released.

13. **RCA LPC-128**   33⅓ EP   BLACK LABEL/DOG ON TOP

Elvis by Request
This is the only 33⅓ EP RCA officially released to the public. It is considered very valuable. (See RCA 33⅓ rpm Extended Play Albums.)

14. **RCA 2006**   33⅓ EP   TAN LABEL
Aloha from Hawaii via Satellite
This record was made for jukeboxes and contained six songs from the "Aloha" show.
One Side: *My Way; What Now, My Love; I'm So Lonesome I Could Cry*
Other Side: *Something; You Gave Me a Mountain; I Can't Stop Loving You*

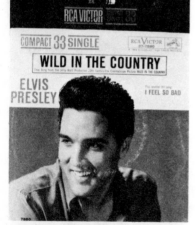

15. Rainbo Records   78 rpm   BLUE LABEL

Elvis Presley: The Truth About Me!

This Elvis interview record came as part of the front cover of the 1956 magazine *Elvis Presley Speaks*. It was originally issued on gold cardboard.

A. Rainbo Records   78 rpm   BLUE LABEL

Elvis Presley: Speaks—in Person!

Another version of the above, this, too, was on gold cardboard. This record, however, is much rarer.

B. Teen Parade   45 rpm   BLUE LABEL

Elvis Speaks!—The Truth About Me

This is the same record as the two that are captioned above (15 and 15A), but this time it came inside *Teen Parade* magazine and was a thin plastic 45 rpm.

C. Teen Parade   45 rpm   BLACK LABEL

Elvis Speaks!!—The Truth About Me

This is the same as 15B, but this time it had a black label.

16. United States Air   45 rpm   GREEN LABEL
Force Presents
Music in the Air

It's Now or Never

Elvis is on one side, and Jaye P. Morgan is on the other side of this super-rare record.

17. United States Air   45 rpm   GREEN LABEL
Force Presents
Music in the Air
Program 159

Surrender

This hard-to-find gem has Elvis on one side and Lawrence Welk on the other.

18. Motion Picture   45 rpm EP   TAN LABEL
Service 1206

Good Rockin' Tonight

Side 1: *Good Rockin' Tonight; I Don't Care if the Sun Don't Shine*
Side 2: *Blue Moon of Kentucky; Shake, Rattle and Roll*

When RCA released Elvis' Gold Standard 45 rpm extended plays, they originally had a maroon label with the dog on the top. They were available with a maroon label for only ninety days. (For song titles on the following extended plays, please see the EP listings earlier.)

19. **RCA EPA-5120**   45 rpm EP   MAROON LABEL/DOG ON TOP

The Real Elvis

20. **RCA EPA-5121**   45 rpm EP   MAROON LABEL/DOG ON TOP

Peace in the Valley

21. **RCA EPA-5122**   45 rpm EP   MAROON LABEL/DOG ON TOP

King Creole, Volume I

22. **RCA EPA-5157**   45 rpm EP   MAROON LABEL/DOG ON TOP

Elvis Sails

23. **RCA EPA-5088**   45 rpm EP   MAROON LABEL/DOG ON TOP

A Touch of Gold, Volume I

24. **RCA EPA-5101**   45 rpm EP   MAROON LABEL/DOG ON TOP

A Touch of Gold, Volume II

25. **RCA EPA-5141**   45 rpm EP   MAROON LABEL/DOG ON TOP

A Touch of Gold, Volume III

26. **MTR-243**   45 rpm EP   SILVER LABEL

Stay Away
Side 1: *Stay Away/U.S. Male*
Side 2: *Guitar Man/Big Boss Man*

27. **MTR-244**   45 rpm EP   SILVER LABEL

Clambake
Side 1: *Clambake/Hey, Hey, Hey*
Side 2: *You Don't Know Me/A House That Has Everything*

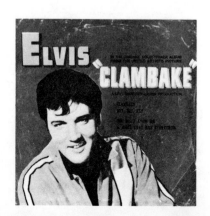

256

28. RCA 7410   (RARE COVER)

RCA 7410 had the same front cover as the *I Got Stung* single. The back cover was a fold-out picture of Elvis aboard the U.S.S. *General Randal.*

29. RCA PB-10191   45 rpm   WHITE LABEL/BROWN LABEL

My Boy/Thinking About You

On the A side of this single, *My Boy* appears on a white label. The B side, *Thinking About You,* is on a brown label.

30. RCA 2458   45 rpm   GRAY LABEL

My Boy/Loving Arms

Thinking About You was the B side of the common release. Not so with this collector's item, as it featured a different picture cover, a gray label, and a different flip side.

31. RCA 74-0769   45 rpm   GRAY LABEL

Burning Love/It's a Matter of Time

32. RCA EPA-992   45 rpm EP   ORANGE LABEL

Elvis, Volume I

This oddball featured the same front cover as EPA-747. (For contents, see the EP listings.)

33. RCA EPA-4387   45 rpm EP   WHITE LABEL

Easy Come, Easy Go

The label read as follows: "RCA Victor Presents Elvis in the Original soundtrack recording from the Paramount Picture EASY COME, EASY GO, a Hal Wallis Production." (For song titles, see the EP listings.)

The most valuable Elvis records in the world had the prefix SP ("special products"). These records were, for the most part, not available to the public. RCA does, however, list them on its official Elvis discography.

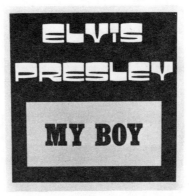

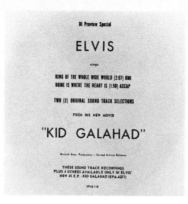

34. RCA SP-76   45 rpm   BLACK LABEL
Don't/Wear My Ring Around Your Neck
The picture cover had the same front cover as LPM-2075; the back cover displayed a telegram to disc jockeys.

35. RCA SP-118   45 rpm   WHITE LABEL
King of the Whole Wide World/Home Is Where the Heart Is
This 45 came in a plastic-paper picture cover.

36. RCA SP-139   45 rpm   WHITE LABEL
One Track Heart/Roustabout

37. RCA SP-162   45 rpm   WHITE LABEL
How Great Thou Art/So High
This came with a black and white picture cover.

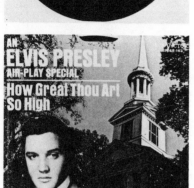

38. RCA JB-50170   45 rpm   WHITE LABEL
Such a Night/Such a Night
This release featured two versions of *Such a Night*. One was from LSP-2231, the other from CPL-1349.

39. RCA SP-15   45 rpm EP   GRAY LABEL
This was from a special ten-record box set and featured four Sun songs.
Side 7: *That's All Right/Baby, Let's Play House*
Side 14: *I Forgot to Remember to Forget/Mystery Train*

40. RCA SP-19   45 rpm EP   GRAY LABEL
RCA issued this ten-record box set as an anniversary package. *Heartbreak Hotel* appeared on side 16.

41. RCA SP-22   45 rpm Double   BLACK LABEL
    EP
This special product featured the same selections as EPB-1254.

42. RCA SP-23   45 rpm Triple   BLACK LABEL
                             Pocket EP

This ranks along with SP-19 as the rarest and hardest-to-find special product. It is the version of EPB-1254 with twelve songs (see the 45 rpm EP listings earlier).
Side 1: *Blue Suede Shoes/I'm Counting on You*
Side 2: *I'm Gonna Sit Right Down and Cry/I Gotta Woman*
Side 3: *One-sided Love Affair/I'll Never Let You Go*
Side 4: *Tutti Frutti/Tryin' to Get to You*
Side 5: *I Want You, I Need You, I Love You/Don't Be Cruel*
Side 6: *Hound Dog/My Baby Left Me*

43. RCA SP-26   45 rpm EP   BLACK LABEL

This ten-record box set had Elvis on sides 6 and 15.
Side 6: *Love Me Tender/Blue Moon of Kentucky*
Side 15: *Mystery Train/Milkcow Blues Boogie*

44. RCA SP-7-37   45 rpm EP   BLACK LABEL

Perfect for Parties
Elvis sang *Love Me* and introduced the songs by the other artists on this sample EP. The only way you could get the EP was to purchase an Elvis Presley RCA 45 rpm record player.

45. RCA SP-7-27   45 rpm EP   BLACK LABEL

Perfect for Parties, Volume 2
Elvis sang *I'm Gonna Sit Right Down and Cry* on this one.

46. RCA EPA 4368   45 rpm EP   WHITE LABEL

Follow That Dream
This SP extended-play came in a plastic-paper picture cover. (For song titles, see EPA-4368 in the 45 rpm EP listings.)

47. RCA JH-10951   45 rpm EP   TAN LABEL

Let Me Be There (mono)/*Let Me Be There* (stereo)
This song could originally be found on the deleted LP *Elvis: Recorded Live on Stage in Memphis*. Al Gallico, the song's publisher, had RCA press a special promo of this song. He sent copies to radio stations with the hope of forcing RCA to release *Let Me Be There* as an Elvis single. His bid failed. What Mr. Gallico did achieve was to make *Let Me Be There* an instant one-hundred-dollar record to collectors everywhere.

As is the case in coin collecting, any error made by RCA in minting an Elvis record makes that record extremely rare and valuable. The following is a list of such RCA errors:

48. **RCA 7000**　　　　　　45 rpm　　　　　　BLACK LABEL
Loving You/Loving You
You're not seeing double! It's a case of RCA's putting the same label on both sides. (*Teddy Bear* is sung on the other side.)

49. **RCA 0769**　　　　　　45 rpm　　　　　　ORANGE LABEL
Burning Love/Burning Love
It's a Matter of Time is sung on the other side.

50. **RCA 6604**　　　　　　45 rpm　　　　　　BLACK LABEL
Hound Dog/Don't Be Cruel
On the *Don't Be Cruel* side, Nipper is the only thing to appear on the label.

51. **RCA 0720**　　　　　　45 rpm　　　　　　BLACK LABEL
Wooden Heart is the only label to appear on this one-sided record. The *Blue Christmas* side has no label.

52. **RCA 8950**　　　　　　45 rpm　　　　　　BLACK LABEL
How Would You Like to Be is on one side; the other side features the RCA logo along with Nipper; the song title (*If Every Day Was Like Christmas*) is omitted.
The following records all have Nipper missing from the label:

53. **RCA 6800**　　　　　　45 rpm　　　　　　BLACK LABEL

54. **RCA EPA-1254**　　　　45 rpm Double　　　BLACK LABEL
　　　　　　　　　　　　　EP

55. **RCA EPA-821**　　　　45 rpm EP　　　　　BLACK LABEL

56. **RCA EPA-965**　　　　45 rpm EP　　　　　BLACK LABEL

57.	**RCA EPA-993**	45 rpm EP	BLACK LABEL
58.	**RCA EPA-994**	45 rpm EP	BLACK LABEL
59.	**RCA EPA-4006**	45 rpm EP	BLACK LABEL
60.	**Reader's Digest Presents Elvis Presley**	33⅓ Single	BLACK LABEL

This extremely rare record was issued on thin plastic to promote the *Reader's Digest* box set. It featured interviews and songs that were considered representative of Elvis' entire career.

| 61. | **RCA** | Original acetate (RCA printed in red) | WHITE LABEL |

The Next Step Is Love/I've Lost You
An "acetate" exists for every record made. Acetates are used for the original pressing.

| 62. | **Special Sun Acetate** | 12″ single |

Mystery Train
This is the actual acetate that was used in pressing the Sun record *Mystery Train*.

| 63. | **March of Dimes Galaxy of Stars** |

This record is known as *March of Dimes Presents Elvis* among Presley collectors. This is a biggie literally, because of its value—$8,000—and its 16-inch size. Elvis sings *Love Me Tender* and can be heard making a pitch for the March of Dimes. This program was to be used between January 2 and 21 of 1957. The radio programmer was instructed to destroy the disc after the one-time use.

261

64. Memphis Flash

Beginnings—Elvis Style—Parts I and II

This record came on a black label and was the first disc to feature the *Memphis Flash* logo. The record contains the earliest documented recorded Elvis interview and features Scotty Moore; Bill Black; Elvis' manager at that time, Bob Neal; and of course the King of western bop, Elvis Presley. This interview was recorded in late 1954.

65. RCA 10857

Moody Blue/She Thinks I Still Care

BLACK LABEL   DOG AT TOP RIGHT-HAND CORNER

Most fans are aware that Elvis' last LP came on translucent blue plastic. However, five copies of the RCA 45 rpm were pressed on the same translucent blue plastic.

66. RCA JB 10998

Way Down/Pledging My Love (stereo)

WHITE LABEL   DOG AT TOP RIGHT-HAND CORNER

This was an advance copy of what would be Elvis' last new single while he was alive. It's so rare that many of RCA's own promotion department are not aware of its existence.

262

LONG-PLAYING ALBUMS

1. **Metro-Goldwyn-
   Mayer Presents
   Speedway**

This 33⅓ LP contained the radio spots for the film *Speedway*.

2. **RCA LPM-1990**   33⅓ LP

This copy of *For LP Fans Only* had the same front and back cover (very rare).

3. **RCA PRS 279**   33⅓ LP

Singer Presents Elvis Singing Flaming Star and Others
This LP was released before RCA began issuing Elvis' LPs on their Camden label. It was issued as a tie-in for Elvis' 1968 TV special sponsored by Singer. It was on sale only at Singer sewing machine centers.

4. **Having Fun with
   Elvis on Stage**

"Boxcar Records" is the name of Colonel Parker's record label. Colonel Parker was given permission to release this LP in 1974 by RCA. He sold it in Vegas and at the other tour stops. It was a talking album, with no music at all. RCA later released it on its own label.

5. **Buddah Records
   Current Audio
   Magazine, Volume 1**

In 1972 Buddah released this LP, which had excerpts from Elvis' historic Madison Square Garden Press Conference. This LP was deleted after being on the market for sixty days.

6. **RCA 0056**   33⅓ LP

Elvis
Brookville Marketing put this special TV package together, selling over three million copies. The LP was available only through TV.

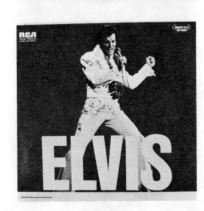

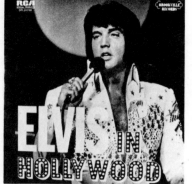

7. **RCA-0168**   33⅓ LP

Elvis in Hollywood

The record-breaking sales of the best-selling Elvis book *Elvis in Hollywood* didn't go unnoticed by the crafty Colonel Parker. In an attempt to cash in on the giant success of the book, Parker called Brookville Marketing. Together they sold the package of *Elvis in Hollywood* on TV. It is a two-record set.

8. **RCA 213690**   33⅓ Double LP

Worldwide Gold Award Hits, Parts 1 and 2

This special RCA release featured half of the four-record set LPM 6401.

9. **RCA 213736**   33⅓ Double LP

Chicken of the Sea Presents Aloha from Hawaii

Naturally, Chicken of the Sea was the sponsor of the Aloha special. It issued this special stereo copy of *Aloha* for its employees.

10. **RCA 0197**   33⅓ 10″ LP

E-Z Pop Programming No. 6

This RCA 10-inch sampler featured one song by Elvis, *I Was the One*. It was issued in 1956.

11. **RCA 9682**   33⅓ 12″ LP

E-Z Pop Programming No. 5

This RCA 12-inch sampler, which featured two songs by Elvis (*Mystery Train* and *I Forgot to Remember to Forget*), was issued in 1956.

12. **RCA SP 33-461**   33⅓ LP

Special Palm Sunday LP

This was a complete half-hour program with spot announcements and selections from LPM-3758.

13. **RCA SP 33-247**   33⅓ LP

December 1963 Popular Sampler

This featured songs from movie soundtracks released in 1963 by RCA. Elvis sings *Fun in Acapulco*.

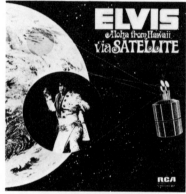

LONG-PLAYING ALBUMS

14. **RCA SP 33-571**   33⅓ Double LP

    Elvis As Recorded at Madison Square Garden
    This special product featured longer songs and was a banded LP.

15. **RCA SP-0606**   33⅓ LP

    Recorded Live on Stage in Memphis
    This is a specially banded LP.

16. **RCA SP-0086**

    The Brightest Stars of Christmas
    Elvis sings *Here Comes Santa Claus* on this special holiday release.

The following list of various artists' LPs does not include any armed forces LPs. Although the number of any particular LP released by the military is small, there are far too many different LPs from every branch of the service to list here.

Also, every album by Economic Consultants has been discontinued. RCA ended up taking the case to the Supreme Court, and finally got a court ruling preventing Economic Consultants from making the records.

17. **Economic**   33⅓ LP
    Consultants

    Journey into Yesterday, 1956
    Elvis sings *Blue Suede Shoes* and *Tutti Frutti* on this LP.

18. **Economic**   33⅓ LP
    Consultants

    Journey into Yesterday, 1969
    Elvis sings *Suspicious Minds* and *In the Ghetto.*

19. **Economic**   33⅓ LP
    Consultants

    Old and Heavy Gold, 1956
    Elvis sings *Heartbreak Hotel; I Want You, I Need You, I Love You; Hound Dog; Don't Be Cruel;* and *Love Me Tender.*

20. **Economic**   33⅓ LP
    Consultants

    Old and Heavy Gold, 1957
    Elvis sings *Loving You; Teddy Bear;* and *All Shook Up/That's When Your Heartaches Begin.*

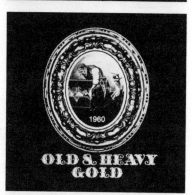

21. **Economic Consultants** 33⅓ LP

Old and Heavy Gold, 1958
Elvis sings *Don't.*

22. **Economic Consultants** 33⅓ LP

Old and Heavy Gold, 1960
Elvis sings *It's Now or Never* and *Stuck on You.*

23. **Economic Consultants** 33⅓ LP

Old and Heavy Gold, 1961
Elvis sings *Surrender.*

24. **Economic Consultants** 33⅓ LP

Old and Heavy Gold, 1962
Elvis sings *Return to Sender* and *Good Luck Charm.*

25. **Economic Consultants** 33⅓ LP

Country and Western Classics, 1955
Elvis sings *Mystery Train* and *I Forgot to Remember to Forget.*

26. **Economic Consultants** 33⅓ LP

Country and Western Classics, 1956
Elvis sings *Heartbreak Hotel; I Was The One; Love Me Tender; Hound Dog; I Want You, I Need You, I Love You;* and *My Baby Left Me.*

27. **Economic Consultants** 33⅓ LP

Country and Western Classics, 1957
Elvis sings *Teddy Bear; Too Much; Jailhouse Rock;* and *All Shook Up.*

28. **Economic**   33⅓ LP
     Consultants

Country and Western Classics, 1958
Elvis sings *Don't.*

29. **Omega Records**   33⅓ LP

Country Super Sounds, 1956
Elvis sings *I Want You, I Need You, I Love You; Hound Dog; Heartbreak Hotel;* and *Don't Be Cruel.*

30. **Omega Records**   33⅓ LP

Country Super Sounds, 1957
Elvis sings *Loving You; Too Much; Jailhouse Rock;* and *All Shook Up.*

31. **Omega Records**   33⅓ LP

Country Super Sounds, 1958
Elvis sings *Wear My Ring Around Your Neck.*

Bootlegs

Although there has been much pressure from Colonel Parker and RCA, bootlegging continues to be a very lucrative and flourishing business. The fact that bootlegs are illegal makes them very hard to come by. This makes the pirated record even more desirable to the avid Elvis collector.

Many of Elvis' bootleg records have professional sleeves and good sound quality. In many cases these records have true historical value. One of the biggest problems concerning the buying of bootleg records is the common practice that has arisen among bootleggers to bootleg bootlegs. In most cases, when this occurs, the bootlegged bootleg loses sound quality, and in place of the original full-color cover, has a plain white cover.

Whatever the morality and the arguments concerning bootlegs, the fact remains that the bootleggers are making up to 1000 per cent profit on each record. They charge top dollar for their product and do not pay the artist or the record company royalties!

The following is a list of the best of Elvis' bootleg records, along with song titles and sound quality ratings.

268

BOOTLEG 45 RPM SINGLES

1. **Please Release Me** 45 rpm

    Baby, Let's Play House/My Baby Is Gone

    This was the first Elvis bootleg single and was derived from the bootleg LP of the same name. The record is on the Sun label and came in a picture sleeve. *My Baby Is Gone* is a slow version of *I'm Left, You're Right, She's Gone*. Credit is given to Aaron P., Scotty and Bill.

    SOUND QUALITY: GOOD   MADE IN ENGLAND

2. **My Baby's Gone/** 45 rpm
    That's All Right

    This record was issued on the Hillbilly Cat label and featured the above-captioned unreleased Sun song along with Elvis' first Sun release (*That's All Right*). The record did not have a picture sleeve, and artist credit was given to Scotty and Bill.

    SOUND QUALITY: GOOD   MADE IN AMERICA

3. **Please Release Me** 45 rpm

    My Baby's Gone/My Baby's Gone

    This record didn't come with a picture sleeve and was yet another boot of the original *Please Release Me*. The same unreleased Sun song was on both sides, and artist credit was given to "The Original Pelvis" with Scotty and Bill.

    SOUND QUALITY: GOOD   MADE IN AMERICA

4. **Elvis Presley Radio** 45 rpm
    Special

    Shake, Rattle and Roll/I Got a Woman

    This is one of my favorite bootlegs because of its historical value. The record came in a beautiful picture cover and was on the White Knight label. Both songs, as well as a bit of *Flip, Flop and Fly*, were from Elvis' first TV appearance on the Dorsey Brothers show. Artist credit is given to the "Blue Moon Boys."

    SOUND QUALITY: FAIR   MADE IN AMERICA

5. **The Satellite** 45 rpm
    Supplement

    Blue Hawaii/Hawaiian Wedding Song

    This record came in a picture cover and was on the Shaker label. Both songs were taken from the studio portions of Elvis' "Aloha" special. Artist credit is given to "The King."

    SOUND QUALITY: FAIR   MADE IN AMERICA

6. **The Satellite** 45 rpm
    Supplement

    Ku-u-i-po/Nostalgia Party

    Ku-u-i-po is lifted from the "Aloha" show, and *Nostalgia Party* is a novelty record from the fifties featuring Elvis with various artists. The record came in a picture sleeve and was on the Shaker label.

    SOUND QUALITY: FAIR   MADE IN AMERICA

7. **Elvis Speaks**   45 rpm

Press Conference, New York, 1972/The Truth About Me, 1956

This record had a beautiful color sleeve and featured Elvis' Madison Square Garden Press Conference (Original Sound label).

SOUND QUALITY: EXCELLENT   MADE IN ENGLAND

8. **Sun Bootlegs**   45 rpm

Sun 209 *That's All Right/Blue Moon of Kentucky*
Sun 210 *Good Rockin' Tonight/I Don't Care if the Sun Don't Shine*
Sun 215 *You're a Heartbreaker/Milkcow Blues Boogie*
Sun 217 *Baby, Let's Play House/I'm Left, You're Right, She's Gone*
Sun 223 *Mystery Train/I Forgot to Remember to Forget*

All of these boots are exact duplicates of the original Sun recordings—the records are perfect copies down to the smallest detail. They were available in red, blue, purple, green, orange, and yellow transparent plastic. Only three sets of all five records were made in multicolored plastic. These are even rarer than the original Sun records.

SOUND QUALITY: PERFECT   MADE IN AMERICA

9. **Sun 224**

Hound Dog/I Want You, I Need You, I Love You

Both of these songs are live versions taken from Elvis' appearance on the Steve Allen TV show on July 1, 1956. They were issued on the Sun label and were available on both black and blue vinyl.

SOUND QUALITY: GOOD   MADE IN AMERICA

270

BOOTLEG EP'S

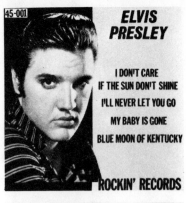

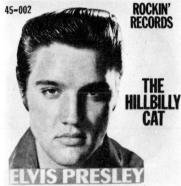

1. **Elvis Presley**   45 EPA

    *I Don't Care if the Sun Don't Shine; I'll Never Let You Go; My Baby
    Is Gone; Blue Moon of Kentucky*

    This EP arrived in a very beautiful color cover and was on Rockin' Records. It was issued with two different back covers.

    SOUND QUALITY: GOOD   MADE IN AMERICA

2. **The Hillbilly Cat**   45 EPA

    Jailhouse Rock (soundtrack); *The Truth About Me; The Lady Loves
    Me; Tryin' to Get to You*

    Once again we have a beautiful color cover and a Rockin' Records label. *The Lady Loves Me* is from *Viva Las Vegas* and features Ann-Margret.

    SOUND QUALITY: GOOD   MADE IN AMERICA

3. **Vegas EPs** (two-
    record set)   45 EPA

    Volume 1: *Never Been to Spain; Lord, This Time You Gave Me a Mountain; Proud Mary; Love Me*

    Volume 2: *Hound Dog* (blues version;) *A Big Hunk o' Love; I'm Leaving It Up to You; American Trilogy*

    This double EP was on Vegas records and did not have a picture sleeve. All the songs were derived from Elvis' 1971 Vegas shows. *I'm Leaving It Up to You* has never been released and so is available only on this record.

    SOUND QUALITY: POOR   MADE IN CANADA

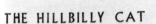

4. **Old Gold**   45 EPA

    Side 1: *Truth About Me; The Lady Loves Me*
    Side 2: *My Baby's Gone; Jailhouse Rock* (soundtrack)

    All songs are repeats of other bootlegs; however, the cover has a great 1950s shot of Elvis. This record was on the Pelvis label.

    SOUND QUALITY: GOOD   MADE IN AMERICA

5. **Mr. Rock 'n' Roll**   45 EPA

    Side 1: *Fame and Fortune; Stuck on You* (from the Frank Sinatra TV Special)

    Side 2: *The Truth About Me;* 1972 Press Conference

    This EP had a nice picture sleeve and was on Pelvis records.

    SOUND QUALITY: FAIR   MADE IN EUROPE

6. **King of Rock 'n'**   45 EPA
   Roll

   Blue Suede Shoes; One-sided Love Affair; Hound Dog; Ready Teddy; Baby, I Don't Care; Got a Lot o' Livin' to Do

   This EP was on the Sunrise label and came in a fantastic cover that opened into pages of great fifties shots. All of the songs were the same as the original versions.

   SOUND QUALITY: EXCELLENT   MADE IN MALAYSIA

7. **(Untitled)**   45 EPA

   My Baby Is Gone; Instrumental version of *I Don't Care; Jailhouse Rock; Treat Me Nice* (soundtrack); *A Cane and a High Starched Collar;* "Ed Sullivan" medley; *Heartbreak Hotel; Love Me Tender; Peace in the Valley*

   This was the first bootleg EP. It came in a plain white cover. The label was white also, with no writing on it. This EP is in great demand by collectors all over the world.

   SOUND QUALITY: POOR   MADE IN PARIS

As should be obvious, the value of a bootleg is not always dependent upon sound quality. In most cases, collectors seek a particular boot because of its rarity rather than its content.

BOOTLEG LP'S

1. **Elvis Live on Stage,**   10″ 33⅓ LP
   Hilton Hotel 1972

   This LP finds the King at his best; it was recorded during Elvis' Summer Festival of August 1972. The cover has an outstanding color action shot. This LP is on the Original Sound label.

   Side 1: *Theme, 2001; See See Rider; You Don't Have to Say You Love Me; Polk Salad Annie; You've Lost That Loving Feeling*

   Side 2: *What Now, My Love; Fever;* Introductions/*Love Me; Blue Suede Shoes; All Shook Up; Heartbreak Hotel; I'll Remember You*

   SOUND QUALITY: EXCELLENT   MADE IN ENGLAND

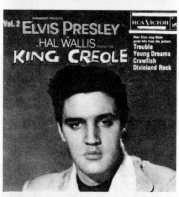

2. **King Creole**   10″ 33⅓ LP

   This LP has the same beautiful cover as the *King Creole* EP, Volume II. The label is Original Sound.

   Side 1: *King Creole; As Long As I Have You; Hard-headed Woman; Trouble; Dixieland Rock*

   Side 2: *Don't Ask Me Why; Lover Doll; Crawfish; Young Dreams; Steadfast, Loyal and True; New Orleans*

   SOUND QUALITY: EXCELLENT   MADE IN ENGLAND

3. **Janis and Elvis**   10″ 33⅓ LP

   A fantastic color photo graces the cover of this beauty. It is a boot of the legendary South African LP *Janis Martin and Elvis Presley.* Once again, the LP is on the Original Sound label.

272

Side 1: *Ooby Dooby; I'm Left, You're Right, She's Gone; One More Year to Go; You're a Heartbreaker; I Forgot to Remember to Forget*
Side 2: *My Boy Elvis; All Right, Baby; Mystery Train; Will You, William; Baby, Let's Play House*
SOUND QUALITY: EXCELLENT   MADE IN ENGLAND

4. **The Hillbilly Cat**   Double 33⅓ LP
    "Live"

   This LP is perhaps the most sought-after bootleg in the world. All songs are from the 1969 Vegas shows. The song *When the Snow Falls on the Roses* has not been released by Elvis.
Side 1: *That's All Right; I Got a Woman; Tiger Man; Love Me Tender; I've Lost You; I Just Can't Help Believin'*
Side 2: *You've Lost That Loving Feeling; Polk Salad Annie;* Introductions/ *Johnny B. Good; Wonder of You; Heartbreak Hotel; One Night*
Side 3: *All Shook Up; Blue Suede Shoes; Whole Lotta Shakin' Goin' On; Hound Dog; Bridge over Troubled Water; Suspicious Minds; Release Me; Can't Help Falling in Love*
Side 4 (bonus songs): *I Got a Woman; Ave Maria; Polk Salad Annie; Heartbreak Hotel; One Night; Hound Dog; When the Snow Falls on the Roses*
SOUND QUALITY: POOR   MADE IN CANADA

5. **Please Release Me**   33⅓ LP

   This LP is on the First label and has the same cover as the single.
Side 1: *Fame and Fortune* (Frank Sinatra show); *Stuck on You* (Sinatra show); *Teddy Bear* (soundtrack); *Got a Lot o' Livin' to Do* (soundtrack); *Jailhouse Rock* (soundtrack); *A Cane and a High Starched Collar* (soundtrack)
Side 2: *The Lady Loves Me; C'mon, Everybody; Dominique* (soundtrack); *Baby, What You Want Me to Do; My Baby Is Gone;* interview
SOUND QUALITY: FAIR   MADE IN ENGLAND

6. **I Wanna Be a Rock**   33⅓ LP
    'n' Roll Star

   This album has a nice front and back cover and is on the Vicktorie label. It featured almost all the tracks of the *Please Release Me* LP along with *Wild in the Country; The Truth About Me*, and *My Baby Is Gone.*
SOUND QUALITY: GOOD   MADE IN ENGLAND

7. **Elvis Presley: The**   33⅓ LP
    Best Years

   This is the same LP, including the label, as the above album. This time the cover had a color photo from the 1968 TV special.
SOUND QUALITY: GOOD   MADE IN AMERICA

8. **Live Experience in**   33⅓ LP
   Vegas . . . February
   1971

This album was made by the same people who made *The Hillbilly Cat "Live"* LP. The record arrived in a beautiful color cover (Elvis wore a black jumpsuit) and was on the Bonthond label. The back cover states that it was made in Holland, but the LP was really made in Canada. The record features live versions of *Get Back* and *Little Sister.* These versions have not yet been releasd by RCA.

Side 1: *That's All Right; I Got a Woman; Jailhouse Rock; Love Me; Mystery Train; Tiger Man; Polk Salad Annie; Sweet Caroline; You've Lost That Loving Feeling; Something; Johnny B. Good*

Side 2: *How Great Thou Art; Don't Be Cruel; Heartbreak Hotel; Blue Suede Shoes; Little Sister; Get Back; Now or Never; Hound Dog; The Impossible Dream*

SOUND QUALITY: VERY GOOD   MADE IN CANADA

9. **From the Dark, to**   33⅓ LP
   the Light!

This LP came in a pink and black cover and featured complete song soundtracks, including rehearsal dialogue, from *That's the Way It Is* and *Elvis on Tour.* The record was on the Tiger label.

Side 1: *That's the Way It Is*

Side 2: *Elvis on Tour ("The King on Tour")*

SOUND QUALITY: GOOD   MADE IN PARIS

10. **The Monologue**   33⅓ LP
    L.P.

This album was issued by Bullet Records and came in a black and white picture cover. All songs are derived from Elvis' opening night in Vegas in 1969. The most interesting thing on the LP is the five-minute monologue that Elvis delivers.

Side 1: *The King Ta'ks About His Career; Jailhouse Rock; Don't Be Cruel; Memories; Lawdy, Miss Clawdy; Until It's Time for You to Go; Oh Happy Day; Sweet Inspiration; More*

Side 2: *Hey, Jude; What Now, My Love; Are You Laughing Tonight?; I John; Baby, What You Want Me to Do; I'm Leaving; What'd I Say*

SOUND QUALITY: FAIR   MADE IN AMERICA

11. **The King Goes**   33⅓ LP
    Wild

Issued on the Wilde label, this LP was the first boot to feature all three Ed Sullivan shows. The cover is outstanding.

Side 1: September 9, 1956—*Don't Be Cruel; Love Me Tender; Ready Teddy; Hound Dog;* October 28, 1956—*Don't Be Cruel; Love Me Tender; Love Me; Hound Dog*

Side 2: January 6, 1957—*Hound Dog; Love Me Tender; Heartbreak Hotel; Don't Be Cruel; Too Much; When My Blue Moon Turns to Gold Again; Peace in the Valley*

SOUND QUALITY: EXCELLENT   MADE IN CANADA

12. **Good Rocking**   33⅓ LP
    Tonight

This is one of the best boots ever made. One side features Elvis, and the other side features various Sun artists. This LP was issued on the Bopcat label and sports a very interesting cover. It contains alternate and unissued Sun tracks. There is some dialogue between takes featuring Sam Phillips and Elvis.

Side 1 (remember, these are all different versions of the Sun classics): *Good Rockin' Tonight; My Baby Is Gone; I Don't Care if the Sun Don't Shine; Blue Moon of Kentucky; I'll Never Let You Go; Mystery Train; I Forgot to Remember to Forget*

Side 2: Unreleased tracks by Jerry Lee Lewis, Warren Smith, and Billy Lee Riley

SOUND QUALITY: EXCELLENT   MADE IN HOLLAND

13. **Elvis**   33⅓ LP

This is a boot of a bootleg. It was issued on the King Kong label and came in a poor cartoon-like cover.

Side 1: Same as Elvis side on *Good Rocking* LP

Side 2: *Teen Parade; Teddy Bear; Got a Lot o' Livin' to Do; Treat Me Nice; Jailhouse Rock;* 1958 interviews

SOUND QUALITY: FAIR   MADE IN AMERICA

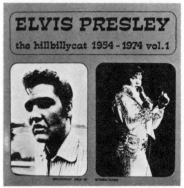

14. **The Hillbillycat,**   33⅓ LP
    1954–1974,
    Volume 1

The cover of this LP featured "then and now" photos. One side of the Brookville label featured two of the Sullivan shows, with a few unreleased RCA songs on the other side.

Side 1: September 9, 1956—*Don't Be Cruel; Love Me Tender; Ready Teddy; Hound Dog;* October 28, 1956—*Don't Be Cruel; Love Me Tender; Love Me; Hound Dog*

Side 2: *Rags to Riches; First Time Ever I Saw Your Face; It's Only Love; The Sound of Your Cry; Come What May; Where Did They Go, Lord; Let Me*

SOUND QUALITY: GOOD   MADE IN HOLLAND

15. **From Hollywood to**   33⅓ LP
    Vegas

This LP is once again issued by Brookville Records and featured unreleased movie material as well as Vegas (live) songs.

Side 1: *Loving You* (soundtrack); *Husky Dusky Day* (soundtrack); *On Top of Old Smokey* (soundtrack); *Dainty Little Moonbeams* (soundtrack); *Girls! Girls! Girls!* (soundtrack); *Auralee* (soundtrack); *Signs of the Zodiac* (soundtrack); *Folsom Prison Blues* (Vegas); *I Walk the Line* (Vegas); *Oh Happy Day* (Vegas)

Side 2: *I Need Your Loving Every Day* (Vegas); *I Ain't About to Sing* (Vegas); *I Got a Woman* (Vegas); *Amen* (Vegas); *Crying Time* (Vegas); *Lovely Mamie* (soundtrack); *Long Tall Sally* (Vegas); *Flip, Flop and Fly* (Vegas) *My Boy* (Vegas); *Hound Dog* (Vegas); "Aloha" Press Conference

SOUND QUALITY: POOR   MADE IN HOLLAND

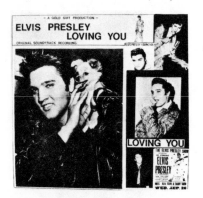

16. **From Las Vegas**   33⅓ Double LP
    . . . to Niagara
    Falls

Here's another double LP from the people who gave us *The Hillbilly Cat "Live"* double LP. The album features Elvis' Las Vegas dinner show of September 3, 1973, and Niagara Falls concert of June 24, 1974.
Side 1: *See See Rider; I Got a Woman; Amen; Love Me; Steamroller Blues; You Gave Me a Mountain; Trouble;* rock medley
Side 2: *Love Me Tender; Fever; Suspicious Minds; My Boy; I Can't Stop Loving You; Teddy Bear; Don't Be Cruel; First Time Ever I Saw Your Face; Can't Help Falling in Love*
Side 3: *See See Rider; I Got a Woman; Love Me; Trying to Get to You; All Shook Up; Love Me Tender; Hound Dog; Fever; Polk Salad Annie*
Side 4: *Why Me, Lord; Suspicious Minds; I Can't Stop Loving You; Help Me; American Trilogy; Let Me Be There; Funny How Time Slips Away; Big Boss Man; Teddy Bear; Don't Be Cruel; Can't Help Falling in Love*
SOUND QUALITY: POOR   MADE IN CANADA

17. **Loving You**   33⅓ LP

This album had a nice front and back cover and was issued on the Gold Suit label. Highlighting the LP is the "Louisiana Hayride" recording and the *March of Dimes Presents Elvis.*
Side 1: All songs from the *Loving You* soundtrack.
Side 2: *Loving You* (soundtrack); *Got a Lot o' Livin' to Do* (soundtrack); *Crawfish* (soundtrack); *Love Me Tender* (cut version); *I Wanna Be Free* (soundtrack); *Love Me Tender; Ready Teddy* (both from "The Ed Sullivan Show"); *Love Me;* Elvis for the March of Dimes; *Blue Moon of Kentucky* ("Louisiana Hayride" show)
SOUND QUALITY: POOR   MADE IN AUSTRALIA

18. **Elvis Talks Back**   33⅓ LP

This album had a horrible cover and consisted strictly of interviews. It was issued on the Sound News label.
Side 1: Interview, 1957
Side 2: Herman's Hermits Interview Elvis; Colonel Parker interview, 1965; *Charro!* interview
SOUND QUALITY: GOOD   MADE IN ENGLAND

19. **TV Guide Presents**   33⅓ LP
    Elvis

What an outstanding album! Everything about this bootleg is first-class. It features an excellent front and back cover and was on the Graceland label.
Side 1: Steve Allen TV show, July 1, 1956 (all songs); *TV Guide Presents Elvis* (interview)
Side 2: Hy Gardener Interview, 1956; Frank Sinatra Timex Special (all songs, including *Witchcraft; Love Me Tender;* duet with Sinatra)
SOUND QUALITY: VERY GOOD   MADE IN AMERICA

20. **The Nashville**   33⅓ LP
    Outtakes and Early
    Interviews

This record is on the Wizardo label and is another example of a bootlegged boot.

Side 1: The same as the *Good Rocking Tonight* LP
Side 2: The same as *The Monologue L.P.*
SOUND QUALITY: POOR   MADE IN AMERICA

21. **Elvis on Stage in**   33⅓ LP
     the U.S.A.

This is another LP from our friends at Wizardo.
Sides 1 and 2: The same as the Monologue L.P., minus the monologue.
SOUND QUALITY: POOR   MADE IN AMERICA

22. **All About Elvis,**   33⅓ LP
     Volume I

This LP featured various artists singing novelty tunes about Elvis.
Side 1: *United Press News—Comments About Elvis; Dear Elvis, Part I;
Dear Elvis, Part II; Hey, Mr. Presley; My Boy Elvis; I'm Lonesome for
Elvis; Bye Bye, Elvis; Marching Elvis*
Side 2: *Elwood Pretzel Fan Club, Part I; Elwood Pretzel Fan Club, Part II;
All About Elvis, Part I; All About Elvis, Part II; Oh, Elvis; Elvis Presley
for President; I'm in Love with Elvis Presley; I Wanna Spend Xmas with
Elvis*
SOUND QUALITY: GOOD   MADE IN AMERICA

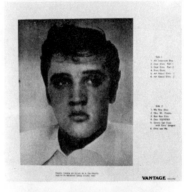

23. **All About Elvis,**   33⅓ LP
     Volume II

Another novelty LP, this one has a great cover that features a picture of
Elvis taken in a twenty-five-cent photo booth in 1952.
Side 1: *All American Boy; Dear Elvis, Part 1; Dear Elvis, Part 2; Elvis
Blues; All About Elvis, Part 1; All About Elvis, Part 2*
Side 2: *My Boy Elvis; Hey, Mr. Presley; Bye Bye, Elvis; Dear 53310761;
Gonna Get Even With Elvis' Sergeant; Elvis and Me*
SOUND QUALITY: GOOD   MADE IN AMERICA

24. **Rock My Soul**   33⅓ LP

This LP was issued on both black and multicolored plastic. It's on the
World label and features the soundtrack from *Elvis on Tour*.
Sides 1 and 2: *Elvis on Tour* soundtrack
SOUND QUALITY: GOOD   MADE IN AMERICA

25. **Elvis King of Las**   33⅓ LP
     Vegas Live

This record is on the Hazbin label and contains the soundtrack to *That's
the Way It Is*.
Sides 1 and 2: *That's the Way It Is* soundtrack
SOUND QUALITY: GOOD   MADE IN AMERICA

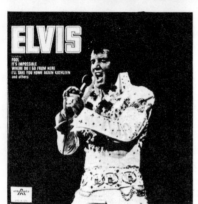

26. Elvis Rock'n Blues   33⅓ LP

Elvis is shown in a beautiful color portrait on the cover of this package. This LP is on the Hal Yen label.

Side 1: *A Mess of Blues; When It Rains, It Really Pours; Shake a Hand; Reconsider, Baby; Stranger in My Hometown*

Side 2: *High-heel Sneakers; Wearing That Loved-on Look; Promised Land; T-R-O-U-B-L-E; Burning Love; Big Hunk o' Love*

SOUND QUALITY: GOOD   MADE IN CHINA

27. The '68 Comeback   33⅓ LP

"Fantastic" is the word for this LP. The sound is so good that I am sure the tapes had to be stolen from RCA. This album features one of the most beautiful covers I've seen. The record is on the Memphis King label. All material is either unreleased or alternate versions of songs from the 1968 TV special.

Side 1: Medley: *Nothingville/Guitar Man/Let Yourself Go/Guitar Man/ Big Boss Man/If I Can Dream; Memories; Let Yourself Go*

Side 2: *It Hurts Me; Trouble; Guitar Man; Sometimes I Feel Like a Motherless Child; Where Could I Go But to the Lord; Saved; A Little Less Conversation*

SOUND QUALITY: RCA-PERFECT   MADE IN AMERICA

28. Elvis   33⅓ LP

This is an Australian boot on the Ambassador label.

Sides 1 and 2: Same as the Australian *Fool* LP.

SOUND QUALITY: EXCELLENT   MADE IN AUSTRALIA

29. Elvis Special,   10″ 33⅓ LP
Volume 1

This is an oddball indeed! The cover is blank, as is the label, on all three volumes.

Side 1: Ed Sullivan Introducing Elvis; *Peace in the Valley;* Ed Sullivan says farewell to Elvis; Army interview

Side 2: *Earthboy* (soundtrack); "Aloha" Press Conference; *Johnny B. Good; Happy Birthday*

SOUND QUALITY: POOR   MADE IN AMERICA

30. Elvis Special,   10″ 33⅓ LP
Volume 2

Side 1: *Peace in the Valley* (live); Uncle Tom's Cabin Interview; *Little Darlin'; Uncle Penn*

Side 2: *Separate Ways* (alternate take); *Burning Love; Ready Teddy; Twelfth of Never*

SOUND QUALITY: FAIR   MADE IN AMERICA

31. Elvis Special,   10″ 33⅓ LP
Volume 3

Side 1: *Little Darlin';* Elvis Speaks; *Stage Fright*

Side 2: *Trying to Get to You* (live, 1957); *Venue; Lonely Teardrops; Ready Teddy; Uncle Penn*

SOUND QUALITY: FAIR   MADE IN AMERICA

278

32. The Magical Rockin' Sound of Elvis Presley   10" 33⅓ LP

This boot came with another beautiful color cover and was on the Jubilee label. Although it claims to have been made in Cambodia, it actually was made in Canada.

Side 1: *First in Line; I Got a Woman; Is It So Strange; I Want to Be Free; Trouble; Lover Doll; Crawfish*

Side 2: *I Love You Because; I Want You, I Need You, I Love You; Dixieland Rock; Don't Leave Me Now; I'm Gonna Sit Right Down and Cry; Young and Beautiful; Any Way You Want Me*

SOUND QUALITY: GOOD   MADE IN CANADA

33. 19 Elvis Presley Great Hits   33⅓ LP

There is nothing new on this LP with the Rex label. The cover is very pretty.

Side 1: *I Just Can't Help Believin'; Love Me Tender; I Gotta Know; Surrender; Are You Lonesome Tonight; Little Sister; Good Luck Charm; In the Ghetto; The Wonder of You*

Side 2: *Don't Be Cruel; One Night; Now or Never; Jailhouse Rock; No More; Moonlight Swim; King Creole; Kiss Me Quick; Life; Devil in Disguise*

SOUND QUALITY: GOOD   MADE IN ENGLAND

34. Sold Out   33⅓ LP

This LP could easily be called *The Best of the Boots, Volume 1*. The material on this album, with a few exceptions, was derived from other bootleg LPs. This is a most interesting LP that features an excellent cover. The record is on the E.P. label.

Side 1: *Burning Love; Lawdy, Miss Clawdy; T-R-O-U-B-L-E; I'm Leavin'; When the Snow Is on the Roses; Need Your Lovin' Every Day; Little Sister/ Get Back; Steamroller Blues; rock medley; Walk the Lonesome Road; Help Me Make It Through the Night; Faded Love*

Side 2: *Heartbreak Hotel; One Night; Reconsider, Baby; Mystery Train/ Tiger Man; Jailhouse Rock; Teddy Bear/Don't Be Cruel; I John; Softly As I Leave; It's Now or Never; My Babe; Sweet Sweet Spirit; I'm Leaving It Up to You; I Got a Woman; What'd I Say*

SOUND QUALITY: FAIR   MADE IN CANADA

35. Elvis Presley Is Alive and Well and Singing in Las Vegas

This album comes in a striking front cover, but don't judge the album by that. It is comprised of Elvis' Vegas appearances of 1974 and 1975. The label is blank.

Side 1: *Big Boss Man; If You Love Me Let Me Know; Until It's Time for You to Go; If You Talk in Your Sleep; Hawaiian Wedding Song; Early Morning Rain; Softly As I Leave You; Amen; How Great Thou Art*

Side 2: *T-R-O-U-B-L-E; And I Love You So; Green Green Grass of Home; Fairytale; Happy Birthday, James Burton;* Glenn D. Hardin solo; *Young and Beautiful; It's Now or Never; Burning Love*

SOUND QUALITY: POOR   MADE IN FRANCE

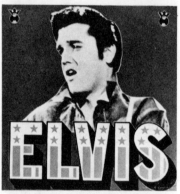

36. Elvis Dorsey Shows

This LP is on the Golden Archives label and was brought to you by the famed Maryland pirate who produced *The '68 Comeback* and *TV Guide Presents*. This album consists of Elvis' legendary appearances on the Dorsey Brothers show.

This bootlegger has excelled again!

Side 1: *Blue Suede Shoes; Heartbreak Hotel; Tutti Frutti; I Was the One; Shake, Rattle and Roll; I Got a Woman*

Side 2: *Baby, Let's Play House; Tutti Frutti; Blue Suede Shoes; Heartbreak Hotel; Money Honey; Heartbreak Hotel*

SOUND QUALITY: EXCELLENT   MADE IN AMERICA

37. Got a Lot o' Livin' to Do!

Although the credits list this LP as having been made in Malaysia, it was in fact, pressed in Los Angeles. The front and back cover contain some never-before-seen photos from the fifties. It is on the Pirate label. Of particular interest are the live excerpts from the Vancouver and Dick Clark shows.

Side 1: *Jailhouse Rock* soundtrack; Dick Clark interviews

Side 2: *Loving You* soundtrack; Vancouver, Canada, excerpts (live performance and short interview)

SOUND QUALITY: VERY GOOD   MADE IN AMERICA

38. Elvis

This 10-inch LP featured a nice cover and a rather interesting label. The label had a line drawing of Elvis, which is the official seal of the German fan club. The release also came with the following warning: "This LP is only for the own use"—it should have read "home use." I guess this proves you don't have to be able to spell to make bootleg records. This LP was issued on the Neuphone label.

Side 1: *Change of Habit* (soundtrack); *Rubberneckin'* (soundtrack); *Spring Fever* (soundtrack); *Girl Happy* (soundtrack); *Shake, Rattle and Roll* (Dorsey show, 1956); *Party* (soundtrack); *Happy Ending* (soundtrack)

Side 2: *Kiss Me Quick; Suspicion; Let Me;* Departure from the U.S.A.; Arrival in Germany, 1958; Arrival in the U.S.A., 1959; *Love Me Tender* (last verse)

SOUND QUALITY: FAIR   MADE IN GERMANY

39. Elvis: A Way of Life, Volume 1

Great title, great cover, and a special 10-inch LP. It's most unfortunate that the material isn't as good as the package. All songs are lifted from earlier bootleg releases. This record was released on the Neuphone label.

Side 1: *Party* (soundtrack); *Shake, Rattle and Roll* (Dorsey show); *I Got a Woman* (Dorsey show); *Girl Happy* (soundtrack); *Spring Fever* (soundtrack); *Happy Ending* (soundtrack)

Side 2: *That's The Way It Is* (rehearsals)

SOUND QUALITY: FAIR   MADE IN GERMANY

40. Trouble in Vegas

The title would indicate that this LP has something to do with Elvis' much publicized scuffle while performing in Las Vegas in 1973. The fact is that this LP has nothing to do with the famous brawl. In spite of this, col-

280

lectors everywhere are willing to pay top dollar for this rare bootleg, issued on a blank label.

Side 1: *C'mon, Everybody; Dominique; Memphis, Tennessee* (Vegas, 1973); *Hound Dog* (Vegas, 1972); *A Big Hunk o' Love* (Vegas, 1972); *Got a Lot o' Livin' to Do; Treat Me Nice;* early interview, 1956; *Witchcraft* (Sinatra show); *Wild in the Country*

Side 2: *An American Trilogy* (Vegas, 1972); *My Baby Is Gone; Baby, What You Want Me to Do* (Vegas, 1969); *A Cane and a High Starched Collar; The Lady Loves Me*

SOUND QUALITY: POOR   MADE IN FRANCE

41. The Legend Lives On

It would be hard to say enough good things about this incredible LP. I'll start by saying that, in my opinion, this album is the best Elvis LP released in the seventies. The gorgeous color photograph used for the front cover must be seen to be fully appreciated. This is without a doubt Elvis' best live recording. A picture of the King can be found on the Presley collection series label.

Side 1: Las Vegas, 1969: Elvis talks about his career; *Yesterday/Hey, Jude* medley; introduction and *Happy Birthday (James Burton); In the Ghetto; Suspicious Minds*

Side 2: *What'd I Say; Can't Help Falling in Love; It's Over* (Vegas, 1972); *A Big Hunk o' Love* (Vegas, 1972); *It's Impossible* (Vegas, 1972); *The Impossible Dream* (Vegas, 1972); *Bridge over Troubled Water* (studio, June 5, 1970)

SOUND QUALITY: EXCELLENT   MADE IN AMERICA

42. Superstar Outtakes

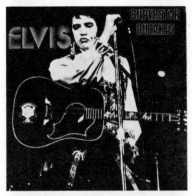

This album came in a beautiful book-like cover. It also featured a picture of Elvis on the EP label. The competition between the bootleggers peaked with this Presleyana release. The entire side 2 was copied from *The Legend Lives On.*

Side 1: Steve Allen TV show, July 1, 1956: *I Want You, I Need You, I Love You; Hound Dog;* Comedy sketch; NBC December 1968 TV special; *Let Yourself Go; It Hurts Me*

Side 2: Las Vegas, August 1969: *Yesterday/Hey, Jude;* Elvis talks; introduction of the band; *Happy Birthday, James Burton; In the Ghetto; Suspicious Minds; What'd I Say; Can't Help Falling in Love; Bridge over Troubled Water* (studio, 1970)

SOUND QUALITY: EXCELLENT   MADE IN CANADA

43. From the Waist Up

A beautiful color photo from 1954 could be found on the front cover. The package included a bonus poster. The subject matter found on this Golden Archives release was from the Ed Sullivan shows.

Side 1: *Don't Be Cruel* (September 9, 1956); *Love Me Tender* (September 9, 1956); *Hound Dog* (September 9, 1956); *Don't Be Cruel* (October 28, 1956); *Love Me Tender* (October 28, 1956); *Hound Dog* (October 28, 1956)

Side 2: *Hound Dog* (January 6, 1957); *Love Me Tender* (January 6, 1957); *Heartbreak Hotel* (January 6, 1957); *Don't Be Cruel* (January 6, 1957); *Peace in the Valley* (January 6, 1957); *Too Much* (January 6, 1957); *When My Blue Moon Turns to Gold Again* (January 6, 1957)

SOUND QUALITY: FAIR   MADE IN AMERICA

44. Rockin' with Elvis New Year's Eve

There are twenty-eight songs on this double LP. They consist of Elvis' entire New Year's Eve performance in Pittsburgh, Pennsylvania, December 31, 1976. This Bicentennial package features sixteen gorgeous color photos of the King in action. These photos were taken by the well-known Elvis photographer Bob Heis. With the exception of LOC-1035 (*Elvis' Christmas Album*) this is the finest Elvis cover release to date. The record appears on the Spirit of America label. One final note: the bootleggers have learned a lesson from Colonel Parker and RCA. The inner sleeve advertises six other great Elvis albums made by the bootleggers. Their slogan: "Be sure you have these great Elvis albums in your collection . . . because you deserve the best!"

Side 1: *2001 Theme; See See Rider; I Got a Woman; Amen; Big Boss Man; Love Me; Fairytale*

Side 2: *Lord, You Gave Me a Mountain; Jailhouse Rock;* Presentation of Liberty Bell by Jim Curtin; *Now or Never* (with introduction by Sherril Nielson); *My Way; Funny How Time Slips Away; Auld Lang Syne;* Introduction of Vernon and Lisa Presley; *Blue Suede Shoes; Trying to Get to You*

Side 3: *Polk Salad Annie;* Introductions to band; *Early Morning Rain; What'd I Say; Johnny B. Good;* Ronnie Tutt drum solo; Jerry Scheff solo; Sonny Brown piano solo; *Love Letters; Hail Hail, Rock 'n' Roll; Fever; Hurt*

Side 4: *Hound Dog; Are You Lonesome Tonight?; Reconsider, Baby; Little Sister; Unchained Melody; Rags to Riches; Can't Help Falling in Love;* Closing vamp

SOUND QUALITY: GOOD   MADE IN AMERICA

There are other bootleg albums in existence; for the most part they duplicate the selections found in this section, and their sound quality is extremely poor. I will list some of their titles and their place of origin.

Col. Parker's Boy	Germany
Elvis for President	America
Memories of Elvis	Holland
Presley Mania, Vol. 1	America
Rockin' in New York City	America
Portrait of a God	America

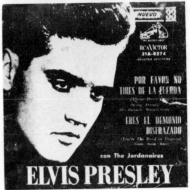

Foreign Records

A few years ago I attended a meeting in Las Vegas with the presidents of Elvis fan clubs from fourteen different countries. The convention was held in my room at the Hilton Hotel. I required an interpreter, as I was the only person present who spoke English. There was one word, however, that was universal—ELVIS! I was amazed how these people who could not speak, read, or write English knew the lyrics to every song Elvis has recorded. This proves beyond a doubt that Elvis is indeed the King of the whole wide world!

I will not attempt to give you a complete foreign discography, as space does not permit that. I will, however, show you some of the rarest and most valuable Elvis records from around the world. To those collectors who have completed their American Elvis collection, and feel that their hobby is over, I can give an assurance that it has only just begun.

ARGENTINA

Here in the United States we are all well aware of how difficult it is to find a 33⅓ single. In Argentina, however, many singles were released as such.

Shown here is the deleted LP *Los Discos de Oro de Elvis* and the 33⅓ single *Devil in Disguise*.

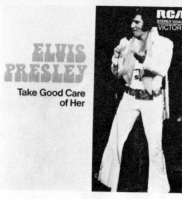

FROM HIS NEW ALBUM "ELVIS" APL1-0283

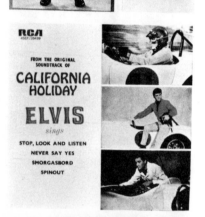

AUSTRALIA

In Australia, singles are released in cardboard picture covers, as are the American EP covers. When an EP is a million-seller, the record company advertises the fact by releasing it with a gold label. The LPs shown here are all SPs (special product). Each features a booklike cover and beautiful artwork.

BRAZIL

Most of this country's LPs and EPs are the same as the American releases. Many of the singles, however, are different.

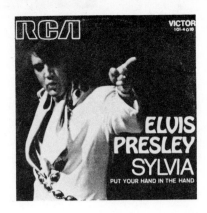

BRITAIN

The HMV label, distributed by Decca Records, preceded the RCA label in England. Elvis had fourteen singles, two EPs, a 10-inch LP, and two 12-inch LPs released by HMV. *His Master's Voice* singles have a purple and gold label, the EPs a blue and gold label, and the LPs a maroon label with a beautiful painting of Nipper. The 10-inch LP is worth about $200, while the 12-inch LPs are worth about $100 each.

Elvis is more popular in Britain than anywhere else in the world. RCA

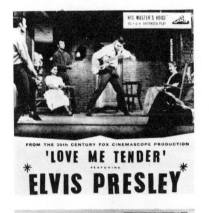
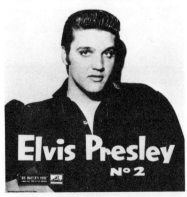

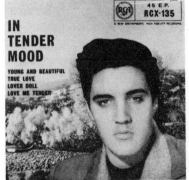

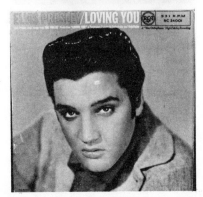
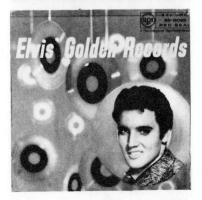

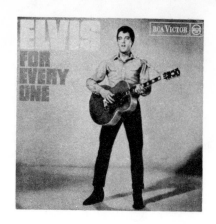

in England is really on the ball. It always seems to find another unique way to market the Presley product. It gave the world Elvis on maxi singles (three songs on a record). *Elvis' 40 Greatest Hits,* issued on the Arcade label, sold one million units in Britain alone. Britain is the only country to have a *Tickle Me, Volume 2* EP. The companies always seem to be deleting Elvis LPs and then reissuing them with different picture covers. The two RCA EPs pictured here, along with the *Such a Night* EP, are the only EPs different from ours. Generally, singles in Britain do not have picture covers. *Elvis' Golden Records* (pictured here) was available with two different covers. Each opened into a book and contained the pictures from our LOC-1035 LP, *Elvis' Christmas Album.* The label on this LP was an RCA Red Seal. This is the only time in Elvis' career that a record he made was on the Red Seal label. In 1975 *Reader's Digest* in England gave us the most unusual Elvis package ever. It was a boxed set of Elvis' greatest hits containing six LPs, all with different color covers. Upon turning the covers over and placing them together, you would have a life-size picture of Elvis.

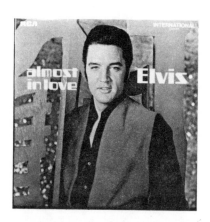

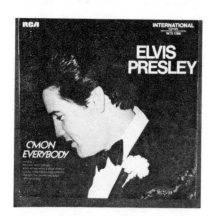

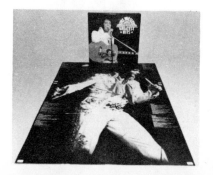

CANADA

Collecting Elvis records can be very confusing if you happen to be in Canada. All record plants in Canada are independent of each other. As a result, if you reside in Grande Prairie, Alberta, and you bought *Elvis' Christmas Album* in 1958, you have the rare one pictured here. If you lived in Montreal and bought the same LP, you've got the same cover as our Christmas LP.

Canada's singles and EPs are the same as those in the United States, though many of its EPs were released with red labels.

CHILE

Chile is another country where the record situation is tight. Its singles, for the most part, do not have picture covers. Its EPs have some of the most interesting covers in the world. The 10-inch LPs shown here have a white RCA label and are worth $3,000 each (happy hunting!).

 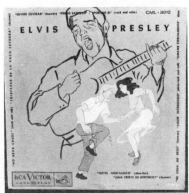 

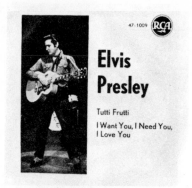

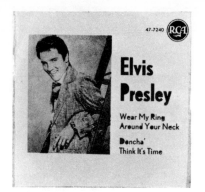

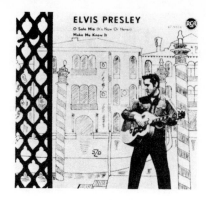

DENMARK

Most of Denmark's releases are the same as the German issues. There are six singles and three EPs that had different picture covers than in any other country.

FRANCE

The French singles come in a cardboard picture sleeve. Most covers are completely different from those issued in other countries. France also has many more EPs, all of which are very beautiful.

Its LPs, with the exception of a few, are the same as in the United States.

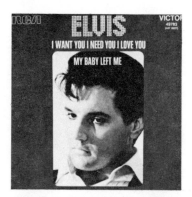

(**France** continued)

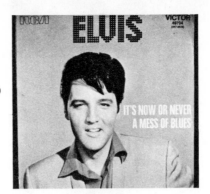

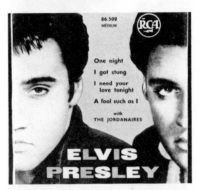

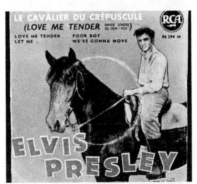

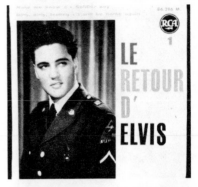

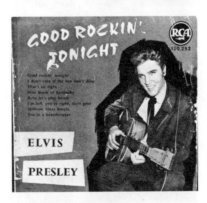

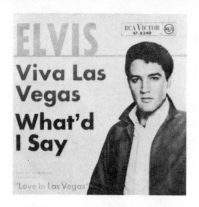

GERMANY

Germany is another country where Elvis' popularity is never questioned. My personal collection contains every 45 ever made in Germany. Many are the same as ours, but in some cases Elvis' singles have different picture covers, along with completely different versions of the songs issued here. *Tonight's All Right for Love* is a fine example. German EPs and LPs are different and interesting. The "Golden Boy" Elvis LP pictured (*Elvis— She's Not You*) was circulated only for a few months; then Colonel Parker had RCA prevent the Hör Zu label from distributing it. "Golden Boy" is on every Elvis collector's list.

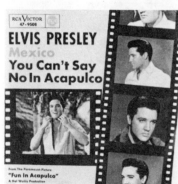

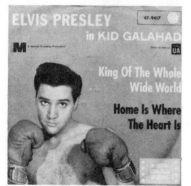

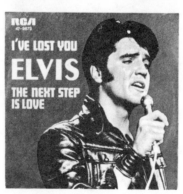

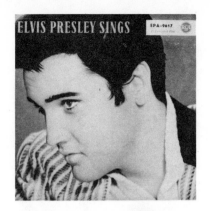

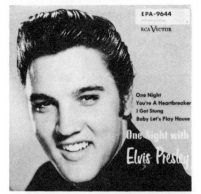

(**Germany** continued)

ISRAEL

Singles and EPs are not available in this country. Israel is the only country in the world to release the *Burning Love* LP as a full-priced, orange-label RCA Victor album.

ITALY

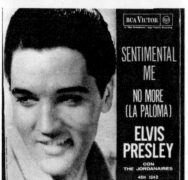

Most Italian singles, EPs, and LPs have different picture sleeves. Italy has an abundance of rare records by Elvis. The *Elvis Presley Show* EP was a special radio station record.

Disco Refrain came inside an Elvis songbook. This 45 EP contains eleven Elvis Presley songs.

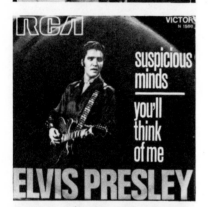

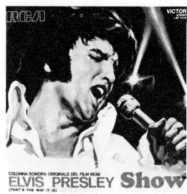

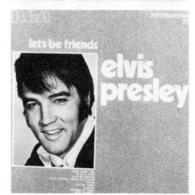

JAPAN

Record-wise, Japan is head and shoulders above any country in the world. Its photography and printing are impeccable. The sound quality of the records is outstanding and their packaging is far superior to what you may find in America. When an LP is in its original release, it is issued in a double book-type cover. Every album contains a book consisting of pages and pages of beautiful color photos accompanied by the lyrics to every song (in both Japanese and English). Here you have the ultimate Elvis package. The EPs and singles, while not as elaborately manufactured, are still better than anywhere else in the world.

Japan is very quick to delete an album and just as quick to reissue it with another title, cover, and book.

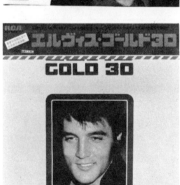

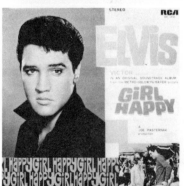

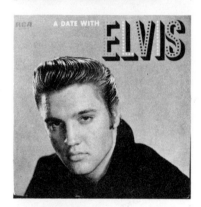

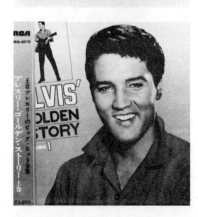
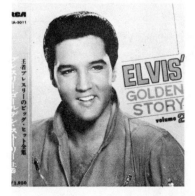
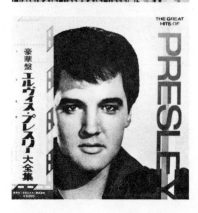

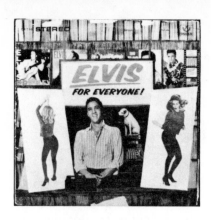
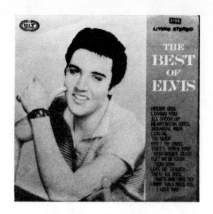

KOREA

Seoul, Korea, issues legal bootlegs. Elvis records are released on Hit and Oscar labels. There are no singles or EPs from this country.

MALAYSIA

RCA does not have a plant in Malaysia, which therefore makes all of Elvis' records released here bootlegs. Malaysian LPs are quite difficult to obtain, and if you should find any, you can expect to pay a high premium for them. The *Elvis on Tour* LP has Elvis' picture on the label. Elvis records are issued on many different labels, the most common being P. S. Records, Sunrise, and Zany.

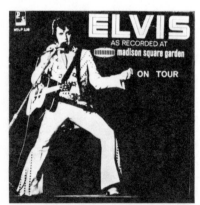

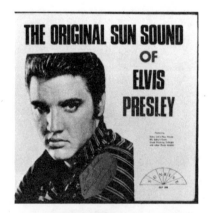

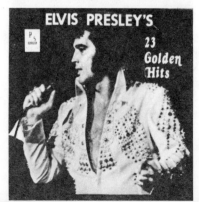

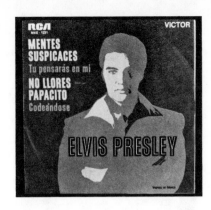  

MEXICO

Although Mexico is a close neighbor, you must travel deep into the country in order to obtain anything other than U.S. imports. If you decide to make the trip, you won't be disappointed, as Mexico has twenty-nine EPs with completely different picture covers and a wide variety of singles and LPs.

NETHERLANDS

This country has a wider variety of releases than those pictured here. Shown are three RCA singles.

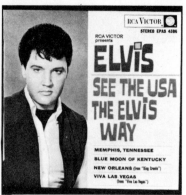

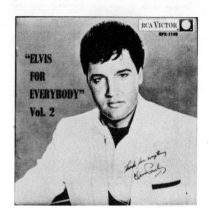

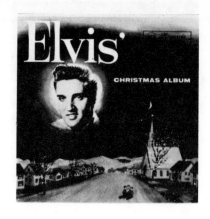

NEW ZEALAND

There are only a handful of different releases in New Zealand. These few are the most sought-after Elvis records in the world. The *See the U.S.A. the Elvis Way* EP was released in both mono and stereo. This EP has a $100 price tag. *Elvis' Christmas Album* and the original *Easy Come, Easy Go* LP in mint condition will cost you somewhere between $300 and $500.

RUSSIA

It is most difficult to obtain records from this country. If you're fortunate enough to obtain any of its Elvis releases, you've got yourself a record that is worth quite a bit of money.

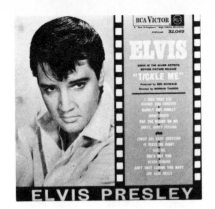

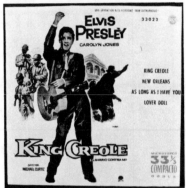

SPAIN

This country has many interesting releases. Pictured here are five of the most unusual Elvis records released in Madrid.

SOUTH AFRICA

South Africa is a country that every Elvis collector wants to conquer. Their singles do not have picture covers, and their EPs are generally the same as the U.S. releases. However, their LPs (or at least a chosen handful) are unique and somewhat expensive. South Africa is the only country in the world to have a *Jailhouse Rock* LP and a *Tickle Me* LP. Other South African releases that are of great interest to the avid collector are *Elvis, King of the Whole Wide World* and *Rock Is Back, Elvis Is King*.

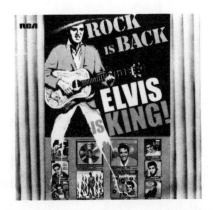

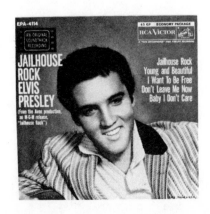

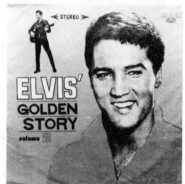

TAIWAN

RCA does not have a plant located in Taiwan, so Elvis records are released on different labels: e.g., C.J.L., Large World, Lyou Fung, Holly Hawk. In Taiwan the LPs are released on a transparent colored vinyl.

The Hollywood Years

While I can't ignore the incredible output of Elvis films over the years, it is impossible to go into all of them in detail here, as they are an entire book in themselves! I know, because I wrote it, and called it *Elvis in Hollywood*. But this book would not be complete without at least mentioning them. There were thirty-three of them; one of the more lucrative outlets for the Presley charisma, they have grossed over three hundred million dollars worldwide.

1. *Love Me Tender* (20th Century-Fox, 1956)
2. *Loving You* (Paramount, 1957)
3. *Jailhouse Rock* (Metro-Goldwyn-Mayer, 1957)
4. *King Creole* (Paramount, 1958)
5. *G.I. Blues* (Paramount, 1960)
6. *Flaming Star* (20th Century-Fox, 1960)
7. *Wild in the Country* (20th Century-Fox, 1961)
8. *Blue Hawaii* (Paramount, 1961)
9. *Follow That Dream* (United Artists, 1962)
10. *Kid Galahad* (United Artists, 1962)
11. *Girls! Girls! Girls!* (Paramount, 1962)
12. *It Happened at the World's Fair* (Metro-Goldwyn-Mayer, 1963)
13. *Fun in Acapulco* (Paramount, 1963)

299

14. *Kissin' Cousins* (Metro-Goldwyn-Mayer, 1964)
15. *Viva Las Vegas* (Metro-Goldwyn-Mayer, 1964)
16. *Roustabout* (Paramount, 1964)
17. *Tickle Me* (Allied Artists, 1964)
18. *Girl Happy* (Metro-Goldwyn-Mayer, 1965)
19. *Harum Scarum* (Metro-Goldwyn-Mayer, 1965)
20. *Paradise—Hawaiian Style* (Paramount, 1965)
21. *Frankie and Johnny* (United Artists, 1966)
22. *Spinout* (Metro-Goldwyn-Mayer, 1966)
23. *Easy Come, Easy Go* (Paramount, 1966)
24. *Double Trouble* (Metro-Goldwyn-Mayer, 1967)
25. *Clambake* (United Artists, 1967)
26. *Stay Away, Joe* (Metro-Goldwyn-Mayer, 1968)
27. *Speedway* (Metro-Goldwyn-Mayer, 1968)
28. *Live a Little, Love a Little* (Metro-Goldwyn-Mayer, 1968)
29. *Charro!* (National General, 1969)
30. *Change of Habit* (Universal, 1969)
31. *The Trouble with Girls* (Metro-Goldwyn-Mayer, 1969)
32. *That's the Way It Is* (Metro-Goldwyn-Mayer, 1970)
33. *Elvis on Tour* (Metro-Goldwyn-Mayer, 1972)

Paul Lichter and
"Nipper" (Nipper
courtesy of RCA
Records and Tempo
Products).

About Paul Lichter

Paul Lichter is a name that has become a household word among Elvis Presley fans. Over the past few years, Lichter's name has been linked with Elvis' as much as Colonel Tom Parker's. Paul has been credited with making Elvis collectible, and rightfully so; but who is this man who, according to Geraldo Rivera, reporting on national television, earns in excess of $30,000 a month through his various Elvis activities? Geraldo has said: "My interview with the world-renowned Elvisologist was indeed enlightening. Paul's mental storehouse of Elvis knowledge should qualify him for the Guinness Book of World Records. You're going to find the things you never knew about Elvis Presley and never even thought you wanted to know when you talk to Paul Lichter. Paul is a thin, dark, sad-eyed young man who looks and talks a bit like a rock and roll idol himself. His black leather hand-stitched trousers and embroidered multicolored shirt make a nice lead-in to the study in hair. There is his long black bob, his double-thick, heavy, black eyebrows, and the masses of coiled black hair on his exposed chest. He is wearing his 500-carat turquoise and silver belt, white moccasin platform shoes, and a massive American Indian bear-claw necklace, along with a matching bracelet of the same huge turquoise stones in silver mountings.

301

'I'm Elvis all the time—100 per cent—that's all I do,' said the thirty-two-year-old author, editor, publisher, and president of the Elvis Unique Record Club. By this time, Paul has become accustomed to being introduced as the man who knows more about Elvis Presley than any other person on earth. The *Memphis Flash* is a bimonthly magazine that is written, edited, and published by Paul. The *Memphis Flash* with its exclusive photos and stories has come to be known as 'the only Elvis magazine that tells it like it is.' The *Flash* has never been available in any store or newsstand, and yet there are over 128,000 subscribers to the magazine. This feat is even more incredible when one stops to realize that Paul has achieved this through word of mouth. According to Lichter, 'Elvis is the most reproduced figure in the world, with the exception of Mickey Mouse. Still, that makes him the most famous human being.'

Paul and Geraldo Rivera in Paul's office.

"Lichter's offices amount to a museum of Presleydom, larded with posters, autographed photos, limited-edition statuettes, and a boggling inventory of records, films, and other memorabilia. There are shelves holding every Elvis publication in or out of print, cabinets containing buttons, bubble gum cards, countless Elvis novelties, and racks stocked with everything Elvis has recorded. These records include every 45 rpm and 78 rpm, extended-play discs, LPs, current and discontinued pressings, foreign versions, and various promotional copies that Lichter has been able to acquire. There are over 210,000 members of the Elvis Unique Record Club, through which these records are made available for sale, and Paul's museum is open to members by appointment only. All correspondence is handled through P.O. Box 339, Huntingdon Valley, Pennsylvania 19006.

"Paul's first book was *Elvis in Hollywood*. To the Presley fan, Paul has become a legend himself. He has done more for the fans than the Presley

Elvis and Paul: painting by Europe's top Pop artist, Ger Ryff.

organization has, and, because of this, Elvis fans are as loyal to Paul as they are to Elvis. Although Lichter has no official connection with Elvis Presley Enterprises, he is looked upon by Presley's manager, Colonel Tom Parker, with benign neglect since Lichter provides what amounts to extensive public relations for free. He is perhaps the organization's lowest-paid press agent.

"Today Paul, his lovely wife, Janice, and their two children, Kyle and Danielle, along with their two dogs (Elvis and Get-lo) live in their country home, Leeland.

" 'My dad prided himself on knowing what was going to be big in entertainment,' recalls Lichter. 'And he was sure about Elvis. I'll never forget the day after he gave me those two Sun records, I went to school in my red corduroy shirt, and for the first time I turned my collar up.' Lichter points out, however, that his interest in rock has never been limited exclusively to Presley. He boasts a private collection of more than four thousand rock albums, but cites Elvis as 'the first, the greatest rock vocalist ever. . . . In fact, Rod Stewart belongs to the club, and so do Elton John and John Lennon. I've spoken with them and they agree that most rock vocal modulations come from Elvis. Besides, he's given generations enjoyment. Right now, I'd say his audience ranges in age from eight to eighty.

" 'There have been contenders, there have been pretenders, but there is only one King—Elvis Presley. Long may he reign.' "